The Modern Firm

The Modern Firm

Organizational Design for Performance and Growth

John Roberts

OXFORD
UNIVERSITY PRESS

OXFORD

UNIVERSITY PRESS

Great Clarendon Street, Oxford OX2 6DP

Oxford University Press is a department of the University of Oxford.
It furthers the University's objective of excellence in research, scholarship,
and education by publishing worldwide in

Oxford New York

Auckland Bangkok Buenos Aires Cape Town Chennai
Dar es Salaam Delhi Hong Kong Istanbul Karachi Kolkata
Kuala Lumpur Madrid Melbourne Mexico City Mumbai Nairobi
São Paulo Shanghai Taipei Tokyo Toronto

Oxford is a registered trade mark of Oxford University Press
in the UK and in certain other countries

Published in the United States
by Oxford University Press Inc., New York

© Donald John Roberts 2004

British Library Cataloguing in Publication Data

Data available

Library of Congress Cataloging in Publication Data

Data available

ISBN 0-19-829376-3

1 3 5 7 9 10 8 6 4 2

Typeset by Newgen Imaging Systems (P) Ltd, Chennai, India
Printed in Great Britain
on acid-free paper by
Biddles Ltd., King's Lynn, Norfolk

To Kathy

Contents

Preface

The most fundamental responsibilities of general managers are setting strategy and designing the organization to implement it. Over the last decades the great value of economics for the study of strategy and the practice of strategizing has become evident. This book attempts to show how economics can contribute in a similar way and at a similar level to organizational design.

I hope that practicing managers will read and benefit from this book. It is not, however, a "how to" book offering the final, simple answer about how to succeed. Instead, it offers ways to think about the problem of designing business organizations for performance and growth. Both students of organizations and management and practicing managers can benefit from having an understanding of the basic principles of the economics of organization and its application to business enterprises. The book tries to offer this. It mixes case studies and shorter examples with fundamental conceptual and theoretical material that is developed and presented in a non-technical manner and then applied to the design problem. It also seeks to explain some of the very great changes in actual companies that are creating the new model of the modern firm.

The lectures on which this volume is based were given at Oxford in the spring of 1997, and it is the summer of 2003 as I write this preface. Clearly, it has taken me a long time to write up my lectures! Yet, I believe the delay was probably worthwhile. In the intervening time, there has been much progress on the subject of how to put together effective organizations, and I personally have learned a lot. Consequently, this volume is radically different than it would have been if I had written it five or six years ago. In particular, three lectures have grown into seven chapters. There is new theory, and there are rich examples of practice that were not available then.

I owe much to many people. First, I am grateful for the honor of having been invited to give the first Clarendon Lectures in Management Studies, and I thank Colin Mayer, the Oxford University School of Management Studies, and Oxford University Press. Second, almost all the work I have done in organizations was collaborative, and I am indebted to each of the people with whom I have thought, taught, and written. I learned from all of them, but especially from Susan Athey, Jonathan Day, Bengt Holmström, Paul Milgrom, and Joel Podolny. They will recognize their ideas here and know how greatly I have benefited from working with them. The Stanford Graduate School of Business provides an unmatched environment for teaching and research in organizations, and I am grateful to the School for its support and to my faculty colleagues and the students in the Ph.D., MBA, Sloan, and Executive programs for their huge contributions to my learning. I am especially pleased to acknowledge my debts

Preface

to Bill Barnett, Dave Baron, Jim Baron, Robert Burgelman, Katherine Doornik, David Kreps, Ed Lazear, John McMillan, Charles O'Reilly, Paul Oyer, Garth Saloner, Scott Schaefer, Eric Van den Steen, and Bob Wilson. During the writing of this book I also spent time at Nuffield College and at McKinsey & Company, London, and I want to express my gratitude to both those institutions and their members. I am also grateful to the executives and managers at the many companies I have been able to visit and study, especially BP, General Motors, Johnson Controls, Nokia, Novo Nordisk, Sony, and Toyota. The cases I co-authored on these companies helped to shape my thinking and are the basis for much of this book. My editor at Oxford University Press, David Musson, has shown immense patience with my tardiness (but not so much that I ceased feeling guilty!) and is owed thanks. Paul Coombes, John McMillan, Andy Postlewaite, Richard Saouma, and especially Jonathan Day read the manuscript and offered useful comments. Ayca Kaya provided valuable research assistance and Jen Smith was helpful putting the manuscript in final form. Finally, my wife, Kathleen Roberts, has suffered my interminable dragging out of this project all these years with her usual grace and humor. Thank you, Kathy.

1

Strategy and Organization

During the first two decades of the twentieth century, managers at Standard Oil of New Jersey, Dupont, Sears Roebuck, and General Motors invented a new way of organizing and managing their businesses. Their creation—the now ubiquitous multidivisional form—involved fundamental changes in the design of the firm. While the most visible change was structuring the organization on the basis of divisions defined by product or geography, rather than functionally, the new form also involved new systems for collecting and recording information, for allocating resources, and for controlling behavior. This new model permitted an efficient solution to the incredibly complicated problem of coordinating and motivating large numbers of people carrying out a complex of interrelated activities, often in different locations. It thus allowed giant, multiproduct business organizations to emerge and function effectively on a continental and then global scale. The new design also led to a huge growth in the number of people working as managers and to the emergence of the set of values and norms that mark management as a profession. In terms of its impact, not just on economic activity, but also on human life as a whole, the multidivisional organizational design must rank as one of the major innovations of the last century.[1]

Yet the last two decades have seen a set of innovations in the organization of the firm that is similarly fundamental and that may ultimately be as momentous. All the elements of the design are not yet in their final form. Managers continue to experiment with improving it as they implement changes in their organizations. Still, some broad outlines are clear. Firms have changed the scope of their activities, typically refocusing on their core businesses and outsourcing many of the activities that they previously regarded as central. These changes are reflected in the immense volume of merger, acquisition, and spin-off activity that marked both the 1980s and 1990s and that may now be building again. Many have also redefined the nature of their relationships with customers and suppliers, often replacing simple arm's length dealings with long-term partnerships. They have eliminated layers of management and associated staff positions, redefined the units into which they divide themselves internally, dispersed functional experts to the business units, and increased the authority and accountability of line managers. By these measures, coupled with improved information and measurement systems and redesigned performance management systems, they have sought to increase the speed of decision-making and to tap the knowledge and energy of their employees in ways that have not been tried before. To facilitate coordination and learning, they have experimented with linking people in different parts of their organizations directly, so that communications are more horizontal and not just up and down the hierarchy. Many have also tried to redefine the nature of the relationship they have with their employees while redesigning jobs and the very nature of work. These changes are aimed at improving the performance of the firms adopting them. Increased competitive pressures drive their adoption, and new technology makes many of them feasible for the first time. Falling barriers to international trade and investment, the rise of information technology (especially the Internet), and improved transportation mean that a firm's competitors are not just the old local rivals, but may be from anywhere. With more competition, the need to improve performance increases. These same developments also open new opportunities to do business far from home, and the new organizational designs support taking advantage of these opportunities. Capital markets, too, are increasing the performance pressures on firms. Especially in the United States, but increasingly elsewhere as well, the increased power of institutional investors and their increased willingness to use this power are pushing companies to do better. In some cases, the changes are also responses to greater competition for talent as more firms seek to attract and retain especially skilled and gifted people. Meanwhile, the massive advances in the technology of communication and computation make feasible many of the key changes in organization and management that are being adopted.

These organizational innovations, when properly applied, do lead to better economic performance, affecting the material well-being of the people of the world. Moreover, they alter the ways work is done, changing people's lives in fundamental ways. Ultimately, they can affect every aspect of how business is accomplished in the modern firm.

Many of the principles underlying this new model are not in fact completely new, however, as the following example will show. The example involves two firms in a service industry—trade. One, the long-established "HB Company," had completely dominated the market for years. Its leaders were politically as well as economically powerful, and the firm was favored by successive governments. The newly established "NW Company," the upstart rival, had none of these advantages. Its leaders were immigrants and refugees, its headquarters was in a distant, provincial town, and it had no powerful friends. In fact, the NW Co. was arguably breaking the law in even attempting to compete with the HB Co. Further, in addition to its advantages in an established customer base, in business experience, and in political and legal matters, HB Co. had vastly superior technology and better access to financing. The result was that HB's costs were estimated to be in the order of one-half those of its rival.

Yet, in a relatively brief time after entering the business, NW Co. had seized 80 percent of the market from its rival and was very profitable, while the once-dominant monopolist was near bankruptcy. How did this happen?

The answer will be unsurprising to anyone familiar with the changes that have gone on in business recently. The NW Co. found a way to serve the customers better by getting closer to them, where it could be more responsive to their differing needs and to ever-changing market realities. It also carried out a number of organizational innovations. It simplified the supplier structure and eliminated traditional middlemen. It avoided excessive bureaucracy while developing systems to ensure that relevant information was shared broadly within the company and that all the relevant parties had a role in and understood decisions. It recruited people for operating positions who were willing to take responsibility and initiative, and then gave them the authority to act on their knowledge and intelligence without checking every detail with hierarchic superiors. Finally, it put in place reward systems that encouraged entrepreneurial behavior. In other words, it developed a new strategy and then put in place the people, organizational structure, managerial processes, and corporate culture to support the strategy. These managerial innovations allowed it to overcome an apparently prohibitive cost disadvantage.

HB Co. was initially unperturbed by the challenge from NW. It knew that its ways had worked for years and that it had tremendous advantages. It probably also failed to see the competitive advantage that NW's new strategy and organization provided. So its response was very slow in coming. Even after the upstart rival had gained a huge market share, the leaders of the old firm did little. This, too, should be a familiar story to those who have followed the experience in a number of different businesses in recent decades.

Eventually, however, HB did respond to the threat, essentially by copying NW's new approach. It did so, however, only after the leaders of the firm had been replaced by new ones who understood the nature of the threat and who were not tied to the old ways that had worked so well for so long.

NW Co. had always known that it would be doomed by its cost disadvantage if HB Co. were to copy its rival's

5

customer-oriented strategy and replace its centralized, command-and-control processes with ones that fit the new strategy. So NW attempted a preemptive takeover of HB before the new leadership could take control. This failed, however, and ultimately HB Co.'s huge cost advantage did overwhelm the NW Co.

The outcome was a deal uniting the two firms that, for public relations reasons, was labeled a merger. But everyone in Canada in 1820 (and those in the United Kingdom who were aware of the matter) knew that the North West Company of Montreal had been absorbed by the victorious, London-based Hudson Bay Company, or more properly, the Governor and Company of Adventurers of England Trading into Hudson's Bay.[2]

The Hudson Bay Company continues in business to this day as one of the leading retailers in Canada. Established by Charles the Second's royal charter in 1670 under the leadership of Prince Rupert, the HBC had been given exclusive rights to trade in the lands draining into the giant Hudson Bay. This monopoly grant covered an area of 1.5 million square miles, more than fifteen times the size of the United Kingdom and significantly larger than the European Union before its expansion in 2004. At that time there were no Europeans resident in this area, which was a trackless wilderness of rocks and trees and water (as much of it still is today!). What it did contain was a relatively small number of aboriginal people and untold amounts of animal furs, especially beaver, which were in high demand in Europe.

The Company exploited its franchise by a very passive strategy: It built half a dozen forts on the shores of the bay and waited for potential customers to come to it, seeking European-made goods for their furs. The trade goods were brought in from England through Hudson Bay in ocean-going ships that made annual voyages, bringing the furs back to England on their return trips. (More frequent trips were impossible because of the technology of shipping and the fact that the bay was frozen solid for most of the year.) The HBC stuck to this approach over the next century, during which a trade network developed in which aboriginal tribes, whose homelands were located away from Hudson Bay, traded with ones nearer the forts, who then traded with the HBC.

This approach to business was hardly very bold, but it was a sensible strategy, given the market conditions and technology of the seventeenth and eighteenth centuries and the risks and opportunities they implied. Moreover, the HBC built an organizational system that fit the strategy very well and that allowed it to be implemented very effectively.

Key decisions were centralized in London. This meant that decision-making was slow and unresponsive to local conditions (especially since none of the senior decision-makers ever set foot in the company's territory, called Rupertsland), but it did ensure coherence and control. Moreover, with an unchallenged legal monopoly, a passive approach to business development, and an unsophisticated, slowly changing market, there was little obvious need for speedy decisions. Rather, the danger was that local employees, far from the oversight of senior management, would fritter away the profits, or, worse yet, misappropriate them. So the Bay's people in Rupertsland were selected as much for their lack of imagination and their ability to bear tedium as for their talent, initiative, and diligence. They were sent out under contracts that were close to indentured servitude, given a specific set of detailed instructions that governed every aspect of their work (including the allowable prices to pay and charge), paid a fixed amount, required to stay near the company's forts, and punished physically for any infractions.

The system seems brutal and stupid, and yet it must be recognized that it worked very well: The Company was very profitable from the outset and remained so throughout its first century of existence.

There was, however, an inherent inefficiency in this system. It did not do a good job of exploiting the opportunities for trade with people far from the bay, leaving their (perhaps unimagined) desires for European goods unmet and the furs they collected in hunting for food underused. Indirect trade through middlemen from the peoples living between the Company's forts and the rich fur areas allowed partial realization of these potential gains from trade, but the system was arguably inefficient. The first reason to expect inefficiency is that the middlemen had monopoly positions that they likely exploited, so that markups were taken on markups and the volumes transacted were too low. The second is that the middlemen were poorly positioned to bear the risk associated with the trade. They lacked access to finance to support their market positions and had to face the uncertainties of demand and supply on their own. Both these effects limited the actual volume of trade to inefficiently low levels.

The founders of the North West Company—recent immigrants to Montreal, either directly from Britain or as refugees from the revolution in the thirteen American colonies—may have seen the profit opportunities that were inherent in these inefficiencies. They probably were aware that French Canadian traders had profitably traded more directly with the native people before the British conquest of Canada, and they certainly saw the profits that the Hudson Bay Company had been racking up for more than a century despite its passive strategy. A decently effective competitor ought to have been able to do very well.

The Nor'Westers' big disadvantage, however, was that they could not ship directly in and out of the center of the fur-trading area: Hudson Bay was closed to them by the HBC's monopoly grant. Instead, they would have to bring the trade goods in from Europe and the furs back out through Montreal, the head of navigation on the St. Lawrence River. But Montreal was thousands of miles from the areas where furs were richest and most plentiful, and, in particular, almost a thousand miles further from them than were the HBC forts. The Nor'Westers could not expect the potential customers to come to them, and so they were forced to go to their customers.

This was the origin of their strategy, and the source of their huge cost disadvantage. In the last decades of the eighteenth century the Nor'Westers set up dozens of trading posts right in the lands where the furs were collected, reaching all the way to the Athabaska region in what is now the far north of Saskatchewan and Alberta. Then, in birch-bark canoes and small open boats paddled by French-Canadian *voyageurs*, they brought the trade goods into the wilderness and the furs out to market, from Montreal to the Athabaska and back, through the Great Lakes and along the untamed rivers of the Canadian North.

Strategy and Organization

This strategy, operating in a now-competitive environment, required very different structures, procedures, and behavior to make it work from those the HBC had used for 120 years. Given the communications technology of the period, coordinating such a complex operation could not be done through central decision-making. Instead, individuals in the field would need to take responsibility for coping with unforeseen eventualities and changing conditions as they arose. To ensure that this was done effectively, the men who actually ran the posts in the fur country were partners in the company ("wintering partners") with broad authority over their operations backed by the incentives of ownership to do a good job. Also, getting the trade goods in and the furs out was a monumental task that relied on near superhuman physical efforts. The wintering partners had the direct incentive of a profit share to ensure that these tasks were fulfilled and the efforts exerted, and they in turn gave strong incentives to the *voyageurs* to carry out the work (including the possibility of becoming a partner). Meanwhile, the Montreal-based partners handled the acquisition of trade goods, sale of the furs, and financing the operations. They also handled getting the trade goods to the company's inland headquarters at the head of Lake Superior, where they met each summer with the wintering partners, who had brought out the furs from the North. This annual meeting of all the partners ensured that information was shared and that decisions were informed and understood.

What are the lessons of this example, other than, perhaps, that there is nothing new under the sun?

First, strategy and organization matter: The North West Company's strategy of eliminating middlemen and getting close to the customer, backed by an organization that implemented this, quickly overcame a 50 percent cost disadvantage, over a hundred years' experience, and a royal grant of monopoly.

Second, there needs to be a fit between strategy and organization and between these and the technological, legal, and competitive environment. The organization of the HBC fit its strategy and the environment that obtained until the entry of the North West Company, and the result was a century of profitability. The Nor'Westers' model similarly showed an internal coherence and an alignment with the strategic, technological, and competitive context. In general, however, finding such a fit would seem a daunting challenge, because there are so many variables and the choice is so complex. Still, it can be done, and it must be if success is to be achieved.

Third, strategic and organizational change is not easy, but it is sometimes necessary and it can and does happen. The HBC took a decade to reform in response to the threat. That is almost as long as it took the American automobile industry to respond to the successful entry of their Japanese rivals! Finally the changes came, although only under the threat of bankruptcy. The HBC put trading posts inland to meet the competition, reformed its organizational processes to support the new strategy, and ultimately triumphed.

Fourth, a more competitive environment favors the sort of organizational design that the North West Company initiated and whose principles are shared in the emergent organizational design of the modern firm.

In this book I will seek to elucidate these principles and show how they apply. In the process I will develop some conceptual frameworks and theoretical constructs that are important for understanding effective organizational design.

My starting point for this exercise is the proposition that general managers must be organizational designers. Just as it is a fundamental responsibility of general managers to devise a strategy that determines how their businesses will compete, it is equally necessary that they design and create an organization through which the strategy will be implemented. And just as we have come to realize that strategy is not solely the responsibility of the chief executive officer, but rather of managers throughout the organization, so too is organizational design.

The second basis for this book is the idea that economics has much to say about the problem of organizational design. In the twenty-plus years since Michael Porter began applying the concepts of industrial organization economics to the field of strategy (Porter 1980, 1985), practitioners and students of management alike have come to recognize that economic analysis is of tremendous value to this field. The methods of economics hold similar promise for the study and design of organizations, as I hope the following will demonstrate. But first we need to set some context.

Strategy, Organization, and the Environment

Achieving high performance in a business results from establishing and maintaining a fit among three elements: The strategy of the firm, its organizational design, and the environment in which it operates. In the conceptualization that has been standard in management studies, the organizational design problem takes the economic, legal, social, and technological environment in which the firm operates as given, presumes that the strategy has been formulated, and then seeks to create an organization to implement the given strategy in the particular environment. This approach follows from Alfred Chandler's dictum (Chandler 1962) that "structure follows strategy"—organization is the mechanism through which strategy is realized.

Although this is a very limited view of the nature of the design problem and of the role of organization, we will place our discussion initially in this context. For the sake of simplicity, then, focus on the traditional Chandlerian formulation and consider a simplified, idealized version of what a firm is and does. The starting point is a business opportunity—an unmet need, a market inefficiency. For the NWC, the opportunity lay in the HBC's inefficient exploitation of the potential gains from trade. More generally, the opportunity might come from having lower costs than the current market participants or a product that better meets the needs of (at least some) customers. This, in turn, might reflect better technology, or more creativity, or previously unexploited economies of scale and scope.

Next, in the traditional view, comes a strategy to exploit that opportunity—a specification of how the firm is going to create value and get to keep some of it. A well-formulated strategy has several components (Saloner, Shepard, and Podolny 2001).

First, a strategy involves a goal against which the firm can measure itself and judge its success. This might be profit or shareholder-value maximization, or it might be something more complex involving the interests of different constituencies and stakeholders. Even when shareholder value is the ultimate objective, the strategic goal might be expressed in more operational (and more motivating) terms. For example, in the 1970s and 1980s, Komatsu, the Japanese heavy equipment manufacturer, had as its aim to "Beat Caterpillar!"

The next key element is a statement of scope—a specification of the business the firm is in, what products and services it will offer, what customers and market segments it will serve, what activities it will undertake, where it will do these things, and what technology it will use. Obviously, the choice of what to do and how, where, and for whom to do it is a directly relevant and significant aspect of strategy. Less obviously, the scope of the strategy determines what opportunities the firm is *not* going to pursue. This is important: Strategy is a discipline device that helps sort out which of the myriad opportunities that will arise the firm should pursue and on which it should pass. It also allows people in the organization to make this determination without a lot of further discussion and debate, so it facilitates coordination. Moreover, it can contribute to motivation by providing clear goals and boundaries for choices.

A third key element of a strategy is a specification of the nature of the firm's competitive advantage, an indication of how the firm's offer will lead others to deal with it on terms that allow it to realize its goals. How will it attract a profitable market? How will it create value, generating a willingness to pay by customers that exceeds the costs of serving them? Will the firm offer a better product at a cost increment that is lower than the additional value of the improvement to customers? Will it offer as good a product for less? A less desirable product but for a much lower cost?

The final component of a strategy is an explication of why the claimed competitive advantage will actually be realized. Why will the firm get to claim some nontrivial share of the value it creates and do so in a sustainable way? How will the firm get a price that exceeds its costs? What will keep actual and potential competitors from eroding its margins and stealing away its customers? What will ensure that suppliers or customers do not manage to appropriate all the value created? This piece is often missing in formal strategy statements, but the existence and validity of such a logic are crucial. Typically, a valid logic will involve a system of implications linking the particular position occupied by the firm and the distinctive capabilities it enjoys to the customers' choices and then back, via the prices, costs, and volumes that result, to the firm's ability to maintain and enhance its position and capabilities.

Had the NWC's leaders enunciated their strategy it would thus have been something like the following:

> The NWC will trade with the native people of the Canadian north, taking furs in return for European goods. The trade will occur at posts established in the fur-bearing regions and the transport between the posts and Montreal will be provided by company employees using small watercraft. The trade goods will be obtained in Montreal and England, and the furs will be sold in London. The NWC will offer terms of trade that are better than the effective net ones coming from the HBC through the middlemen who are between it and the people actually collecting the furs. The NWC will

also be more responsive to the customers' needs than is the competition. Together, these will make it the preferred trading partner. This positional advantage and the savings from eliminating the middlemen will allow the NWC to serve its customers on terms that still leave a profit margin, despite the Company's higher costs. It will be able to offer such terms and keep these profits as long as the HBC does not match its offer [which the established firm's strategy, organization, and management initially prevented it from doing]. This will allow the NWC to achieve its goal of profitably dominating the fur trade in British North America.

In a multi-business firm, there is another level to strategy, that of corporate strategy. A corporate strategy identifies the set of businesses the firm will encompass and the logic of why doing so will allow it to create extra value over and above what a collection of stand-alone businesses can create. Thus, it is essentially a portfolio choice combined with a theory of the role of the corporate center.

A strategy implies a set of activities that need to be carried out to realize it. In a typical firm these include the "value-chain" activities that must be undertaken in meeting customers' needs, such as product design and development, input procurement, manufacturing, distribution, sales, and post-sales service, as well as "support" activities such as human resource management, management information systems, and finance. In the NWC the value chain was acquisition of trade goods, their transport to the customers, the actual trade, and transport of the furs out to Montreal and thence to London for sale.

The organization is then the means through which these activities are to be carried out and the strategy is to be implemented. Any firm's organization is multifaceted,

16

and the range of organizational variables is mind-boggling. Thus, even a bit of classification may be of some use. One taxonomy identifies the organization as a collection of *people* and an array of organizational features. These, in turn, can be sorted into *architecture*, *routines*, and *culture*, giving rise to the acronym "PARC."

First is the set of people who are part of the organization. What sort of talents and skills do they have, what tastes, what beliefs, what objectives? How hard are they prepared to work and for what ends? What sorts of risks will they accept and what sorts of rewards do they value? How are they connected to the firm? As owners? Employees? Contractors?

The architectural features include what is on the organization chart: the vertical and horizontal boundaries of the firm; the assembling of tasks into jobs and jobs into departments, business units, and divisions; the reporting and authority relationships; and so on. It also includes such matters as the financing, ownership, and governance structure of the firm. These are relatively "hard" features, often with an explicit contractual element. However, architecture also includes the personal networks that link people throughout the firm and across the firm's boundaries. These can, in fact, be as important and more than the formal architecture.

The routines include all the managerial processes, policies, and procedures, official and unofficial, formal and informal, that shape how information is gathered and transmitted, decisions made, resources allocated, performance monitored, and activities controlled and rewarded. The allocation of decision authority within the firm—what decisions are made by which people at what levels, with what oversight or review—is a key element here. The processes also include the routines through which work is done and the mechanisms through which these are altered. These features may involve explicit contractual elements as well as "implicit contracts," more or less formal, shared understandings about how things are to be done.

Culture is the "softer" stuff, but it is not less important for that. It involves the fundamental shared values of the people in the firm, as well as their shared beliefs about why the firm exists, about what they are collectively and individually doing, and to what end. It also encompasses the special language used within the firm, which shapes thought and action. Culture also involves the fundamental mindsets of the firm's members and the mental models they have, which determine how they see themselves and the firm and how they interpret events. Most significantly, it involves the norms of behavior that prevail in dealing with other members of the firm and with outsiders. Culture defines the context in which the relations among people develop and operate and sets the basis for the implicit contracts that guide and shape decisions. It operates as a social motivation and control system.

Along with the strategy and the organization, the third determinant of performance is the environment in which the firm operates. This includes its competitors and their strategies and organizational designs, the state of other relevant markets and firms (suppliers of inputs, complements, and substitutes), and the customers, as well as the ambient technology, the legal and regulatory context, various political, social, and demographic features, and so on.

The Design Problem: Setting Strategy and Organization

If we now apply a design perspective, the job of the general manager is to craft a strategy—objective, scope, competitive advantage, and logic—and create an organization—people, architecture, routines, and culture—in light of the environment to maximize performance. In the longer term, the designer might also try to shape the environment, but we will largely leave this aside in our discussion. The model is captured in Figure 1.

Performance thus depends on the strategy, the organization, and the environment. This formulation leads to a contingent theory of strategy and organization. There is no uniquely best strategy, and there is no one best way to organize. The attractiveness of a strategy is defined only in terms of how well it works in the environment in which it is operating with the organization that is trying to implement it. Similarly, the value of an organizational

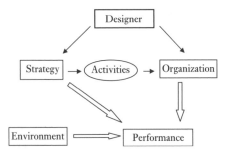

Figure 1. The design problem is to select the strategy and organization to achieve maximal performance in the context of the environment

19

design depends completely on how well it matches the particular environment and strategy. What is good is what works, and we should expect that what will work in different contexts may depend on the context. The key is in finding and establishing a fit among strategy, organization, and the environment and then maintaining the fit over time in the face of change.

What, however, is "performance?"

Firms are institutions created to serve human needs. Performance ultimately is how well the firm does at serving these needs. This raises the issue of whose needs are to be served. Is the firm simply a mechanism for creating shareholder returns? Or is it (also) to provide meaningful experiences, secure employment, and valued opportunities for its members; valuable goods and services for customers; tax revenues and jobs for communities; positive effects on the environment; and so on?

We will, for the most part, take the point of view that the purpose of the firm can be expressed as "value creation." This is not an uncontroversial position, either on prescriptive or descriptive grounds. Indeed, it should not even be immediately clear what it means. The value created by economic activity is the difference between the maximum that people would be willing to pay for it, less the opportunity costs of the activity. Under rather specific and somewhat special conditions, value and value maximization are well defined and would be uncontroversial objectives. These conditions are that (1) there is a medium of exchange that is valued by everyone, (2) that this "money" is freely transferable in any amount between people, and (3) that the amount of money that just compensates any individual for any change in his or her circumstances does not depend on how much money the individual already holds. Under these conditions, the value created in any act of production or trade is just the extra amount of money that all parties in aggregate would pay (or need to be paid) in order to induce unanimous agreement for the action from all affected parties. This amount is unambiguously defined and, further, maximization of the value created in this sense is equivalent to achieving full economic efficiency. If the value-maximizing course of action is adopted, it will be impossible to find any alternative that all parties would unanimously prefer, and if there is another course of action that creates greater value, then it will be possible to make everyone better off by adopting this alternative and distributing the gains appropriately.[3]

Under these conditions, then, value maximization is arguably an appropriate goal from a social point of view. Further, to the extent that those in whose interests the firm actually operates are able to claim the value created, they would want it to be run so as to maximize value. Of course, the conditions are restrictive, and they surely are not fully met in the real world. Even if we treat financial wealth as the universally desired good (as seems most natural), the second condition may fail if the winners from some move do not have enough money to compensate the losers, and in this case the condition of maximizing value may not win unanimous support. It is also necessary that all the relevant interests are recognized and taken into account. Moreover, the third condition requires that there be no "income effects" in demand, which is surely false.

Nonetheless, with a reasonably complete, well functioning system of markets and contracts, the assumption that the owners of firms want their companies run to maximize the owners' long-term wealth is likely to be descriptively accurate (at least to a first approximation). Further, if there are adequate mechanisms for taking care of concerns that are not reflected in market prices, value maximization is unlikely to be an obviously undesirable objective from a social point of view. For example, effective markets will mean that employees have good outside opportunities and so owners will not find it worthwhile to exploit the workers, and effective contracting will ensure their ability to protect themselves and perhaps claim a share of the value created. Meanwhile, the effective laws and regulations will lead the owners to want the firm not to abuse the environment or collude with competitors against the customers' interests.

There is still a problem with measuring long-term value or wealth creation. If stock market prices immediately and accurately reflected all the available information about the firm and its prospects, then stock market valuations would be a fine measure, and maximizing the market value of the firm would be an appropriate goal for managers. Of course, markets do not necessarily work this well, especially in the short run. Moreover, if information is deliberately withheld or manipulated, they cannot work well. Still, over the long haul, honest managers who pursue the maximization of firm value are likely acting to create the most possible value for their shareholders. Then the problem becomes one of selecting the (long-run) value-maximizing strategy for the particular environment and then creating the organization that will best realize it. This problem of organizational design is the subject of this book.

Strategic and Organizational Change

The foregoing formalization of the process of establishing a fit between the environment, the strategy, and the organization is clearly appropriate for a start-up enterprise deciding for the first time what it is going to do and how it is going to do it. The design approach applies as well in an ongoing firm, although some interesting complexity emerges.

At any point in time for an established firm there will be an issue of whether the existing strategy and organization generate the highest performance available in the environment in which the firm finds itself. Since the environment is changing, there is a likelihood that what may once have been a good fit has since deteriorated. This means that there can be a need for strategic and organizational change.

Strategy can be changed relatively quickly: In principle a new strategy can be developed and announced in a short time. Organizations, however, show a lot of inertia, in two distinct senses. First, successful organizations tend to persist, becoming long-lived assets in which firm's strategic capabilities are embedded. Thus, the existing organization shapes the opportunities for future strategic choice and for responding to environmental change. Second, organizations cannot be changed as surely and quickly as can strategy. While it is easy enough to change the formal architecture, it certainly takes real time to change the set of people in the firm and the networks among them, to redefine the fundamental beliefs they share, and to induce new behavioral norms. Yet these may be the most important elements to the realization of the strategy. Thus, effective implementation may not be immediately possible. This will affect what strategic choices are best in a particular context.

The interesting complexities arise from the interplay between the speeds of change of strategy, organization, and the environment. In the traditional view of management scholars, the environment has often been taken to be relatively stable, changing only slowly and infrequently. This may well have reflected reality in an earlier day—it was certainly true in the case of the HBC in the first century of its history—and it may still apply in some industries today. If it is an approximately accurate assumption, then the approach already outlined applies more or less as indicated. Once the environmental change has occurred, the new environment can be taken as given and likely to persist. A strategy can then be developed to address the new opportunities the environment offers, and an organization put together to implement the strategy in the new environment, just as the traditional recipe directs. Should the environment happen to change again, the strategy can be altered and all aspects of the organization restructured to fit the new environment. Because some aspects of the organization will not adapt instantaneously, there may be some period of misalignment. Such a period would also result if the right organizational design is not immediately obvious, but has to be discovered through a process of search and experimentation. However, in either case the misalignment ought to be brief compared to the period over which the strategy and the implied organization are in place and functioning.

BP Exploration (BPX), the "upstream" part of the company then called British Petroleum that was responsible for finding and producing crude oil and natural gas, operated essentially according to this recipe in the late 1980s and first half of the 1990s (Berzins, Podolny, and Roberts 1998*a, b*). When John Browne took over as head of BPX in 1989, "petropreneurs"—smaller energy firms operating in a relatively narrow range of activities—often outperformed the major integrated oil companies. Browne reformulated the strategy at BPX to seek cost advantage by focusing on what the oil industry called "elephants"—very large hydrocarbon deposits—that offered possible economies of scale and took advantage of BP's technical capabilities and financial strength. This led to a redirecting of exploratory activities and the sale of a variety of productive assets that did not meet the test of being sufficiently large. This strategy remained in place throughout the succeeding years.

Meanwhile, at the corporate level, BP had been organized as a complex matrix, with geographic and stream (exploration and production, refining and marketing, and chemicals) dimensions, large central staffs, and heavy centralization of authority. A shift in corporate organizational design beginning in 1990 then moved significant decision power from headquarters to the streams. Beginning in 1992, in the context of a corporate financial crisis that saw BP on the verge of bankruptcy, Browne in turn radically redesigned his part of the business. He eliminated the regional structure in the upstream, as well as most of the managerial center that set direction and oversaw operations. Decision rights were reallocated between an extremely lean Executive Committee consisting of Browne and two other senior leaders and the managers of individual production units or "assets." (The typical asset was a single oil field.) The asset managers were empowered to determine how they would deliver performance against negotiated contracts, which initially specified targets for costs, capital expenditures, and volumes, and rewards were linked strongly to the performance of the individual assets. Meanwhile, the centralized functional staffs were largely dispersed to the assets. The objective was to increase performance by empowering those closest to the relevant information to act upon it and motivating them to do so, and the size of the individual assets meant that there was significant payoff from efforts aimed at improving performance at the asset level.

Employing this basic organization design resulted in a great improvement in performance from the outset. Still, over the next five years, while the strategy remained unchanged, there were important adjustments in the organization on an ongoing basis as the company experimented with improving the design. Some of these changes were explicitly intended to overcome shortcomings in the original model. Chief among these was the introduction of "peer groups" that linked assets facing similar technical and commercial challenges to provide mutual support and spread learning. This structure proved necessary because the absence of middle managers and the limited functional expertise at stream headquarters meant that the asset managers could not look to the center for help with problems. Other changes were made in the organizational architecture and routines to take advantage of the evolving culture. Norms of trust, of helping other businesses, and of delivering promised performance became thoroughly embedded in BPX under Browne's leadership. These shaped behavior and thus allowed shifting the basis of compensation to promote other objectives than simple individual asset performance. They also permitted passing responsibility to the peer groups for allocating capital and for meeting the aggregate of the performance contracts of the member assets. These changes, in turn, permitted further performance improvements.

Strategy and Organization in Turbulent Environments

When environmental change becomes extremely rapid and ongoing, however, the sequential approach to strategy and organization exemplified by BPX may no longer be viable. An extended process of adaptation is not going to work—by the time a new strategy is generated and the organization restructured, the environment will have changed many times again.

In fact, many management scholars and practitioners have asserted in recent years that, in sufficiently turbulent environments, *ex ante* strategizing from the top becomes nearly pointless. The necessary information about markets and technologies is not directly available to top executives and it cannot be communicated to them and comprehended with sufficient speed and clarity to be used for top-down strategy formulation.

This position tends to confuse detailed, short-term tactics and formalized strategic plans (of the sort that get bound in fancy covers and then set on shelves, never to be read) with strategic thinking of the sort embodied in a strategy statement. Still, to the extent that the argument has some validity, then the nature of the design problem is altered in another interesting fashion.

In very turbulent environments, many of the specifics of the firm's strategy are likely to emerge from a multitude of decisions taken at various levels within the organization. The most that can be done from the top is the setting of broad strategic direction or intent. The design of the organization then determines in large measure what decisions will get made. Thus, reversing Chandler, strategy follows organization.

The solution, then, is to try to set the relatively slow-moving elements of the organization appropriately and then to take them more or less as given. What is appropriate in this context clearly involves some forecast of the evolution of the environment and of the basic strategic direction. Then the idea is to alter the strategy and some of the more formal but malleable elements of the organization to keep up with the changes in technology and markets.

Yet the design perspective remains valid, even in this context. Now, however, the role of the designer is to shape the relatively inert elements of the organization, like the culture, that will exert a persistent effect on the strategic and organizational choices that are made by the people in the firm, and to design a set of processes that will allow them to make good decisions. The designer should also set broad strategic intent to inform and shape the dispersed strategic decision-making. Finally, the designer must adapt the strategic intent and the controlled elements of the organization over time.

Nokia Corporation, the Finnish manufacturer of mobile telephones and network equipment, followed this latter model during the 1990s (Doornik and Roberts 2001). This was a decade that saw massive environmental change in the mobile telephony business: Deregulation and privatization, the entry of new service providers, an unforeseen explosion of demand, the emergence of digital technologies, and, at the end of the decade, the beginnings of convergence between the Internet and mobile phones. Nokia was the big winner in all this—it went from nearly bankrupt in 1992 to being Europe's most valuable company in 2000.

The top executives of Nokia set the broad intent that gave the context for the hundreds of dispersed decisions that became the firm's strategy. In 1992 the intent was expressed in four criteria—"Focused," "global," "telecommunications-oriented," and "high value-added"—under a vision that "voice will go wireless." This led the company to exit the broad range of businesses that had contributed 90 percent of its revenues only a few years previously and to focus on mobile handsets and network equipment. The leaders also set a stretch goal of doubling Nokia's market share by the end of the decade. When the objectives for 2000 had already been realized in 1997, the earlier strategic intent was replaced by the statement that Nokia wanted to become the leader in the most attractive telecom segments. (At the time, Motorola was the clear industry leader.) By 1999, Nokia had indeed become the industry leader in mobile phones, while the possibilities for the Internet being accessed via mobile phones were becoming evident. The 1997 objective in turn was replaced by the stated intent for Nokia to lead the development of the "mobile information society" by being the company that would "bring the Internet to everyone's pocket." Note that these are not strategies. While they do address the scope issue broadly, they are not very precise and they give little of the logic of why the firm is going to be able to create value or keep some of it. They do, however, set the context for strategy to emerge.

Meanwhile, the leadership of Nokia was very conscious of the importance of culture in motivating people to act in the needed ways. It thus worked hard to keep the crucial features of the culture fresh and effective, even as the company grew at 30 percent per annum and spread its activities around the world. As for the more formal elements of organization, these were kept very fluid: "We hate organization charts, and if forced to create one, we will draw it only in pencil!" Formal structure was shifted almost constantly to keep up with emerging needs and networks were used heavily to share knowledge and get work done. At the same time, the increasing size and complexity of the firm were met by an increased reliance on regularized processes in place of earlier informal routines that had differed across the firm.

BP and Nokia were both extremely successful in the 1990s, and they continue so today. Each adopted a distinct organizational model that was well suited to the environment in which the company operated and the strategy it pursued. The resulting fit between environment, strategy, and organization was key to the two firms' successes: Like the HBC and NWC centuries ago, and the firms that developed the multidivisional form at the start of the century, each solved the organizational design problem, and success followed.

Notes

1. The standard reference on these developments is Chandler (1977). See also Chandler (1962).
2. The discussion here draws heavily on Newman (1985, 1987). See also Newman (1991) for the history of the

company after the merger, and Spraakman (2002) for a more detailed discussion of aspects of the control systems at each company, before and after the merger.

3. For more on the concept of value and its applicability, see Milgrom and Roberts (1992: 35–9) and Roberts (1998).

2
Key Concepts for Organization Design

The problem of strategic choice and organizational design is, in principle, immensely complex. Selecting a strategy is complex already, but when one considers all the elements of an organization design, the problem becomes mindbogglingly complicated. Indeed, the "rugged landscapes" literature in strategic management (Levinthal 1997) is built around the idea that the problem is arbitrarily complicated, essentially without logic or regularity.

While this presumption captures some of the difficulties of finding a good design and, even more, of successful imitation, it is too strong. There is a logic underlying the idea of "fit." Certain strategies and organizational designs do fit one another and the environment, and thus produce good performance, and others do not. Moreover, there are frequently recognizable, understandable, and predictable relations among the environmental features and the choice variables of strategy and organization that determine which constellations of choices will do well and which are less likely to do so. These relations arise for both technological and behavioral reasons. Recognizing these relations and understanding their implications can guide the design problem.

Further, when these relations are present there will often be a quite restricted number of coherent patterns among the choice variables. The design problem then is to identify and select among well fitting, often quite distinct arrays of choices on the many dimensions. Thus, the problem becomes much more tractable when we have some understanding of the factors that generate fit.

We have already seen one example of these ideas. The HBC's organizational policies fit with one another and with the strategy and the environment (until the environment changed with the entry of the NWC). So too did the NWC's choices. They each had an internal logic to which they adhered in all crucial dimensions. Moreover, "mix and match" would not have worked. For example, performance pay would not have been particularly valuable at the old HBC, given that the range of allowed behaviors was tightly circumscribed. Thus, there was really a limited set of alternatives that were apt to be of interest.

But why are there a limited number of coherent patterns? What defines them? Why does mix and match not work?

The idea that strategy and structure need to fit with one another and with the business environment is an old one, as is the recognition that there may be several distinct patterns among these variables that are coherent, but not necessarily equally good. These ideas have, however, rarely been formalized. Recent developments in economics allow doing so in a simple, intuitive, and powerful way. The key ideas are *complementarity* among choice variables, *non-convexity* in the set of available choices, and *non-concavity* in the relationship between choice and performance. Complementarity gives rise to clear patterns of coherence in design. Non-convexity and non-concavity mean that there can multiple coherent patterns that are quite distinct. Together these ideas give great insight into the problems of designing and changing an organization. In this context we will especially explore some of the difficulties of organizational change. This leads to considering another feature, the extent of *tight coupling* in the design, which reflects the extent to which the organization is finely tuned to maximize performance against a particular strategy and environment or, instead, is designed to work reasonably well in the face of change.

Complementarity

Complementarity involves the interactions among changes in different variables in affecting performance. Consider any pair of variables that the designer might determine or influence in attempting to realize the firm's goals. Prices, service levels, frequency of product redesign, the debt–equity ratio, intensity of performance pay, the allocation of decision authority to subordinates, and aspects of the culture are all possible examples of such choice variables. Then the two choice variables are complements when *doing (more of) one of them increases the returns to doing (more of) the other*. In more mathematical language, the incremental or marginal return to one choice variable increases in the level of any complementary choice variable.[1] Thus, if one of a pair of complements is instituted or increased, it will be more attractive than before to introduce or increase the other.

For example, price and product quality are complements if higher quality makes demand less sensitive to price increases (less elastic). Then an improvement in quality renders a higher price more attractive because a price increase leads to a smaller fall in the quantity sold than it otherwise would.

In contrast, activities are substitutes if doing (more of) one reduces the attractiveness of doing (more of) the other. For example, direct monitoring of employees' behavior and the use of performance-based incentive pay may be substitutes. If introducing performance pay gives stronger incentives for good behavior, because the results of this behavior are rewarded, then value of monitoring to enforce the desired behavior directly is probably lower at the margin, and the level should be reduced.

Another example of substitution concerns make-to-stock versus make-to-order. Producing output in response to specific customer orders is a substitute for making to stock, where output is produced in advance of receiving orders and held in inventory until the demand materializes (Milgrom and Roberts 1988a). The claim here is not just the obvious one that these two approaches seem to be alternatives. Rather, if we look at the fraction of output produced under each regime, then the higher is the fraction made to order, the more attractive it is to increase this fraction even more (and, correspondingly, to lower the fraction made to stock). The reason is that producing to stock is subject to economies of scale with regard to the level of inventory needed to maintain reliability in meeting demand as it emerges. Consequently, if it is worthwhile producing a little bit to stock, it is even more worthwhile to do the next increment (and correspondingly cut the share made to order).

35

Key Concepts

These ideas of complements and substitutes can be extended to relations among aspects of the environment and the designer's choice variables. For example, a choice variable is complementary with an element of the environment if an increase in the level of the environmental variable increases the returns to introducing or increasing the choice variable. So, if income tax rates are lowered, it may be more attractive to increase the use of explicit performance pay, since the cost to the firm of providing a given intensity of incentives is reduced. Performance pay and the negative of the tax rate are complements. The ideas can also be extended to groups of choice variables: Several choice variables are complementary if each of them is a complement for each of the others.

The substitution and complementarity relations among choice variables give structure to the problems of organizational design. In particular, complementarity results in very clear patterns, with all the complementary choice variables tending to be done together and at comparable levels.

This may be intuitively clear, but to see the logic more clearly, consider another example of complements: the flexibility of a firm's manufacturing system and the variety of its product offerings. We might measure flexibility by the speed with which the firm can change over from producing one product to another, or by the (inverse of the) cost of changeovers. Variety could be represented either by the breadth of the product line at a point in time or by the frequency of product changes. In any case, flexibility and breadth should be complements in normal circumstances. Broadening the product line presumably increases the total demand facing the firm but lowers the potential sales of each individual product as customers sort themselves among the wider set of alternatives. Unless average inventory levels are to increase dramatically, this means shorter production runs and more frequent changeovers. This, in turn, increases the value of being able to do changeovers more quickly and cheaply—of more flexibility. (In general, doing more of any activity and lowering the activity's marginal cost are always complements.) So having more variety increases the returns to increased flexibility, and the two are complements. Conversely, a more flexible production system lowers the cost of realizing the demand advantages of having a broader product line, so the relationship holds in that direction as well. This symmetry is no accident—it is always true that if the returns to increasing one variable are nondecreasing in the level of a second variable, then the returns to increasing the second are also nondecreasing in the level of the first.

Complementarity gives rise to systems effects, with the whole being more than the sum of the parts (in a precise sense). Consider increasing each of a collection of choice variables. Suppose we look at the effect on performance of increasing each one in isolation, without raising the others, and then sum these estimates. Then complementarity among the activities means that the total effect on performance of increasing all the variables together exceeds the sum of these individual impacts. This is because complementarity means precisely that, once we have raised the level of one of the activities, the impact of raising any of the others is now greater than it would have been when the first variable was at a lower level.

Indeed, when the variables are complements, it is quite possible that changing any one of them alone would worsen performance, yet changing all together would increase it substantially. In this regard, Eric Brynjolfsson and his colleagues[2] have studied the impact on productivity of the huge investments of the last decades in information technology. They find that the costly investments had little impact on productivity on their own, which matches Nobel Laureate Robert Solow's quip that one saw computers everywhere except in the productivity statistics. However, when the investments are matched with complementary changes in the organization design, there are very significant productivity effects. Neither the investments nor the organizational changes might be worthwhile on their own, but together they have a huge positive effect on performance.

Coherence among a set of complementary choice variables tends to result in all of them being set at a high level or all at a low level. Consider the flexibility and variety example. When we allow for choices to be either high or low on each dimension, we might expect that there would typically be two coherent choice patterns in the variety/flexibility problem: Lots of variety and lots of flexibility, or little of either. This is because it will be worthwhile to bear the costs of flexibility only if the desired variety is high, and a high level of variety will be worthwhile only if the production system is quite flexible.

The automobile industry provides an example of each pattern (see Figure 2). Famously, in the first decades of the twentieth century, Henry Ford would sell you any car you wanted, as long as it was a black Model T. Thus, Ford's product line was very narrow, and it did not change often—Ford kept the Model T in production for decades. On the flexibility side, Ford's plant was completely specialized to the Model T. It was so inflexible that it had to be gutted when the switch was finally made to the Model A. These features of organizational design and strategic choice obviously fit with one another.

On the other hand, Toyota in the last decades of the twentieth century had extremely flexible factories and a broad product line. For example, in the early 1990s Toyota's Kamigo engine plant on any given day produced over 350 different engine/transmission/fuel-system combinations (including both single and dual camshaft engines) on a single line, in batches of one—each successive item coming off the line was different from the one before. The product line was broad, and the factory was very flexible.

Each of these patterns has an internal logic. Further, each was, in its environment, arguably optimal. Ford's strategy allowed it to build and dominate an industry: At one point more than half the cars in existence were Ford Model Ts. In the 1990s, when flexible automation was much more readily available than it had been in the early years of the century and when customer tastes had become more diverse, Toyota was viewed as the leading firm in the global auto industry and as perhaps the best manufacturing firm in the world.

While there may be multiple coherent patterns for complementary organizational features, what typically does not work is "mix and match" among elements of different patterns. The high variety/low flexibility combination is probably not even worth considering in most manufacturing contexts. Either production runs would be kept short, implying immense costs from the frequent changeovers, or long production runs would be employed to avoid costly changeovers, implying that the firm would

Key Concepts

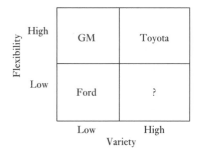

Figure 2. Complementarity can lead to discrete coherent patterns

face financing gigantic inventories. The other off-diagonal point is less problematic in some ways, but can be disastrously expensive. It is, in essence, where General Motors found itself in the 1980s. In that decade GM spent more than the combined market values of Toyota and Nissan on flexible automation and other, related capital expenditures that increased potential flexibility. It did not, however, adequately speed up its product development processes, adjust its product mix and production scheduling, reform its human resource practices, and take a variety of other actions that are complementary with increased production flexibility. Indeed, its assembly lines still often produced only a single model of car, even when the machinery would have permitted producing several models on a single line. GM at the end of that decade set a new record for the amount of money lost by any corporation in one year, and then it broke the record the next year. While other factors contributed to this disaster, GM's long, painful decline through the 1980s was in significant part due to this mismatch in its organizational design choices.

40

In fact, GM was far from alone in making these mistakes. For example, Jaikumar's work (1986) on the adoption and use of the innovation of computer numerically controlled (CNC) machine tools in the United States and Japan gives another example of failure to adapt fully. He found that Japanese firms had rapidly seen the complementarity between the flexibility afforded by the CNC tools, shorter production runs, and greater variety. They were producing an increased variety of products in very small batches. In the United States, however, many firms initially used the highly flexible manufacturing equipment just as they had used the older, inflexible machines, to produce huge numbers of single items.

Another, richer example of complementarity among choices involves the unique set of practices that mark the Lincoln Electric Company (Berg and Fast 1975, see also Milgrom and Roberts 1995). Lincoln Electric's primary product is arc-welding equipment and the consumables, such as flux, used in welding. Lincoln long dominated the industry in the United States, leading major firms such as General Electric and Westinghouse to exit rather than attempt further to compete with it. Moreover, Lincoln enjoyed an unbeaten record of performance—it was profitable every quarter, year in and year out, for almost a century, and its U.S. operations have never lost money or had a layoff. The basis for Lincoln's success was its execution on a strategy of pursuing ever higher productivity and lower costs and then passing on some of these benefits to customers in lower prices. It was able to improve productivity and costs so consistently because of a set of organizational policies that supported these aims. Together, there was a high complementarity between its strategy and organization and among the elements of its organization design.

The centerpiece of Lincoln's organizational design is very extensive use of piece-rate compensation. Whenever possible, workers are paid piece rates, that is, a fixed amount for each unit on which the individual worker completes the assigned tasks. Indeed, at one point typists were even paid by the keystroke (until one was discovered sitting her desk at the lunch break, repeatedly hitting the same key while she ate) and overhead crane operators were paid by the number of objects moved (until safety concerns arose about the speed and height at which heavy items were being moved around the plant).

Piece rates give very strong, straightforward incentives, not just to work hard but also to seek ways to increase one's output further. They are easy to understand and administer. At one time they were a very common method for paying industrial workers. Yet they are now a comparative rarity. There are several reasons for this. First, if the pace of work cannot vary between individuals, then the possibility for responding to the piece-rate incentives is limited and they are not of much use. Thus, individual piece rates have little value in such contexts as assembly line operations or team-organized work. The second difficulty is that by giving strong incentives for quantity, a piece-rate system discourages spending time and effort on other valuable activities. Most directly, if skimping on quality allows the worker to increase the number of pieces made, there is a perverse quality incentive from piece rates. Moreover, other desirable activities that cannot be paid at piece rate—such as helping other workers or accepting temporary reassignments to deal with emergencies—are discouraged. The third difficulty is that workers often distrust managers and fear that the piece rates will be lowered if they respond fully to the incentives that the piece rates appear to offer and they thus reveal just how productive they can be. Consequently the piece rates are not as effective motivators as they would otherwise be. (This may in part explain why unions have usually opposed piece rates: They fear that some workers will respond and then all will be subjected to higher standards.) Finally, there is the problem of selling all that might be made and of maintaining the system when sales slump.

Lincoln responds to each of these difficulties with policies and processes that make the piece rates more effective. The production system is designed to allow work to be individually paced, so that workers will have the freedom to increase their output rates in response to the incentives. To facilitate this, significant amounts of work-in-process inventory are tolerated. To overcome the "multi-tasking" problems with quality and cooperation, Lincoln uses an individual bonus scheme. The amount of the individual bonus is determined by the employee's supervisor and is based on the quality of the employee's output and such factors as perceived cooperativeness. These bonuses normally double the employee's base earnings from the piece rate. In addition, each employee's name is stencilled on each welding machine on which he or she works, so that responsibility for quality problems can be assigned. If a piece is found to be defective on inspection, the responsible worker must repair it on his or her own time. If a machine fails in the field as a result of a worker's skimping on quality, the worker's bonus is docked by as much as 10 percent.

Lincoln has also adopted a whole range of organizational features that help overcome the trust problems and thereby make the piece rates credible. First, the company promises that the rates will not be adjusted unless there is a change in the product or work methods, and it allows an employee to challenge any new rates and have them recomputed.[3] What makes this promise credible, however? First, the firm is essentially employee-owned. For a long time, the employees and managers and the founding Lincoln family held most of the stock, and when Lincoln issued new equity to the public in the mid 1990s, it was offered without voting rights. This ownership arrangement reduces the danger than investors who do not understand the value of the commitment or are too impatient will force reductions in the rates. Second, early in its history the company adopted a set of measures that encourages two-way communication between workers and management. Such schemes are not uncommon today, but they were an innovative rarity when Lincoln adopted them. Third, Lincoln was run by the founder and his brother until 1965 and then, for the next three decades, by career Lincoln employees. They were personally committed to the system, and they well understood its logic and the need to honor the workers' trust. Fourth, Lincoln has a number of policies that are symbolic of the relative positions of management and workers, including no assigned parking spaces for executives, low executive compensation levels, no separate executive dining facilities, and Spartan managerial offices. These factors increase employees' trust of the management and reduced the danger of an "us versus them" mentality.

Finally, to deal with the problems of matching output to demand, Lincoln normally rations the time that workers can be at their posts while demanding mandatory overtime when it is needed.

Each of these features of Lincoln's design may or may not be attractive on their own, but together they are powerful because they complement one another. Work-in-process inventory is often viewed as anathema in modern, "lean" production systems, but Lincoln's tolerating it permits the flexibility in the pacing of individuals' work that must be present to allow workers to respond to the piece rates. Absent offsetting incentives for quality and cooperation, piece rates can be disastrous, and so Lincoln's piece rates are made more effective by the complementary bonus scheme. The effectiveness of the piece rates is also increased by the high levels of trust that are supported by the open communication policies; the ownership structure; the long-term, internally recruited leadership of the firm; and the symbolic acts and policies. The relative rarity of some of these features suggests that they are not valuable in more standard models of organization. They are, however, important elements of the model that underlies Lincoln's success. Finally, Lincoln attracts and retains employees who like the Lincoln model, and this makes it more effective. Judging from interviews with Lincoln's employees, they are oriented towards material success and are willing to work hard to achieve it, they are attracted by the individual responsibility and autonomy that Lincoln offers, and they do not want a union.

Lincoln's organization permits it to achieve remarkably high levels of productivity, which is key to realizing its low-cost strategy. But Lincoln actually aims not just for low costs, but also for constantly reducing costs. A major potential barrier to doing this would be the workers' concern that increasing productivity might endanger employment, because the same output could be produced by fewer people. This helps explain another of Lincoln's very unusual policies, a promise to avoid layoffs. It has stuck by this promise even in severe recessions, when it put production workers to painting the factory rather than lay them off. This policy also probably contributes to the trust that supports the credibility of the piece rates. So another policy that might be of questionable attractiveness in isolation becomes very valuable in the context of what Lincoln seeks to do and how it seeks to do it.

Thus, the features at Lincoln together yield much more than would be estimated by looking at the impact of doing any one of them in isolation, exactly because they are complementary with one another.

As this example suggests, the range of variables over which complementarity can spread can be very broad and the corresponding patterns very rich. Other examples can be found in the literature, especially in the context of human resource management (HRM). Pfeffer (1996) and Baron and Kreps (1999) have argued for the existence of complementarities among rich sets of HRM practices. Baron, Burton, and Hannan (1996) have found evidence for these complementarities in the practices of Silicon Valley start-ups, identifying limited numbers of patterns that are actually adopted out of the thousands that are conceivable. Ichniowski, Shaw, and Prennushi (1997) have documented patterns in the HRM systems used in specialty steel finishing lines that are best explained in terms of widespread complementarities among manufacturing and HRM practices. Bresnahan, Brynjolfsson, and Hitt (2002) have found complementarities among investments in information technology, workplace organization, product innovation, and a number of HRM practices in a large sample of U.S. industrial firms.

Perhaps the broadest set of complementarities studied so far involves traditional mass production versus modern, lean manufacturing (Milgrom and Roberts 1990*b*, 1995).[4] Mass production and lean manufacturing represent two coherent patterns of choices over a very large set of policy variables, where a move of any one element from the mass production model practice to the lean model is complementary with the corresponding move on each of the other variables. (See Tables 1 and 2.)

While examining all the interactions among such a rich set of variables would be too much of a digression, we can sketch some of them. The connections between the flexibility of capital equipment, the length of production runs, the levels of inventory, the breadth of the product line, and the frequency of product changes have already been discussed. The approach to marketing and to communicating with customers is then driven largely by need for them to fit with the product strategy. The frequency of changes in products drives the value of speed in the product development process. Drawn-out, sequential approaches to product development work in the Mass Production model but are infeasible in the Modern model, which requires the use of cross-functional teams to get new products designed and manufactured speedily. Frequent changes in products and frequent process innovations favor having a highly skilled workforce that can both handle the complexity and solve problems as they emerge (rather than waiting for the managers and engineers to do this), so ability and training are complementary with innovation.

Key Concepts

Table 1. Characteristic features of mass production

Logic: The transfer line, interchangeable parts, and economies of scale

Specialized machinery
Long production runs
Infrequent product changes
Narrow product lines
Mass marketing
Low worker skill requirements
Specialized skill jobs
Central expertise and coordination
Hierarchic planning and control
Vertical internal communication
Sequential product development
Static optimization
Accent on volume
High inventories
Supply management
Make to stock, limited communication with customers
Market dealings with employees and suppliers
Vertical integration

To take full advantage of the workforce's abilities, it is then more worthwhile to elicit their involvement in developing process improvements, so empowering the workers and looking for continuous improvement are complementary with their being more skilled. With skilled workers who are particularly knowledgeable about the firm's activities and needs, it is desirable to establish long-term employment relations in order to help retain this valuable human capital. Meanwhile, the flexibility of the manufacturing equipment reduces the dangers of lock-in to particular

Key Concepts

Table 2. Characteristic features of modern manufacturing

Logic: Flexibility, speed, economies of scope, and core competencies

Flexible machines, low set-up costs
Short production runs
Frequent product improvements
Broad product lines
Targeted markets
Highly skilled, cross-trained workers
Worker initiative
Local information and self-regulation
Horizontal communication
Cross-functional development teams
Continuous improvement
Accent on cost and quality
Low inventories
Demand management
Make to order, extensive communications with customers
Long-term, trust-based relationships
Reliance on outside suppliers

---

suppliers and customers and so favors external sourcing relative to internal supply. This is further supported by the adoption of long-term relationships with suppliers.

Modern, lean manufacturing is supplanting mass production in many industries and having strongly positive effects on performance. This is an example of one coherent pattern of strategic and organizational choices becoming more effective than another that had previously seemed best. Such changes occur in response to changes in the environment. Complementarity is also valuable in understanding when different patterns will be more or less effective.

Key Concepts

When choice variables are complementary, any environmental change that increases the attractiveness of raising one of the variables tends to result in all of them being increased. This gives rise to systematic, predictable patterns in how the choices move in response to environmental changes. To see this, suppose, for example, that a set of initial choices among a group of complementary productive inputs actually maximizes performance. This means that, in particular, no decrease or increase in any of the input levels from this point is worthwhile. Suppose then that the cost of one of the inputs falls by enough that it is now worthwhile to raise this variable. But doing so raises the attractiveness of an increase in each of the complementary choice variables, and so we expect that all the other input usage levels will increase in response to the increase in the first one. This, in turn, raises the returns to increasing the level of the first input further, and doing so again increases the returns to raising the others. The final result is that all the choice variables have increased in response to an environmental shift that initially favored increasing only one of them.

Applying this logic, the move from mass production to lean manufacturing that has been occurring in the last decades could be a response to a number of environmental changes. Certainly the cost of flexible manufacturing equipment—computer-aided design and manufacturing equipment, numerically controlled machinery, and industrial robots—has fallen: Indeed, these did not exist until recently. The first effect of this is to encourage the use of more flexible manufacturing systems, and the adoption of these then favors the other elements of the overall shift. Also, the cost of communicating with customers and suppliers has fallen with improvements in communication and information technology, which favors a make-to-order approach and, indirectly, all the features that are complementary with it. It may also be possible that, with rising incomes, consumer tastes have shifted towards greater variety, and this too would favor the move to the new model. Again, the increases in the level of formal education in the workforce that have occurred over the decades would favor a shift to making more use of workers' brains (and not just their brawn), and this too is complementary with the other elements of the lean model. Finally, as a firm's suppliers and competitors move to the new model, its incentives to do the same are increased.

This raises the issue of moving between patterns of strategic and organizational design change. The mathematics of complementarity indicates that, in a system of complements, any change in the environment that favors increasing a particular variable then also leads to increases in all the other variables. Thus, when the choices are complementary, the direction of desired change is unambiguous. Yet, organizational change seems, in fact, to be very difficult. The reasons why this is so are many, but one element of the answer lies in understanding more deeply the nature of the relationship linking the environment, the strategy, and the organizational design to performance. Here is where the second idea, failures of convexity and concavity, comes in.

Non-convexity and Non-concavity

Traditional models in economics and the social and managerial sciences have usually made particular mathematical assumptions—formally, convexity of the choice set and concavity of the objective—that were borrowed from the physical sciences. They were used because they facilitated analysis of the models by the methods of differential calculus. Such models often underlie the intuition that both scholars and practicing managers use in trying to understand the world. Yet, these mathematical assumptions are often quite inappropriate when dealing with problems of strategic and organizational choice, and the intuition they yield often is quite wrong. Replacing them opens up important new insights.

The first assumption, convexity of the set of alternatives, is that if two options are available, then any intermediate choice is also possible. In particular, this assumption implies that choices are infinitely divisible. The second assumption, concavity of the objective function, deals with nature of the relationship between choice and performance for a given environment. In the case where choice is represented by a single variable, concavity means that the impact on performance of successive increments to the choice is decreasing, perhaps ultimately becoming negative. More generally, it requires that if two distinct choices lead to the same performance, then any choice intermediate between the two would lead to a higher level of performance. These properties (plus some boundary conditions that were also typically assumed) imply that there is a unique performance-maximizing choice for any environment.

This sort of situation is illustrated in Figure 3, where the relation is graphed between choice (assumed to be one-dimensional to allow graphical representation) and performance for a given environment. As the choice

Key Concepts

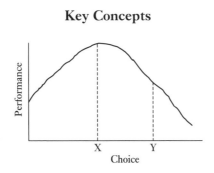

Figure 3. The classic model of choice and performance

increases, the realized performance increases, reaches a maximum at choice marked X, and then declines.

The first implication of this sort of modeling has already been noted: There is a single best way to do things (denoted X in the figure). Further, if the current choice is not at the best point, then small changes in its direction will improve performance. For example, at the point Y in Figure 3, any move towards X improves performance. More generally, if there is some other point that offers better performance, then a small adjustment in the choice in the direction of the new point, will be performance enhancing. Thus, the task of finding the best choice is relatively simple, because local experiments that improve performance will eventually lead to the optimum. This remains true even when there are multiple dimensions to the choice. When choice is multidimensional, concavity means that the optimum can be found by very uncoordinated, local, decentralized experimentation and search. Change any element of the design, on its own, by a small amount in a direction that increases performance, and continue to make such adjustments as long as any are possible. Then when the process stops, the performance-maximizing design has been found. So there is no

53

coordination problem in decentralized search for improvements in performance.

A second, subtler implication concerns the task of maintaining the optimal choice as the environment changes. Suppose changes in the environment reshape the connection between choice and performance, so that the optimal choice changes, but that the general concave shape of the relationship is maintained. Then it seems a relatively simple matter to track the changes and keep near the moving target. A little local experimentation, *kaizen*-like, will reveal whether an improvement is possible and in what direction to change. Start moving the choice in that direction, and when no further improvement is possible, the new best point has been found.

Suppose, for example, the initial relationship between choice and performance is shown by the solid curve in Figure 4, and the firm manages to put itself at X, the optimal strategy and organization. Now suppose the environment changes, so that the dotted line reflects the connection of choice to performance. Performance at X has not changed in this example, although in general it might have. The new optimum is at X', involving a higher level of the choice. Experimenting by changing the choice just a little at X signals that the new optimum lies at higher levels, because increasing the choice increases performance, and decreasing it hurts performance.

The problem with such models and the intuition they generate is that the maintained assumptions underlying them are quite implausible in thinking about strategic and organizational choice. Indivisibilities abound (the firm cannot have a fractional number of plants; it either enters a market or it does not). These are inconsistent with

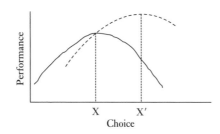

Figure 4. Shifting the relationship between choice and performance

convexity. Further and more crucially, increasing returns to scale, learning effects, and indivisibilities are all inconsistent with concavity of the objective. For example, with increasing returns, zero profits would result both from not operating at all and from operating at some positive, break-even level of output. Yet, operating at an intermediate level would produce losses, because the costs per unit are higher there. This directly counters the definition of concavity, so performance is not a concave function of choice. In fact, if there are multiple elements to the choice and these show strong, pervasive complementarities, then mathematically it is impossible to have the conditions that underlie these models.

A number of important insights into management problems follow from recognizing these simple facts and embracing the possibility, and even the likelihood, that convexity and concavity will not hold.

The first is a basis for understanding why some firms seem to be constantly changing their organizations, going from centralized decision-making to decentralized and then back again, apparently aimlessly. This has puzzled numerous observers of organizations and has been raised

55

as an objection to the very idea that organizational design is actually done in any rational way. In fact, this can be a very effective response to indivisibilities.

The key lies in recognizing that one who has the authority over a decision is inherently indivisible; either the authority rests with headquarters or it is delegated to an operating unit. Now suppose that the organizational designer cannot directly control some of the less formal elements of the design, like the operation of personal networks or some of the elements of corporate culture. Instead, these evolve in ways determined by the formal aspects of the organization, including the allocation of decision authority. In particular, suppose that if decision-making is centralized certain norms weaken, while the reverse is true under decentralization. These norms might govern behavior like risk-taking or the allocation of effort among tasks. Finally, suppose that the norms are what really matters for performance and that the best performance comes when the norms are at some middling level of strength, between the limits to which they would tend under permanent centralization or permanent decentralization. Then if organizational change is costly, the optimal solution is to alternate intermittently between centralized and decentralized decision-making. When the norms drift too far in the direction induced by the current allocation of decision-making authority, performance starts to suffer. The solution is to switch to the other allocation, thereby reversing both the drift in the strength of the norm and the declining performance. The analogy is with a furnace being only on or off, and the temperature in the house drifting in the direction determined by the state of the furnace. When the house gets too hot, the thermostat shuts off the furnace, and when the temperature falls far enough, it turns it back on.[5]

A second, more fundamental, major insight is that there may be multiple choices (or patterns of choice, when there are many choice variables) that are coherent. Yet, among these multiple coherent patterns, some may yield much better performance than others.

Here "coherence" has a double meaning. First, it requires that no small adjustment in the set of choices can increase performance—the choice is "locally" best. So if a choice is coherent, then *kaizen*-type seeking for a little better way to do things, even if coordinated across decision-makers, yields no improvement (unless the environment changes). Second, when choice is multidimensional, then no change, however big, in just some proper subset of the choice variables can improve performance. Thus, if the organization is at a coherent point, even if it shows poor performance, it is still possible that managers cannot find a better solution unless *every* element of strategy and organizational design is changed in a coordinated fashion.

The first sort of coherence—local optimality—is illustrated in Figure 5. The horizontal axis shows the choice (assumed again to be one-dimensional to allow graphical representation), and the vertical the resulting performance. The point Z is not coherent—indeed, any small change from Z improves performance. There are two distinct points, X and Y, from which no small change yields an improvement and so which meet this local optimality criterion for coherence. Yet, Y clearly has better performance. This could not happen if the relationship between choice and performance were concave, because then there could be only one local maximum.

Key Concepts

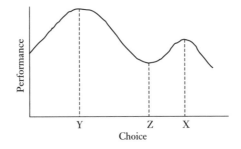

Figure 5. A non-concave performance relationship

To illustrate the second aspect of coherence, consider a situation where organizational performance is the minimum of the performance levels of the different units in the firm. This is essentially the case when output is produced by different people or units working in sequence, each doing an operation, as in an assembly line. (Note that in such a situation, the actions are complementary: One person working harder is more valuable if others do the same.) Then any pattern where all the units are all operating at the same level has the second element of coherence: No change, however large, in any subset of the activity levels can increase performance. This is because some of the activities will not have been changed and so, even if we increase all the others, the minimum is still the same, and overall performance is unchanged. For example, if there are three organizational units, all operating at level 2, then the organizational performance is $\min\{2, 2, 2\} = 2$. Increasing the first two activities to level 3 still leaves organizational performance at $2 = \min\{3, 3, 2\}$. Actually increasing performance requires all the activity levels to increase. (Note, however, that small coordinated changes can be performance enhancing in this

58

set-up, so we do not necessarily have the first element of coherence.)

More dramatic, and more important managerially, are situations where there are multiple patterns that meet both tests for coherence. To illustrate these we need to consider several choice variables—at least two. Rather than drawing the relationship between the two dimensions of choice and performance in a three-dimensional picture, we look just at a contour map, as in Figure 6. The map there shows a "mountain" with two "peaks," one to the northeast of the other, and a "high pass" across a ridge between them. The curves connect choices with equal performance, and the arrows point "uphill."

There are two points here that are local maxima, each of which lies inside one of the smallest oval contour lines. One (marked A) has relatively low levels of the choices and the other, B, has both choices at higher levels. They are the peaks. Each of A and B has the first element of coherence in that any small change, even in both choice

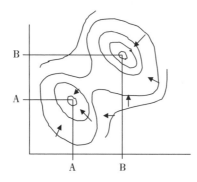

Figure 6. Non-concavity allows multiple, distinct coherent points

variables, lowers performance. They each also have the second property, that no move parallel to an axis (i.e. no change in just one of the choices, no matter how large) can improve performance. Yet, either peak might have a higher level of performance than the other. If the firm finds itself at the wrong one, then any improvement requires large, coordinated changes on all (i.e. both) dimensions of choice.

An important implication for management is that, when complementarities and non-concavities abound, decentralized local experimentation is not enough. Search and change must be coordinated. This does not mean they must be driven from above, in a command and control way. But leaving individual managers in charge of particular elements of the organization to find improvements on their own can fail miserably, as can experimentation that is limited in scope. Both can fail to find the better solution and instead leave the firm stuck at an inferior coherent point. This means either that realizing the best design must be centrally coordinated—there needs to be a designer—or else that the different parties making the choices need to communicate intensively with one another.

Why or how would a firm end up on the wrong peak? One answer is that it simply made the wrong choice. A deeper answer is that it can get trapped in the inferior position by environmental change. For example, the environmental change brought on by the entry of the NWC suddenly rendered the HBC's model inappropriate, even though it had worked very well for more than a century. Strikingly, however, the change need not be radical or discontinuous. Continuous change in the environment

Key Concepts

can, in the presence of non-concave performance functions, result in discrete, substantial changes in the optimum configuration of strategy and organization.

Consider Figure 7. The vertical and horizontal axes are as in Figures 3 through 5 and show choices and the resulting performance. (If possible, however, think of choice as being multidimensional, as in Figure 6.) On the third axis is time. Over time, as technology, the behavior of competitors, suppliers, and customers, or other factors gradually change, the curve linking choice and performance changes too. The diagram plots the relationship at three points in time. Initially, at time T_1, the choice of Y_1 is best. X_1 is a coherent choice, but worse than Y_1. As time and change gradually proceed, the two coherent points move somewhat, from Y_1 to Y_2 and then Y_3, and from X_1

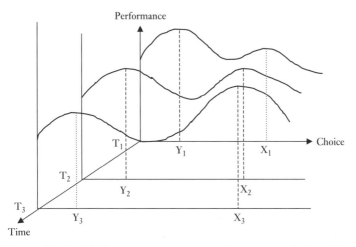

Figure 7. A shifting, non-concave performance relationship results in discontinuous change in the optimum

to X_2 and X_3. A firm that started at Y_1 could probably track the change in the locally optimal configuration and adjust its strategy and organization on an ongoing basis, moving to Y_2 and then to Y_3 without too much difficulty. But note that, over time, the attractiveness of the Y positions is slipping relative to the X's. It need not be that Y_3 has lower performance than Y_1 offered, although this might be the case. But if the technological, competitive, regulatory, or social changes favor the X configuration enough, then it will pass the Y's in performance terms.

In the figure, at time T_2, the X_2 configuration is as good as Y_2. By T_3, X_3 is clearly better than Y_3. A firm that was following its basic Y strategy, skillfully adjusting it as needed at the margins, would then suddenly find that it was poorly adapted to the environment: There is a much different way, and it is now a much better way. The firm is then faced with sticking with its old ways, which may not ultimately be viable, or undertaking radical strategic and organizational change.

Such changes are not easy, which can be seen as one of the reasons for dysfunctional organizational inertia, that is, failure to adopt changes that would seem worthwhile. To bring them about requires several elements of leadership.

First, there must be *strategic recognition*. The most basic problem is to recognize the need or opportunity for change. The HBC's leaders failed to appreciate the need for change to meet (let alone deter) the entry of the NWC. Similarly, Jack Smith, the former CEO of General Motors, has said that the automaker was "in denial" through the 1980s, failing, somewhat willfully perhaps, to see that the Japanese competitors had fundamentally changed the nature of the business, and thus to see the need for basic change in GM's strategy and organization. Here, past success becomes a trap.

The second required element of leadership is *vision*, in order to see the other, better pattern, at least in broad outline. This first requires an understanding of what sort of change is required. When American auto company managers and engineers went to Japan in the late 1970s and early 1980s, they saw lots of differences between practices in the Japanese auto plants and theirs. There were no visible work-in-process inventories; the workers could (and did) stop the production line to deal with problems at any time by pulling a cord; there seemed to be no rework area where mistakes in assembly could be corrected (the rework area was typically a quarter of the floor space in a traditional U.S. auto plant); the day began with exercises and a company song; workers wore uniforms; there were teams for various purposes; and so on. Which of these mattered? Why? It took a long time to figure this out. Lacking a good theory about which of these mattered and how the pieces fit together, the American experts brought back a few of the novel features, especially quality circles. These flopped resoundingly because they were not supported by a commitment to quality, by workers' being empowered to experiment with and change work methods, and by guaranteed employment (so that workers did not need to fear that improving productivity would hurt employment), all of which are complements to getting workers involved in improving things.

What this points to is the need for theory. Of course, the problem is even greater when organizational innovation is required, rather than just mimicry. Then the organization must engage in the search for a new way. The sort of global search that is involved in developing radically different models has little in common with local search for improvements within a given paradigm, and even firms that are very good at the latter may struggle with the former. Still, theory can help by suggesting where to focus the search.

In this regard, it is important to accentuate that the new way need not be understood in all its complexity from the outset. Indeed, what we would expect is that, as opportunities arise, companies adjust their policies and add activities that are complementary with what they already have. Thus, they would evolve towards patterns of strategy and organization that are marked by a high degree of fit among complementary activities, even though initially no one fully comprehended all the complexity of the design that finally emerged. Lincoln Electric's system, in fact, developed over many years, with features that complemented what was already in place being added seriatim. The piece rates were instituted when the company started at the end of the nineteenth century, the bonus system was implemented in 1934, and the no-layoff policy was not formalized until 1958. What was constant was the vision of James Lincoln, the company's long-serving president, who believed strongly in providing individual incentives to increase productivity.

Similarly, the Toyota Production System (TPS), which is the basis for the modern, lean manufacturing model, developed incrementally (Ohno 1988). As postwar Japan emerged from defeat and destruction and Toyota sought to resume automobile manufacturing, the creators of TPS, Eiji Toyoda and Taiichi Ohno, saw that they could not compete on the basis of mass production, because the Japanese market was too small and the demands (for trucks, limos, taxis, etc.) already too fragmented. They then started building a new approach that might allow them to succeed without the efficiencies of large-scale operations. The basic theme was to save costs through the ruthless elimination of *muda*—waste—and the crucial insight was to view inventory as *muda*. Efforts to reduce inventory led to the just-in-time approach to parts supply. This both raised the importance of flexibility and revealed the possibilities for improving quality when problems could be caught immediately and corrected. Doing so, however, required empowering workers to act on local information. Eventually, the whole modern model was developed.

The third element of leadership needed in bringing about change is the ability to *communicate*, to explain the new way, what its general features are, and how to get there. The leader cannot in fact design the new system in all its detail and implement it single-handedly. People throughout the organization must be involved. So they must understand what needs to be accomplished. With communication there must also be *persuasion*, to convince people of the need for change and of the gains that it will yield.

Finally, there must be *courage* to try for the distant and difficult and not to turn back when the transition is not easy and performance actually suffers. Such performance declines are almost inevitable during a major change operation. First, unless the firm can nimbly and accurately leap from peak to peak, the path from one to the other must lead downward in terms of the maximum attainable performance. Refer again to Figure 5: If the organization cannot instantly change from X to Y, but must instead track over the points between, performance goes down. Such tracking would reflect an inability to change people, processes, and culture instantaneously. Even if the firm can execute giant leaps (which means changing everything overnight, including values, norms, and reputations!), unless it is extremely accurate in its jumps, it will likely come down some distance from the other peak. Then performance will not be all that was expected.

Moreover, there is reason to expect that a firm in the midst of a major change will not realize even the maximum performance possible from its imperfectly aligned organization. Thus, it will be below the curve, rather than on it. First, the organization's resources and attention are diverted from getting work done to figuring out what to do and how to do it. Second, even once "what to do" is determined, it is not likely to be done with full efficiency. Changing established patterns of behavior means learning how to operate in new ways and how to communicate with new people about different things. This is likely to be a slow, costly process. Third, resistance to changes that endanger the positions, power, perquisites, and pay of those in the organization may further degrade performance. Change is almost always a threat to at least some of the people in the organization. It threatens to break the implicit contracts that have guided past behavior, removing the promised rewards; it upsets the established allocation of power; it may destroy the value of established skills and positions; and it may put jobs and careers at risk. In these circumstances, people may actively resist the changes. At a minimum, they are likely to eat up a lot of their time and others', worrying about what will happen. This makes undertaking change costly.

Further, the prospect of change creates opportunities to influence the new distribution of resources, power, and rewards, and members of the firm will have every incentive to attempt to ensure that they and their allies do well. They will expend time and resources campaigning to have the change structured to their advantage, and they will misrepresent information to twist decisions in their favor. So simply putting change on the agenda creates influence costs that would otherwise not arise. This may mean that changes that would, organizational politics aside, be worthwhile are actually delayed or avoided.

This logic suggests one reason that change is easier to accomplish in a crisis situation. The gains to resisting change or attempting to influence its shape and direction are dependent on the continued survival of the firm. Then, worsening prospects and the threat of collapse can reduce the influence costs occasioned by strategic and organizational change. This means that changes that would not be worthwhile to attempt in good times will actually be implemented when survival is in danger (Schaefer 1998).

Tight and Loose Coupling

The difficulties of organizational change imply that there is value in an organizational design that will perform reasonably well in a variety of environments, even if it is not perfectly adapted to the current context. This factor introduces a trade-off in the design problem. In a static context with a given environment, solving the design problem largely involves recognizing complementarities among different features and adjusting the different aspects of the design to take advantage of these. When the inherent uncertainty about the environment is recognized, the designer must also decide on how tightly to link the different aspects of the design. A system that is "tightly coupled," so that changing any aspect of the design or the environment will compromise performance severely unless numerous other aspects are also adjusted, may work very well if all goes according to plan. A tight fit among strategic and structural choices and with the environment can yield great performance. The danger comes when an unintended or unforeseen change knocks everything out of alignment by forcing a change in some choice variables or making the previous choices no longer fit with the environment. Performance then may suffer dramatically. Further, finding a new pattern may be difficult, and implementing it even more so.

Thus, a less fully optimized, more "loosely coupled" design may offer flexibility and be favored when changes in the environment or autonomous change in the organization are likely. Then adjustments can be made where needed and performance maintained, without incurring the costs of massive restructuring of the whole system.

For example, a standard assembly line is the ultimate example of a tightly coupled system: No one on the line can reduce the pace of his work without affecting everyone else. Lincoln Electric's design is more loosely coupled by virtue of the work-in-process inventories that it maintains between different steps in the production process. Holding these inventories is very costly, and their levels could be lowered significantly if everyone always worked at a constant pace. However, they are useful because they permit individual variations over time in the pacing of work. The research program of the typical academic department is almost entirely decoupled—what one professor does, or does not do, can change with little or no impact on the other faculty members' activities. Of course, there is little direct gain on the research side from having these faculty grouped in the same department.

These ideas offer one explanation of the difficulties that Japan has been experiencing since the early 1990s. The system that marked the Japanese economy and major Japanese corporations through the 1980s was characterized by a dense, rich web of complementarities that extended through demographic and cultural variables to national policies and on to corporate design and management in an economy-wide example of tight coupling.[6] The key element was a growth orientation in the way firms were run that fed off and supported the high growth and savings rates in the Japanese economy. This focus on the long-run survival and growth of the firm in turn fit with the permanent employment policies, the heavy investments in human capital, and the reliance on long-term supplier relations. The accentuation of growth over profitability was supported by the governance system, where shareholders had little power and boards of directors were completely dominated by inside, executive directors; the financing by affiliated banks that would support the long-term orientation; and the restrictions on Japanese individuals' investing their savings outside the country. Social attitudes legitimized the system, accentuating hard work, loyalty to the employer, the development of the nation from its postwar destitution, and savings over consumption. Every element of the model was finely

adjusted to every other, and together they gave an exquis-
ite fit with the prevailing environment and produced outstanding economic performance for several decades.

Then a series of shocks hit. Japan reached the technological frontier and could no longer rely on net imports of
technology as a source of growth. Population growth
slowed and the population started to age rapidly.
Successful corporations accessed the Eurobond markets
for financing, depriving the main banks of a key part of
their traditional business, driving them into real estate
loans. These helped create the bubble in asset prices
in the late 1980s and then went sour when the bubble
burst. Social attitudes changed in ways that reduced the
willingness to work for the good of the corporation and
country. Foreign political pressures concerning trade
increased, meaning that growth could no longer be so easily
achieved by exporting more. The system had presumed
the way things had been on all these dimensions, and now
they had changed. The other elements—growth-oriented
strategies, permanent employment, firms being run
essentially in the interest of their permanent employees,
main-bank monitoring in place of stock market and outside director oversight of management, and so on—no
longer fit, and performance has suffered now for a decade.
But it is no easy task to change all the elements of the
pattern to find a new one that works, especially in a
democracy, where no one is empowered to play the role of
designer. Indeed, it has taken a long time for leaders there
to begin to realize that the problems were not simple
macroeconomic ones, but fundamental structural ones.
Japan is still struggling to find a new way.

Firms, in fact, can vary the tightness of coupling of different elements of their organizational designs. Some elements, like financial controls or IT platforms, could be absolutely standardized throughout the organization, with no variation permitted. Meanwhile, marketing or human resource practices might be allowed to vary across different geographies to respond to local variations in tastes, market conditions, and regulations. Such variegated coupling is, in fact, probably best. The issue is which parts to couple tightly, which to allow to be completely decoupled, and how loose the loose coupling should be to permit adaptation to change.

The tightness of coupling in the organizational design has a second effect in a dynamic context. It affects not only how performance varies in the face of environmental change, but also the ability of the organization to learn and improve. Learning in an organization involves three somewhat distinct processes. First, there must be *variation*, the identification of new alternatives. This can come from experimentation in the organization itself or from observing what other organizations are doing. Internal experimentation might occur in the laboratory or product development if it involves new or improved products, but it could just come about from the actions of different people and units in the business trying to solve emerging problems or acting on new insights. Then there is the process of *selection*, of determining whether the new alternatives are indeed better than the current way. Finally, if something better has been identified, the new ways must be *transferred and retained* in the organization.

Obviously, the more loosely coupled the design, the easier it is to experiment with changes in any aspect of the organization. Indeed, with different parts of the business facing different opportunities and challenges and operating in different environments, variation will come automatically if the units are sufficiently free from mandated central control of their architectures and routines. Thus, loose coupling supports variation.

However, loose coupling makes selection and transfer more difficult. It may be hard to determine whether something new that works in one part of the organization will also work in another part that has other routines and perhaps a different culture. Moreover, if the different parts of the organization are each allowed to do what they think best, then getting them to adopt a new practice or product may be much harder than if the center can simply order that currently defined best practice must be followed.

Thus, there is a second trade-off in determining the ideal amount of tight versus loose coupling. Not only is there a trade-off between getting optimal performance in a particular context versus doing better in the face of changes in the strategy or environment, but there is also a trade-off in supporting learning. A company that mandates operating strictly according to currently defined best practice and has operations manuals that are always followed will have a very hard time generating potential improvements in that best practice. One that allows more variation will rarely be using best practice at any given point in time in all its operations, but may do better on average.

So we now have a way of thinking about strategy and organization in the modern firm. Success involves strategy and organization that are coherent, fitting with one another and with the environment. However, environmental change implies a need to change strategy and structure—there is no one universal answer to the design problem. We understand that change will be difficult, and some reasons why this is so. But we also understand that the choices are among coherent systems, not individual policies and features. This accounts for the fact that the changes that firms have been adopting in recent decades have definite patterns—they are not random, but rather consist of general moves towards a new coherent pattern of organizational design.

Notes

1. Hidden in this definition is the requirement that doing more of one activity does not automatically prevent doing more of the other. Note that complementarity is conceptually different from a positive spillover. A positive spillover occurs when the overall benefit from some activity (rather than the returns to increasing the activity) is increasing in the level of the other activity.

2. See Brynjolfsson and Hitt (2000) for a survey and an extensive bibliography.

3. The rates are intended to be set so that a worker producing at the standard rate would earn an amount that would be competitive with standard industrial wages in the geographic area.

4. These papers also develop much of the theory of complementarity more formally. The 1990 paper contains formal mathematical statements and derivations of the key results, while the 1995 paper provides a more accessible verbal exposition.

5. For a formal model of these ideas, see Nickerson (2003).

6. For a fuller discussion, see Milgrom and Roberts (1994). A more easily accessible source for some of the argument is Milgrom and Roberts (1992: 349–52).

3

The Nature and Purpose of the Firm

Why are there firms? What is their fundamental nature and purpose? The answers to these seemingly very academic questions are actually of practical significance. Our objective is to understand the problem of designing the business enterprise and to gain some insights into some of the changes we see in the way firms are being organized and managed. Having a clear understanding of the nature and purpose of the firm as an institution is fundamental to reaching the desired objective.

The primary answer is that firms exist to coordinate and motivate people's economic activity. As Adam Smith (1776/1937) noted in his famous discussion of a pin factory, scale economies and learning effects imply that there are tremendous gains in efficiency if individuals specialize in their production activities (the division of labor). But once people specialize, they become mutually dependent, because no one produces by herself all the things she needs even to survive, let alone to prosper. Indeed, in most contexts in a modern economy, an individual in her job actually produces nothing that she wants personally to consume.

Instead, she must exchange the limited set of things she does produce for the vast variety of goods and services that she actually wants and that others make. These interdependencies mean that there is a need to coordinate different individuals' activities and to motivate them.

Coordination means, at a minimum, that all the needed tasks are completed without pointless duplication. Better yet, it seeks to ensure that the tasks are done efficiently, by the right people, in the right way, and at the right time and place. Ultimately, full coordination also requires that the tasks actually undertaken are the right ones. In the context of the firm, this means that the activities indicated by the strategy are carried out in a cost-minimizing fashion and that execution on the strategy creates as much value as possible. Finding a solution to the coordination problem is clearly a major task, even in relatively simple contexts. The coordination problem for the economy as a whole is mind-bogglingly complex.

Motivation becomes a problem too, because it may not automatically be in the self-interest of individuals or groups to act in ways that promote realizing an efficient solution to the coordination problem. Generally, we might expect that people are somewhat selfish. This is not to deny elements of altruism, but just to assert that pure altruism is unlikely. Most people most of the time would like to receive more of the things they value, even if in so doing they might deny others the benefits of these things. Further, they will want to avoid as much of the costs of economic activity as they can, even if others have to bear somewhat higher costs as a result. In the presence of interdependencies, individuals' attempts to grab more of the benefits and duck the costs can make everyone, including themselves, much worse off than if they behaved differently. The issue is then to motivate people so they choose to behave in ways that are conducive to realizing a coordinated solution.

Of course, as Smith also noted, markets are one very prominent mechanism for solving the problems of coordination and motivation that arise with the interdependencies of specialization and the division of labor. Market institutions leave individuals to pursue (narrowly) self-interested behavior, but guide their choices by the prices they pay and receive.

A well-functioning market leads the interdependencies among people to be fully "internalized." Interdependence means that one person's choices and actions have an impact on other people. Selfish behavior would then potentially lead to inefficiency, because the decision-maker takes account of only some of the costs and benefits of his actions, namely, those he experiences personally. With well functioning markets, however, each person is led to take full account of the aggregate costs and benefits of his actions, no matter to whom these accrue, because these are reflected in the prices that he faces. Prices in well-functioning markets simultaneously reflect the benefits of an extra unit to buyers and its cost to sellers; so price-guided choices bring these marginal costs and benefits into equality (as they must be for efficiency). In essence, market prices signal what needs to be done, when, where, how, and by whom. In so doing, markets achieve a remarkable level of coordination without any conscious central planning or control.

In fact, one of the central results of economic theory is the demonstration that if all the relevant markets exist and are competitive, then the allocation of resources that emerges from full market clearing is actually an efficient one—there is no rearrangement of economic activity that would be unanimously preferred. Instead, any change from what the market generates must hurt at least one person.

Moreover, markets provide intense individual incentives for innovation, investments, and effort; they require minimal amounts of formal communication about opportunities, needs, and resources; and they allow for unmatched individual freedom and personal discretion. The case for using markets to coordinate and motivate is strong.

Further, as Nobel laureate Ronald Coase (1960) has argued, even if formal, organized, competitive markets do not exist, direct bargaining among the interdependent parties can produce the same efficient outcomes, again without conscious central planning and control and again with each pursuing only his own self-interest. The logic is simple. Suppose that all the affected parties can meet and bargain freely and that the consequences of failure to agree are clearly established (e.g. through freely enforceable property rights). Then the different parties have every reason to reach an agreement that is efficient in the sense used above—one where it is impossible to make one of the parties better off without hurting one of the others. Otherwise, there are gains to be had from revising the bargain.

If voluntary dealings between distinct parties work so well, however, why then do we use firms to coordinate and motivate economic activity, particularly as extensively as we do? After all, as Nobel laureate Herbert Simon (1991) has noted, even in the most market-oriented of economies, the vast bulk of economic activity occurs within formal, managed organizations rather than through market exchanges. In fact, John McMillan (2002: 168–9) estimates that less than a third of all the transactions in the U.S. economy occur through markets, and instead over 70 percent are within firms. Coordination and motivation are predominantly achieved through firms, rather than the price system or bargaining among individuals on their own account. Why?

The basis for the answer was put forward by yet another Nobel laureate, Kenneth Arrow (1974). Arrow's answer is that sometimes markets simply do not work: There is "market failure." It can happen that markets fail to exist, or are not competitive, or do not clear properly. In these circumstances, interdependencies among people will not be fully internalized—people's self-interested behavior does not account for the costs borne and benefits received by others. Consequently, possible changes in the allocation of resources that would benefit all parties may remain unrealized. When markets fail to yield an efficient solution to the problems of coordination and motivation, other mechanisms for coordinating and motivating may be better and may come to supplant the market. The firm is the principal such alternative.[1]

By this logic, economic activity should occur within the firm when it represents a better way to coordinate and motivate than does the market. To understand when this is likely to be the case, we need to understand the nature of market failure as well as when firms might be expected to work better.

Sources and Nature of Market Failure[2]

Microeconomics identifies a number of circumstances when market failure is likely and thus other arrangements may be preferred. The most familiar include situations where monopoly or other forms of imperfect competition prevail, whether through collusion or because barriers to entry or regulation limit the number of competitors. In such circumstances, supply is typically restricted to increase profits. This hurts efficiency because customers' losses in higher prices and foregone surplus typically exceed the extra profits that are generated for the monopolist. If internal provision of the monopolized good is reasonably cost efficient, then internal procurement may be better for the customer.

Public goods are another traditional example where markets do not work well. A public good is one where one party's consuming the good does not diminish the amount available to others; indeed, in the extreme, making the good available to one person may even require that it be available to all. The first property is called nonrivalry in consumption; the second is called non-excludability. An example of a non-excludable public good is national defense—if one person in an area receives it, all do. Television broadcasts are an example of an excludable public good. One person's viewing the signal does not diminish its availability to others, so consumption is not rivalrous, but the signal can be scrambled to prevent its being viewed by those who do not have a decoding device. Simple market arrangements do not work well for public goods because one person's purchases are automatically available to all (in the non-excludable case), and there will then be a temptation to free ride on others' contributions. Alternately, the individual benefits that will drive someone's decision to purchase or provide a public good are only a fraction of the aggregate benefits, leading to undersupply. The inefficiency with excludable public goods is that, in order to induce people to pay for the good, resources are expended to deprive non-payers of the benefits. Yet, once the good has been created, these extra benefits could be made available to all at no cost to anyone, increasing the total benefits realized from the good at no direct cost.

Since information often has the characteristics of an excludable public good, it is to be expected that markets for information are likely to be problematic. In fact, the problems of selling information are especially intense. How is the buyer to evaluate the value of the information being offered? With a private good she can examine it and try it out. But if the seller of information offers these options, the buyer has gotten the value for nothing, because the information cannot be taken back on her refusal to pay. Sometimes the information can be codified and packaged in a way that makes it more easily excludable. For example, potential customers can be allowed to try a database or computer program and if they do not agree to pay, then the sample can be taken back. At other times a patent may be created and enforced. But generally problems remain and inefficiencies can persist.

Public goods are an extreme form of externality. An externality exists when a person's actions affect others' welfare and the first party does not have an incentive to recognize this impact in decision-making, so that he or she does not account for all the costs and benefits in selecting actions. Because of this, externalities lead to inefficiencies.

The classic examples have to do with such choices as a decision to drive to work on congested roads using a polluting vehicle, but externalities arise in business too. For example, there is a danger that different business units will ill-use a common corporate asset that is available to all, such as a common brand. Because the benefits of protecting the brand are spread among all those that use it, whereas the costs of taking actions to protect and build it are borne by the individual units, there will be inadequate incentives to invest in brand building and maintenance.

Coase's argument that direct bargaining can replace impersonal market dealings to achieve efficiency was formulated explicitly to deal with externalities—he cites examples such as soot from a train raising the costs for a laundry that dried clothing outdoors or sparks from the train causing fires (Coase 1960). Coase argued that if property rights were well established and enforceable, then bargaining would lead to an efficient outcome. For example, if the train owner has a property right to pollute but it is cheaper to reduce the emissions than for the laundry to rewash soiled items, then the laundry will pay the train owner to reduce the pollution. A similar point applies to the example of monopoly: There is no obvious reason for a monopolist to adopt value-destroying behavior. Instead, let it bargain with potential customers. If Coase's arguments apply, then the parties will reach an efficient outcome.

The issue then is why such bargaining might not work. Part of an answer lies simply in the costs of identifying the relevant parties, bringing them together to negotiate, establishing the terms, and then enforcing the agreement. Many of these are, in turn, tied up in information problems. In fact, recent research has given much attention to informational problems as a source of market or bargaining failure, and the originators of this work, James Mirrlees, George Akerlof, Michael Spence, and Joseph Stiglitz, received Nobel prizes for their contributions.

Nature and Purpose of the Firm

One especially important class of circumstances generating market failure arises when there are informational asymmetries among different parties. For example, suppose potential sellers are better informed than the buyers are about the quality of the items they are offering. Think, for example, of used cars: The original owner's experience with the vehicle makes him much better informed about the car's quality than is any potential buyer. Then the buyers must be wary that they are not being stuck with a really low quality car—a "lemon"—at a high price, because sellers with low quality items may be tempted to misrepresent the quality of their wares. Thus, buyers will expend resources to determine the quality of the goods they are offered, and sellers of higher-quality goods will attempt to demonstrate that they really do have good products that will command premium prices (Spence 1973). Each of these activities involves costs but directly creates no value and so results in a less-than-efficient allocation.

The inefficiency can be even more substantial than simply the waste of resources in screening and signaling quality: Trade may break down almost completely (Akerlof 1970). If eliminating the asymmetry of information is not possible, then buyers will refuse to pay more than the expected value of the goods, averaged across the different quality levels they expect to be offered. Then the best quality goods may not be offered at all, because they command only a middling price that does not reflect their true value. Consequently, the distribution of qualities that are actually offered is worse than what is potentially available. Since the selection of products on offer is not representative of the underlying distribution of quality, but instead is an *adverse selection*,[3] buyers will rationally lower their willingness to pay even further. Then, even more potential sellers of relatively high-quality items may no longer be willing to sell at the lower price. The overall result may be that nothing but very low quality items are available—only lemons are on offer— and markets fail to exist for high-quality products, although buyers are anxious to have such goods and would happily pay enough for them to compensate the sellers if they were sure to get what they paid for.

A second form of informational asymmetry that may cause market failure involves limitations on the ability to observe others' actions, and thus to determine whether they are adhering to agreements. This leads to the problem of *moral hazard*.[4] Is a salesperson in the field actually calling on customers or playing golf? Is a knowledge worker really thinking about the job, or about something else? Is my lawyer giving me an honest best effort or a perfunctory, half-hearted one? Similar problems arise when the information that individuals have gathered and upon which they are acting is not observable by others in whose interests the actions are to be taken. Is my broker's recommendation to trade really a good one, or does he just want the commissions? Am I being denied a possible treatment for my medical condition because it really will not be worthwhile or because the insurance company does not want to pay for it?

In such circumstances parties cannot write contracts that directly address their concerns, and markets for the directly relevant goods and services then cannot exist. Instead, parties must content themselves with mea-suring performance indirectly and imprecisely and with contracting on proxies and signals rather than directly on the value-creating choices and actions. This can create various sorts of inefficiencies: Misdirected effort, a misallocation of risk, inefficiently low levels of effort, expenditures on monitoring and on manipulating the performance measures, and so on. (We will deal with the problem of moral hazard in detail in Chapter 4.)

Bringing transactions that are subject to adverse selection and moral hazard out of the market and under some other form of organization does not automatically solve the problems. However, the fact that market dealings do not work well does mean that other arrangements may do better than the market and are worth exploring.

Much recent research has focused on another problem of enforcing agreements. Even if there are no informational asymmetries between the directly affected parties that prevent contracting on the relevant variables, relying on third parties to enforce a contract requires that these parties must be able to determine whether the agreement has been breached. It is easy to imagine situations where such external verifiability might be problematic: Both parties to an agreement might be fully aware of what each has actually done, and yet there is no unambiguous way of demonstrating the facts to others. In such cases, there are two options. Either useful agreements cannot be reached regarding the nonverifiable matters, or else the agreements must be "self-enforced"—the parties must find it in their interests to adhere to the agreement, even in the absence of the incentives that might normally come though outside enforcement. Simple market-like arrangements can rarely provide such self-enforcement options.

Somewhat related are problems of commitment. A simple instance arises when contract enforcement is costly. These costs might be legal fees, court costs, and managers' time, which in some cases might exceed the gains that could be realized by winning. If the parties to an agreement do not have an incentive to insist on its enforcement, contracts again may lose their efficacy. If enforcement is costly, then both sides may lose from punishing transgressions. Absent some means for the aggrieved party to commit to punishing the transgressor, some violations of the agreement will then go unpunished. They consequently cannot be prevented. This in turn affects what can be achieved by contract.[5]

A subtler but also more important commitment problem arises when actions taken under the agreement alter the incentives to adhere to the remaining terms. This may result in a situation where both parties would be happy to renegotiate. Yet, understanding that the renegotiation may occur will affect the incentives to abide by the original agreement. For example, suppose that to motivate an employee, her pay is made very highly dependent on her performance. Suppose too that performance is not completely under the employee's control but instead is also subject to random, uncontrollable variation. Once the job has been done, but before the results are realized, there is no further value to having the employee bear all the risk that making her pay depend on her performance entails. At this point there is nothing more to motivate, and yet her continuing to face risk in her pay is costly if she is risk-averse and the firm is not (as might reasonably be the case). Both the employee and the firm would gain by replacing the original payment scheme with a fixed payment that was somewhat lower than the expected value of the original reward. The firm saves money in expectation and the employee avoids the risk. Yet, if the employee forecasts that renegotiation of this sort is likely, she may no longer be motivated to exert effort in the first place.

While both sides are happy to renegotiate in this example, there can also be situations where the renegotiation essentially occurs under duress. For example, suppose that two companies enter a supply relationship in the course of which the buyer becomes locked into dealing with the seller because no competing supplier can meet the buyer's needs. Then the seller may be able to use its power to hold up the buyer, forcing a renegotiation of the original contract terms to deprive the buyer of many of the benefits it forecast when the relationship began. This bargaining may be costly, and it may lead to a breakdown in the relationship. Moreover, foreseeing the possibility of opportunistic renegotiation may prevent the relationship ever being formed (Williamson 1975; Klein, Crawford, and Alchian 1978).

The source of difficulties here is that it is not possible to commit not to renegotiate. Why should there be such commitment problems? In the first instance, the courts (at least in the United States) generally will not enforce a "no renegotiation" clause in a contract—if the parties agree to renegotiate, they are free to do so, no matter what they may have previously agreed. There is some question about the desirability of such a policy, but even in its absence, preventing renegotiation may be difficult. In many cases, there is no third party that would have an interest in enforcing the prior agreement, and neither contracting party would want to do so if the renegotiation is mutually beneficial.

Moreover, since any real contract is necessarily incomplete, there will very likely be situations that arise that were not foreseen in the original contract's terms. These may require some sort of after-the-fact negotiation. Contractual incompleteness can arise for a variety of reasons. If actions or outcomes are not verifiable by third-party enforcers, there is no point to contracting on them explicitly. Bounded rationality can prevent parties from foreseeing all the relevant contingencies that might arise. The costs of negotiating terms of agreement concerning contingencies that are not thought very likely to occur can rationally lead to their omission from the contract. The inherent limitations of natural language may prevent describing terms unambiguously. In any of these circumstances, after-the-fact renegotiation may be needed in particular situations. This means that there is a cost to applying bans on renegotiation unconditionally. Meanwhile, distinguishing situations where renegotiation is to be allowed and where it is forbidden could be extremely problematic.[6]

Generally, if contracts are ineffective or markets simply fail to exist, they clearly cannot guide efficient resource allocation. Coase's bargaining might be a solution in some circumstances where organized markets do not come into being. Yet, the same informational asymmetries that undercut the working of the market would plague bargaining, preventing it from reaching fully efficient agreements.[7] Meanwhile, in many of the cases of imperfect competition or public goods, the costs of organizing all the relevant parties to bargain and of enforcing any resultant agreements might be overwhelming.

When markets do not work, other institutions may be created that do a better job. In particular, the firm can be such a mechanism.

Firms versus Markets

When might firms be better than markets? Much of economists' current understanding of the answer to this question traces to another element of the work of Ronald Coase. Almost 70 years ago, Coase (1937) asked explicitly why some economic activity is carried out through market transactions while other parts are organized under hierarchic authority relations within firms. His answer is that there are costs to organizing economic activity, to achieving coordination and motivation, and that economizing on these *transaction costs* explains the patterns of organization that are adopted. In particular, a transaction is removed from the arm's length contracting of the market and brought inside the firm precisely when it is cheaper to organize it this way. Thus, we are to understand the boundaries of the firm and, more generally, observed patterns of organizational design as being efficient ones— ones that create the most possible value.

There are at least two aspects of Coase's answer that need elaboration. One is why efficiency—rather than, say, the pursuit of monopoly power and profits—should be determinative. The second is the origin and nature of transaction costs.[8]

The basis for efficiency arguments is simply that if arrangements are not efficient, then (definitionally) it is possible to make everyone better off—not just to increase the size of the total pie, but instead actually to increase the size of each person's slice. Presuming that the potential improvements can be identified and the gains can be shared, we should expect such changes to be made. So if an arrangement persists, there is reason to suspect that it is efficient, at least for the parties who are in a position to have their interests represented.[9]

This argument might seem Panglossian—that everything we observe is the best it could be—but there are important qualifications and subtleties that render it less problematic.

Note first that the requirement that the relevant parties can identify any potential improvements limits what is achievable. Thus, the efficiency of actual arrangements is constrained by informational and observational limitations.

An example is the "Market for Lemons" problem of adverse selection considered earlier. The result of the informational asymmetry may be that only the very worst cars are offered and sold, even though there are many potential trades that would make both sides to the transaction better off. Gains from trade are not realized because informational asymmetries prevent identifying their magnitude and sharing them in a satisfactory way. So this situation may, in fact, be the best that can be achieved (provided we continue to respect private property and allow each side to decide whether it wants to trade). Thus, it is efficient in the limited sense that we use the term, although this mainly demonstrates how weak a notion efficiency actually is, or just how constraining the informational limitations are.

Similarly, strikes and other costly delays in reaching agreements need not be seen as inefficient waste and evidence against the efficiency hypothesis. Rather, they may be interpreted as the best options available under the circumstances for credibly communicating the value of an agreement to each side (Kennan and Wilson 1993). For example, a firm's willingness to suffer a strike signals that an agreement is not so valuable to it as might have been believed. Thus, the union learns that it cannot hope for as rich a settlement as it had desired. For if an agreement were really very important and valuable to the firm, it would be anxious to settle.

We now turn to the second point: the nature of trans-action costs. In a market setting, transaction costs are the costs of finding and qualifying trading partners, of estab-lishing specifications and prices, of negotiating and drafting contracts, and of monitoring and enforcing agreements. They are also the opportunity costs of lost benefits that are occasioned by the difficulties of develop-ing complete, enforceable agreements between separate parties.

To a large extent, the informational and commitment issues discussed already underlie the transaction costs of using markets. However, one particular example has a cen-tral place in the research in this area. The example involves hold-up and specialized investments (Williamson 1975, 1985; Klein, Crawford, and Alchian 1978).

Williamson (1975) argues that many business dealings involve lock-in—even if there are initially lots of potential trading partners, once one is chosen and the parties start to work together, there is a "fundamental transformation" of the relationship that makes changing to another partner very difficult. In such circumstances, if contracts are incomplete, then the parties may have to negotiate after the lock-in has occurred. These negotiations may be costly and acrimonious in the best of circumstances. Moreover, they present an opportunity for one party to act opportunistically to attempt to extract more of the returns to cooperation than it was due under the original agreement. Both the bargaining costs and potential benefits that are lost if the bargaining breaks down and cooperation does not occur are transactions costs of dealing with another party.

Lock-in is actually inevitable when assets are specialized. An asset is specialized to a particular use when the value it can create in its next-best alternative use is substantially lower than what it yields in the current one. For example, the dies used to shape materials in manufacturing are very specific to that use: If they are not employed for this purpose, they are just scrap metal. Firm-specific human capital—knowledge that is only (or especially) valuable in the context of employment with a particular firm—is another example. When assets are specialized, they are subject to hold-up—attempts by trading partners to appropriate some of the returns that the assets' owners expected when they invested in them. This can lead to a variety of inefficiencies.

Suppose two firms have an opportunity to trade, but the seller needs to make specific investments to serve the buyer's needs in the best way possible. Once the investments are made, the costs are sunk. This means that even if the price ultimately received by the seller were cut almost to the level of variable costs, so that almost no contribution to covering the costs of the investments would be realized, it would still not be worthwhile to withdraw from serving the buyer. The reason is that the sunk costs must be borne in either event and the asset has no other good use. A portion of the returns to the asset are then *quasirents*, returns in excess of what is needed to keep the asset in its current use once it has been created.[10] The seller is then subject to the danger of hold-up.

If there is a prior contract, but it is sufficiently incomplete that negotiations over terms need to take place after the investments have been made, then the bargaining over terms will very likely give little protection to the seller's investments. This is because the sunk costs are irrelevant in determining how much value is created by cooperation versus breaking off the relationship, which is what the parties effectively bargain over. Even if the terms are nominally fixed in advance, the buyer may still be tempted to force a renegotiation of the terms of trade, appropriating a portion of the quasirents that the seller had hoped to enjoy. This is possible because the seller has little recourse: To refuse to renegotiate and break off the deal leaves him or her with only the nearly worthless asset. Meanwhile, forcing a renegotiation may be quite simple. For example, the buyer could claim business conditions have changed in way that justifies a lower price, or that service or quality has not been acceptable, or any of a number of other things, depending on the particular circumstances.

Thus, the seller cannot expect to receive the full returns on the specific investments it has made. Anticipating this, the setter may be reluctant to commit resources to the specific assets. For example, if the specificity arises from the seller's learning the particular needs of the buyer, the seller might underinvest in this knowledge, so that less of a loss is suffered in case of a hold-up. Thus, less value is created. Alternatively, the seller may expend resources for protection against the anticipated hold-up. Making the assets more flexible in their uses, so that they can be redeployed at less cost, might do this. This is a waste, for the resources are being expended to improve the value of the asset in a use to which it ought not to be put.[11]

One solution to this problem is for the buyer to pay a part of the cost of the investment up front—essentially the buyer pays *ex ante* for the amount to be (mis)appropriated later. This will work, however, only if the agreement to undertake the investment is enforceable. Otherwise, for instance, the seller might just pocket the buyer's money and still make only the investment that seems individually optimal given that the terms will later be renegotiated. Another solution may be for the transaction to be brought within a single firm. Empirically, this has been an important element in vertical integration.[12] This is can be costly in a number of ways, however, as we will soon see. Thus, the enforceability problems create transaction costs in markets.

What are the transaction costs of organizing economic activities inside the firm? This is still a controversial issue. One might think first of the costs of communicating information up and down through the hierarchy, of information overload at the center/top, and of slow decision-making that is based on limited and possibly outdated information. Organizational decentralization may sometimes provide an effective response to these phenomena, however, as the developers of the multidivisional form discovered (Chandler 1977). (Generally, it is a good idea not to rely on explanations that are based on inefficiency—managers are awfully good at creating new and better ways to do business more efficiently!).

In this vein, Oliver Williamson (1985) has pointed to the policy of *selective intervention* as a response to any inherent disabilities of the centralized, hierarchic organization of a firm. The idea is to replicate the workings of the market within the firm whenever this yields efficiency, while top executives intervene selectively in the subunits and the relations among them only when this yields a better outcome than market dealings.

If selective intervention worked, then it would be efficient to have everything in one gigantic firm. Yet, even the ideologues of the old Soviet economy never dreamt of a system that was so extreme in its centralization. There must be something that prevents effective application of selective intervention.

One response is that it is impossible to generate the same intensity of incentives within a single integrated firm as when units are separately owned. In this regard, Williamson himself suggested that, while it might be easy to promise as strong incentives to employees as to outside contractors, it is hard to do so *credibly*. The problem is that the owner controls the performance measures[13] and would always be tempted to fudge them. This could happen both when the employee has done very well and is due to be paid a lot, and when there have been bad results despite apparently good effort, in which case the owner may be too forgiving. Either possibility blunts actual incentives and can imply that the firm does not achieve the levels of efficiency that the market might realize.

This argument clearly rests on the difficulties of effective contracting. Reputational concerns may help counter it. As well, it may be possible in some circumstances to use third-party monitoring and auditing. For example,

BP used "self-help" figures—essentially, improvements in earnings not resulting from changes in crude oil prices or exchange rates—in its performance pay. It then employed an outside auditor to attest to the accuracy of the self-help numbers it calculated. Equity carve-outs and tracking stocks may be an especially interesting possibility here. For example, Thermo-Electron Corporation sold stakes in its business units to the public explicitly to "outsource performance evaluation." Outside equity investors are strongly motivated to act as monitors because their own funds are on the line, and the stock prices they generate become low-cost, objective performance measures that may have more credibility and integrity than any internally generated ones.

The "property rights" approach to the theory of the firm, developed by Sanford Grossman and Oliver Hart (1986) and Hart and John Moore (1990),[14] suggests another reason why it may be harder to give strong incentives in a larger, integrated organization. This logic is most applicable when thinking about owner-managed firms. Suppose such a firm is selling to an industrial customer. If the relationship is severed, the owner of the upstream firm still owns the assets in his firm (machines, brand name, etc.) and can redeploy them as he sees fit. In contrast, suppose the customer owns the assets, with the upstream manager now an employee running a business unit corresponding to the original firm. Now if the relationship collapses, the manager does not get to keep the assets.

As Grossman, Hart, and Moore (GHM) argue, this difference affects the relative bargaining position of the two parties in dividing up the value created by their cooperation. (Assume that it is impossible to specify the division of value contractually in advance, so that it must be determined by bargaining after the value has been realized.) Thus, the ownership of assets determines the payoffs the parties receive.

These payoffs in turn affect the strength of the incentives the parties have to undertake investments that are complementary with the assets of the firm/business unit, such as learning how to work with the assets more effectively or developing a brand that increases the value of the goods that the buyer produces using the services of the assets. Getting a larger share of the return motivates investing more to create greater returns. So, who owns the assets affects investment and thus the value created. If there are two separate firms interacting through the market, the supplier owns the assets and has strong incentives to invest, but the buyer's incentives are weak. If there is vertical integration and the buyer owns the assets, then the employee–manager has weak investment incentives, although the buyer has strong ones. With incomplete contracts it simply is not possible to give the same incentives to an employee as an owner receives.[15]

Note the importance of incomplete contracts to this theorizing. If binding agreements were possible, then the division of the value created could be set contractually to provide incentives, or, indeed, the investments themselves could be governed by contract. (In this, the GHM theory is like the hold-up analysis discussed earlier.) Then equally strong incentives could be given inside the firm as outside—ownership and the boundaries of the firm would not matter.

Bengt Holmström and Paul Milgrom (1991) have argued that the issue is not just offering incentives that are strong enough, but offering ones that are appropriately *balanced*. The full details are in their model of multi-tasking in agency relationships, which is discussed in detail in the Chapter 4, but the theory rests on two observations. First, they note that typically there are multiple ways that someone can spend time, many of which might be of value to an employer. But if these activities compete for the person's attention,[16] then the incentives offered for different activities must be comparable. Otherwise, the person will focus disproportionate amounts of her effort on those things that are especially well compensated and ignore the others. The second observation is that providing strong financial incentives is costly if the person is risk-averse, because it loads extra risk into pay. Further, the cost is greater the more difficult it is to measure performance. This means that, other things being equal, tasks where performance is hard to measure should not be given as intense incentives as ones that are more accurately observed.

Suppose now that two activities are desired. Think of one as producing output, which is easily measured, implying that the costs of providing strong incentives (in terms of the risk that the person bears) are low. In isolation, this activity should then be given strong incentives. The other can be thought of as some form of investment, where effort is hard to measure accurately and in a timely fashion. For example, it is hard to determine precisely the change in the long-term value of a division occasioned by its manager's efforts and decisions. Providing strong incentives for this investment activity is very costly. This is because doing so makes her pay highly random, since it is not determined solely by the manager's actions but also by the other uncontrolled factors that affect measured performance. The manager will have to be compensated for bearing this risk, so the costs ultimately are borne by the employer.

It is obviously desirable that the manager both increase current performance and undertake the right investments that increase long-term value. If, however, strong incentives are given for improving current costs and revenues and weak ones for investments (as might be optimal if there were no interaction among tasks), then problems arise. The manager is tempted to mortgage the future, ignoring good investments, and concentrate on getting current performance up, even if this reduces total value created. The solution must be to provide balanced incentives. There are two ways to do this.

One solution is to sell the operation to the manager, who then bears the long-term consequences of her investment choices as well as the current effects of improving performance. This may, in fact, be a factor in the management buyouts that first became prominent in the 1980s. The second is to treat the manager as a salaried employee, giving relatively weak incentives for both short- and long-term performances. (These incentives might be implicit and subjective, perhaps through the opportunities for promotion.) The first solution means that the manager receives as strong incentives for generating future returns as current ones. The second means that both sorts of effort get equally muted incentives. In either case, the incentives are appropriately balanced, and both activities get some attention (but less, of course, in the low-incentives, employment regime).

The key point for the present discussion, however, is that if the employing firm continues to own the investment opportunities, the employee must be given weak incentives for other activities—weaker than what would be received as owner of a separate firm. Thus, the market solution cannot be replicated inside the firm.

A fourth approach to the issue of why selective intervention does not work questions whether senior management will—or whether they even can—limit their interventions to those that are efficiency enhancing (see Milgrom and Roberts 1988*b*, 1990*a*, *c*, 1992: 192–4 and 269–77, 1998). A defining characteristic of the firm is that its executives have the unchallenged legal right to intervene in lower-level operations and decisions, to direct that very specific actions be taken, and to enforce these directives. (Indeed, they must have this power if selective intervention is to occur.) In contrast, outsiders (even the courts or regulators) cannot easily make such detailed interventions. So moving an activity out of the market and into the firm increases the opportunity for interventions, including ones that are not efficiency enhancing.

Excessive or inappropriate interventions might come for a number of reasons. First, senior managers may be tempted to intervene when they should not because, after all, it is their job to manage. They may also be too impatient, intervening when they see that at lower levels people might not do the absolutely best thing. This is understandable—mistakes are being made, after all—but costly. The intervention destroys both the opportunities and the incentives for the lower levels to learn. It also undercuts their autonomy and the very real performance incentives that come from that (Aghion and Tirole 1997). The senior managers can also have an overblown estimate of their own abilities, not trusting others to take the appropriate actions (i.e. those that they would take themselves). Finally, implicit bribery of various forms might lead them to intervene.

But even if the executives are scrupulously honest and superbly competent, there may still be excessive interventions. The problem is that lower-level people will care a lot about the decisions that the firm makes, and they will have every reason to attempt to influence the executives to intervene, making the decisions in the way they like. For example, someone in the organization has to be assigned to Paris, Texas, and someone to Paris, France. One can imagine that candidates would exert huge amounts of effort to affect this decision. Similarly, one person will be promoted and another not, or one division's investments will be funded and another's not. There will be strong incentives for the interested parties to try to influence these decisions, and not necessarily in directions that increase overall value creation. Further, to know when and how to intervene, the senior executives will have to rely on information from the potentially affected parties.

Among the techniques of influence are biasing information provision, misdirecting effort (e.g. towards building the case for your side rather than attending to ongoing responsibilities), politicking, and worse. Collectively, these *influence activities* have three sorts of costs. First, resources are directly expended on influencing decisions, even when all that is accomplished is to shift their distributional consequences (which means that no extra value is created). Note that such efforts will also call forth defensive expenditures from those who are threatened. The second is that, to the extent that the influence activities are successful, bad decisions may be made. The third is that the firm may be led to change its organizational design from what would otherwise be ideal in order to control the influence activities.

There are a variety of methods that can be employed to limit influence activities. One is to limit communication between executives and lower-level people. This limits the opportunity for politicking and strategic information provision, although it brings an obvious cost that some useful information is not transmitted. The "three strikes and you're out" policy employed at ABB Asea Brown Boveri, the Swiss–Swedish electrical power equipment and industrial products company, is of this sort (Bartlett 1993). Two managers who disagreed could take their issues to a higher level for resolution, but only twice. If they did it a third time, one or both was replaced.

A second approach is to structure decision processes so they are less susceptible to influence. Firm adherence to bureaucratic, inflexible rules can be an example. If salaries are completely determined by seniority and job assignment, then there is no point in politicking for a raise. The airlines' policy of assigning cabin crews on the basis of seniority similarly minimizes influence opportunities. Promoting on objective measures of past performance rather than on the apparent (i.e. less objective and more manipulable) qualifications for the new post can be rationalized as reducing the incentives for influence (as well as motivating current performance). A very lean headquarters is one means to commit not to intervene too often— HQ simply lacks the resources to mess around in the lower levels' business. Executives may also attempt to establish a reputation for not intervening in order to deter attempts at inducing interventions. Note, however, that this may require not intervening even when it might seem appropriate in a particular instance.

A third approach is to limit the distributional consequences of decisions, so individuals will have less at stake. For example, pay compression and uniformity of treatment, even when other factors argue for differentiation, have this effect. This may explain the pressures that are common in organizations to apply standard procedures even when differentiation and special treatment might seem appropriate—to do otherwise is to invite everyone to try to make the case that he qualifies as an exception.

A final method of controlling influence takes advantage of the fact that the boundaries of the firm set limits to such internal influence activities. Putting activities in separate firms limits influence activities. For example, different pay and promotion policies can be employed in connection with the different activities if they are in different companies, whereas differential treatment within a single firm might lead to huge amounts of politicking and influence activities. The reason the boundaries of the firm matter is that it is pointless to campaign with one's boss over assignment to another firm, but it may be quite reasonable to do so if the transfer is within the corporation. Similarly, one advantage of using outside suppliers rather than in-house ones is that trying to discipline or replace the in-house supplier for poor performance invites influence costs, as do the establishment and adjustment of transfer prices.

Once it is established that there are costs to internal organization, the boundaries of the firm are determined by the Coasian formula: Organize transactions internally if and only if the costs of doing so are lower than organizing through markets. We know quite a bit about market organization. How then to think about internal organization? What characterizes a firm? Why and how are firms different from markets? When will the firm be the favored form?

The Nature of the Firm

Many authors, including Ronald Coase (1937) and Herbert Simon (1951), have identified the essential nature of the firm as the reliance on hierarchic, authority relations to replace the inherent equality among participants that marks market dealings. When you join a firm, you accept the right of the executives and their delegates to direct your behavior, at least over a more-or-less commonly understood range of activities. Simon argued that this may be an efficient response to the impossibility of foreseeing and contracting on what tasks will need to be undertaken—the need for coordination—and to the impossibility (high costs) of bargaining anew each time there is a change in the required activities. It is not a perfect solution, because the boss will not have an automatic incentive to take account of the employees' interests in choosing how they spend their time. Still, it can be better than a rigid prespecification of activities, as under a simple market contract.

Others—most notably Armen Alchian and Harold Demsetz (1972) and Michael Jensen and William Meckling (1976)—have challenged this view. They argue that any appearance of authority in the firm is illusionary. For them, the relationship between employer and employee is completely parallel to that between customer and butcher. In each case, the buyer (of labor services or meat) can tell the seller what is wanted on a particular day, and the seller can acquiesce and be paid, or refuse and be fired. For these scholars, the firm is simply a *"nexus of contracts"*—a particularly dense collection of the sort of arrangements that characterize markets.

While there are several objections to this argument, we focus on one. It is that, when a customer "fires" a butcher, the butcher keeps the inventory, tools, shop, and other customers she had previously. When an employee leaves a firm, in contrast, she is typically denied access to the firm's resources. The employee cannot conduct business using the firm's name; she cannot use its machines or patents; and she probably has limited access to the people and networks in the firm, certainly for commercial purposes and perhaps even socially.

The firm's control over access to resources comes ultimately from ownership of the assets and from being the unique common party to all the employment contracts with the members of the firm. By controlling access, the firm can offer or deny people the opportunity to create value and earn rewards by being part of the firm. This gives the firm power, and it uses the power to specify the "rules of the game": To prescribe and proscribe behavior, to set rewards and punishments, and to control relations among members of the firm and with outsiders. The point of doing so is to create value by making the firm an effective mechanism for coordination and motivation— a more effective mechanism than simple market relations.

These ideas (due to Bengt Holmström 1999—see also Rajan and Zingales 1998) bring us back to Arrow's conception of the firm as a mechanism for dealing with market failures. This is actually a somewhat more general conception than the transaction costs approach, because we can think of the market as effectively failing when the costs of using it are higher than the costs of non-market organization. Note too that the central role for power harks back to the idea in the property rights literature that ownership is important because it conveys power.

One striking insight from this line of reasoning is that it is not necessarily a disability of the firm that it offers weaker incentives. Rather, one reason the firm exists is specifically to provide weak incentives when those the market provides are too strong!

What does it mean for incentives to be "too strong"? This is best understood in the context of the Holmström–Milgrom multi-tasking model discussed earlier: Incentives for some activity are too strong if they cause excessive diversion of effort and attention from other valued activities that, for whatever reason, cannot be given similarly strong incentives.

As an example, consider the question of whether to sell through an outside distributor or use an in-house sales force. Suppose that, in addition to generating current sales, the sales people (whether employees or not) can also gather customer information that could, for example, be useful in product development. If an outside distributor is used, it must be offered strong incentives for current sales, for example, via a large commission that is perhaps the full difference between wholesale and retail prices (as with a independent retailer). Otherwise it will be inclined to divert its attention to selling other clients' products.

This means that the outside distributor must also get intense incentives to gather and transmit information if it is to be motivated to do this as well. Providing such incentives is likely to be difficult, however: How do you measure performance in this activity?

Thus, if information gathering is important, so that balanced incentives are crucial, it may be better to give weak incentives for sales that match the weak incentives that can be given for information gathering. But this cannot be done except by bringing the sales activity inside the firm, where the sales force can be paid a salary, asked to gather information as well as to sell the product, and told not to sell other firms' products (Anderson 1985; Anderson and Schmittlein 1984; Holmström and Milgrom 1991).

Cooperation and Initiative

More generally, Holmström has pointed to a fundamental multi-tasking problem and associated set of trade-offs that are involved in organizational design. Generally, two broad sorts of behavior might be desired from people in an organization: Call them "initiative" and "cooperation." The former refers to intelligent, honest, diligent, imaginative pursuit of individual goals and responsibilities—increasing your unit's sales, lowering costs, making successful product innovations, and so on. Cooperation refers to promoting others' well-being and common goals—improving another unit's profits, developing the overall brand, creditworthiness, and customer reputation of the firm, and so on. Clearly, both sorts of behavior are desirable. Initiative leads to better individual and unit performance, both immediate and longer term. It is obviously valuable. But as long as there are any externalities, cooperation is needed too, so that the interactions are accounted for and managed. For example, we want to avoid hold-ups of other parts of the company, cheating on unobserved quality on internal sales, and depreciating the value of common assets and to encourage sharing knowledge and helping other members of the firm.

The problem is that we are in a multi-tasking context. Providing incentives to induce more of one sort of behavior may then involve getting less of the other. For example, if skimping on quality increases my profits but hurts yours more, then initiative drives me to skimp, while cooperation means I do not. The two are incompatible.

Typically, for any given level of expenditure of resources on coordination and motivation, there will be a maximum amount of initiative that can be induced for any given amount of cooperation that is desired. Further, we might expect that in most situations the frontier is downward-sloping: Once we have induced the most initiative possible for a given level of cooperation, getting even more initiative is possible only by lessening cooperation. This might occur, for example, because providing stronger incentives for own goals makes people more focused on these and less willing to devote time to doing things to help other people. This is shown in Figure 8. The frontier in the figure shows the maximum initiative available for any specific amount of cooperation, given a level of expenditure on inducing these. Devoting more resources presumably pushes the frontier out, allowing more of both desired behaviors.

Nature and Purpose of the Firm

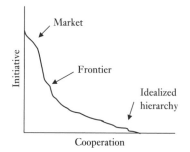

Figure 8. Cooperation and initiative

In this framework, arm's length market dealings typically give the maximal incentives to pursue own goals and so the most initiative, but they provide little incentive for cooperation. So organizing through market arrangements gives a point on (or close to) the vertical axis. The idealized rational bureaucracy with centralized decision-making and weak performance incentives arguably would get little initiative but might achieve high levels of cooperation. Actual organizations get less cooperation than the idealized hierarchy but more than the market. Of course, real companies need more cooperation than arm's length dealings would induce, because interdependencies abound. The cost is that they do not generate the initiative that market organization would generate.

A well-designed and well-managed organization will be on the frontier—otherwise, it could get more of both cooperation and initiative for free. Of course, this does not mean that actual organizations are there—this is one of the big tasks of management! The design of the organization determines the mix of cooperation and initiative that will actually be achieved. The people, the architecture, the processes and routines, and the culture all affect the behavior that is induced. Where an organization should want to position itself depends on the activities it is undertaking and what it is trying to accomplish, that is, on its strategy. Correspondingly, a shift in strategy might be expected to lead to a change in organization. The strategy will also determine how much the firm should want to spend on organization, and thus where the frontier will lie.

For example, beginning in the late 1980s ABB Asea Brown Boveri attempted a complex strategy that required it to achieve, simultaneously, global efficiency, responsiveness to the particulars of each of the hundreds of distinct national product markets in which it competed, and the spread of learning worldwide. All this had to be done while merging and integrating two predecessor companies and numerous acquisitions. To do this, ABB needed both strong initiative from its managers in pursuit of their own objectives and, at the same time, a willingness to help out other units and contribute to the whole.

This imperative led ABB to adopt a very complex and expensive organizational form. ABB was made up of some 1,300 operating companies, each with its own income statement and balance sheet. The operating companies in turn contained some 5,000 profit centers. The small size of the business units (the profit centers averaged perhaps thirty-five employees each) meant that responsibility could be clearly assigned and that the people in a unit could readily see the impact of their actions on results. This contributed to generating initiative in pursuit of unit performance. A powerful financial and operational reporting system gave senior managers the information necessary to track results and to motivate and control behavior.

Each operating company was matrixed under a dual reporting relationship. On the one hand, the manager of an individual ABB company—for example, the steam turbine manufacturing operation in Germany—reported to a country head whose role was to ensure local responsiveness and to coordinate across the ABB companies in the country, thus supporting cooperation on this dimension. Since many of the customers were governments or government-owned electric and railroad companies, this local responsiveness was especially crucial. The country heads also played a major role in postmerger integration. At the same time, the individual company head also reported to a global product area executive, who sought to achieve global efficiency by coordinating investments and allocating production across countries and to promote learning by developing cross-national linkages among engineers and functional specialists. Both bosses had a say in performance evaluations and compensation.

Holding the whole together was a cadre of global managers who traveled almost constantly among different business units. Particularly important among these were the Executive Committee members, each of whom oversaw a variety of product areas and countries. This design required huge amounts of managerial time and energy: CEO Percy Barnevik famously quipped that he was in the office two days a week—Saturday and Sunday. Such a design would not have made sense under a less ambitious strategy.

As its strategy evolved, ABB adjusted its organization to affect the mix of behaviors its people supplied. In the early 1990s, the strategy moved to accentuate expansion in Eastern Europe and Asia while correspondingly shrinking the level of production in the West. This required more cooperation from the country heads in Western Europe, who would lose employees and investment and, with them, influence inside the firm and with the national governments where they operated. The response was to create a regional structure at the top level of the firm, so that one top manager oversaw all of the European country heads and could make sure that the managers in Western Europe supported the efforts in the East. This was to ensure that the needed cooperation of the country managers could be induced.

A change in the environment can also change the needed mix of cooperation and initiative. Johnson and Johnson, the huge pharmaceuticals, medical equipment, and consumer health care products company, organized itself to generate very high levels of initiative (Pearson and Hurstak 1992). It was divided internally into roughly 150 separate, product-based companies, each fully self-sufficient and fiercely independent. In the 1980s, there were thirteen different J&J companies serving the hospital market for medical equipment, each aligned with a different medical or surgical department. These units had their own sales forces, their own logistics and distribution, and their own billing. This was inconvenient and inefficient for their customers, which under cost pressures had transferred procurement from the individual departments to central purchasing managers. The obvious solution was for J&J to consolidate at least the distribution and billing for the thirteen companies. Yet it took J&J fifteen years to even try to establish such a system, because it would require more cooperation from the companies and threatened to undercut their independence and initiative.

Note that technological and organizational innovations can move the cooperation–initiative frontier, making it possible to have more cooperation and more initiative simultaneously. Information technology is an obvious source of such movements. By allowing finer performance measurement and better communications, it facilitates getting more initiative (through lowering the cost of providing incentives) and more cooperation (by making coordination easier and increasing contact among units). Another important determinant is the technology of organization and management. For example, the development of the multidivisional form for internal organization and of long-term relations with suppliers are both innovations in management that shifted the frontier.

Using this framework to examine a company's organization design does not require actually measuring the amounts of cooperation and initiative that are being generated. Rather, it simply requires evaluating the sorts of behavior being shown against what is needed. Two examples illustrate this.

At BP Exploration, the disaggregation of the business into discrete, empowered business units with clear performance responsibilities and the elimination of layers of middle managers and central functional staffs had the intended effect of increasing initiative, which John Browne saw as critical to improving performance. But the changes also created a great need for the business units to cooperate in sharing best practice and in supporting one another in solving technical and commercial problems— activities that were previously handled by the center, but that it now lacked the resources to undertake. The solution was to link collections of business units facing similar technical and commercial challenges into peer groups, each of which had around ten members. The members of these peer groups developed norms of sharing information and of helping one another resolve problems. Central to this was the practice of peer assists, under which a unit facing technical or business difficulties could call on other units and they would respond by sending experts to help resolve the problem. It became a strong norm to ask for help if in trouble and to respond wholeheartedly if asked for help. This cooperation was crucial to BP's success.

Novo Nordisk, one of the two global leaders in diabetes-treatment drugs, faced a crisis in 1992 when communication problems inside the firm led it to be out of compliance with new U.S. Food and Drug Administration regulations (Kamper, Podolny, and Roberts 2000). Novo had to withdraw temporarily from the U.S. market and to destroy a large amount of insulin. In response to the crisis, it instituted a new organizational design. It continued to allow large amounts of discretion to individual units in determining the exact routines and procedures they would use, but it increased their accountability for adhering to broad company policies. The intent was to maintain the initiative that had marked the highly decentralized organization but to get more cooperation in supporting overall policy and performance. Crucial to this was the creation of a group of "facilitators." The facilitators were experienced managers from around the organization who were charged with the internal audit function of providing assurance that individual units were adhering to company policies. When a unit was found not to be in compliance, the facilitators would agree with the unit head on the needed changes. In this process they came to know managers all over the company and they became very knowledgeable about the experiences different managers had had. This allowed them to connect managers facing problems with others who had resolved similar issues and to help the managers build networks that would support cooperative behavior.

Generally, the problems of effectively measuring cooperation mean that it is difficult to provide formal incentives for it. Thus, to induce cooperation, it is better to look to the softer elements of organization, including social networks and norms, as was done at BPX and Novo Nordisk. Meanwhile, architecture and process can be manipulated in the first instance to encourage initiative.

Many firms have, in fact, decided that they are not getting enough initiative, that increased competition demands that their people work more effectively in delivering performance in their jobs. Correspondingly, they are moving towards more market-like solutions to the organization problem. Within the organization these involve delayering, using stronger performance pay, empowering managers, creating clearer business unit boundaries, and ceding authority over operations and even elements of strategy to the units. These changes involve moving upwards in terms of Figure 8, getting more initiative, but they may also have the effect of moving left, reducing the cooperation. To counter this effect, the firms are seeking new ways of relating to and motivating their employees and of connecting their people to one another. These firms are also moving activities across their boundaries via outsourcing, spin-offs, and carve-outs, which also typically increase initiative while perhaps limiting the willingness to cooperate. At the same time, they are not settling for the inadequate cooperation that arm's length market arrangements usually engender. Instead, they are seeking more cooperation by using novel ways to connect to suppliers, customers, and other firms, including relational contracts, joint ventures, and alliances. We will explore these changes more in later chapters.

Notes

1. This is not a claim about historical patterns—that markets were tried but failed, and then firms were created. Rather, that the division of activity between firm and market has changed over time in complex ways.

2. See Milgrom and Roberts (1992: chapters 5, 6, and 9) for a more detailed discussion of many of the topics addressed in this section.

3. This term originates in the insurance industry, where it refers to the fact that those who know they are bad risks are more likely than the average person to buy insurance.

4. This term also comes from the insurance industry, where it refers to the tendency of people with insurance to take greater risks than they would if they bore the full impact of their choices.

5. For explorations of contracting with costly enforcement, see Doornik (2002, 2003).

6. There is a large literature in economics on incomplete contracts and renegotiation. See Williamson (1975, 1985), Grossman and Hart (1986), Hart (1995), Hart and Holmström (1987), and Hart and Moore (1990) for some of the early explorations of the institutional effects of these features. Later work is mathematically more demanding. Milgrom and Roberts (1992: 127–33) has a discussion

that, while still nontechnical, is more complete than that offered here.

7. Myerson and Satterthwaite (1983) show that, unless there is common knowledge between buyer and seller that the buyer's willingness to pay for the object on sale exceeds its value to the seller, there must be inefficiency. This can manifest itself in trades that do not occur although they should, or in protracted negotiations and costly delays in reaching agreements.

8. See Milgrom and Roberts (1992: chapters 2 and 5) for more detail.

9. The strong form of the argument is that efficiency alone determines what will occur. This is true, however, only if the size of the pie is independent of its distribution: Formally, that there are no income effects and that wealth is freely transferable. These may be decent assumptions in many circumstances, especially in thinking about relations between firms, and theorizing built on them has been very successful in explaining observed practice. When they fail, however, efficiency alone does not fully determine the patterns of organization and the allocations of resources that are viable. The predictive power of the theory is then reduced.

10. In contrast, "rents" are returns that are in excess of the minimum needed to attract a resource to a particular use in the first place. Note that once an investment is sunk, some of the returns may be quasirents even though there were no rents (excess returns) being earned *ex ante*. This situation occurs exactly when there is specificity but competition obtains before the lock-in occurs.

11. For more on the hold-up problem, see Milgrom and Roberts (1992: 136–9).

12. See, for example, Monteverde and Teece (1982), Masten (1984), Joskow (1985, 1987, 1988), and Masten, Meehan, and Snyder (1989) for studies where asset specificity seems to explain patterns of vertical integration and long-term contracting.

13. Unless the measures are completely objective, which is rare, and contractible, in the sense that third parties can observe them, which is necessary for courts to enforce contracts written upon them.

14. See Hart (1995) for an exposition of these ideas and Whinston (2003) for an evaluation of their empirical implications.

15. Concluding that the incentives inside the unified firm are actually weaker requires an additional assumption: That the marginal impact of the investments is greater when the relationship is intact than if it breaks up. In particular, this means that the investments should not have more of an effect at the margin on outside opportunities than on the person's value in the firm.

16. Formally, if the marginal cost of doing one increases in the amount of the other being undertaken.

4

Motivation in the Modern Firm

Firms, like other economic organizations, serve to coordinate the actions of groups of people and to motivate them to carry out needed activities. The problem of motivating people in organizations comes from the fact that their own self-interest may not automatically lead them to act in the ways that the organization would want. This divergence of interests arises because the individual members of an organization typically do not bear all the costs and benefits of the actions they take and the decisions they make within the organization. Consequently, when they make decisions—about how to spend their time, how hard to work and on what, what risks to take— the choices that appear best from their personal point of view may not maximize the total value generated for the organization. Even if they are cognizant of the larger interests, they may not automatically take these fully into account.

From an organization design perspective, the motivation problem is to shape the organization—the people, the architecture, the routines and processes, and the culture—to bring a closer alignment of interests between the organization and its members and thereby increase the efficiency of the choices they make. In this task, the designer in a firm can have access to all the levers of organization design—people, architecture, processes, and culture—and in many contexts all these should be used. In particular, motivation is not just a matter of monetary incentives, as important as these are in some cases.[1]

The Source and Nature of Motivation Problems

In general, motivation or incentive problems arise when individuals'[2] organizational decisions and actions affect others in ways that the individual does not fully take into account—when there are *externalities*. There are basically two ways that a disparity can arise between the costs and benefits that an individual bears versus those that accrue to the organization as a whole. Perhaps most often, individuals in organizations receive only a small fraction of the benefits that result from their taking various actions, but bear a disproportionate part of the costs that are involved. In this case, their decisions are likely to involve too little activity for organizational efficiency. The other possibility is that the fraction of the benefits that they get exceeds the share of costs that they bear. Then they are likely to choose too much of the activity in question.

In the simplest example of the first sort of problem, someone employed for an hourly wage or a fixed salary directly experiences the physical and emotional effects of working harder and longer. The direct gains resulting from his extra effort are the increased output he generates, but these gains accrue to the firm, not the worker, whose earnings do not change. There may, of course, be some gains to him: A decreased likelihood of being disciplined or fired, a possible increase in the chance of promotion or a raise, and perhaps social approval (or opprobrium!) from fellow workers. He might also experience some feelings of individual satisfaction, from a job better done. Yet, because he does not directly receive the full benefits of the increased output, he is unlikely to be motivated to work as hard as he would have if he received the full fruits of his labor. Indeed, there may be temptation to slack off, and if the shirking is not too obvious and egregious, he is unlikely to bear any great consequences. Thus, there is a real temptation not to work too hard—certainly not as hard as might maximize total value created.

Similarly, a manager may avoid taking risks that are worthwhile from the point of view of the shareholders. This happens because she receives little of the gains that would accrue to success, but faces the risk to her career that failure would bring. As another example, a shareholder who does a diligent job of monitoring corporate management bears the all the costs of this activity. However, the benefits in terms of improved performance are shared among all those holding the firm's stock. In this case, we would expect less monitoring than would be optimal.

The motivation problem can also arise because the gains accrue to the actor but the costs are borne elsewhere in the organization. For example, a CEO who enjoys the increased status that comes from heading a bigger company may be tempted to make acquisitions, even if they destroy value.[3] The executive gets the benefits, and the costs are borne by shareholders. Note that other members of the organization may support the CEO in this empire building because their career prospects are enhanced by the firm's growth.

It is important to understand why motivation problems arise in managed organizations—why there are systematic divergences between the costs and benefits that accrue to the organization and those that its decision-makers face. After all, we do not worry about motivation issues in all transactions, even though the interests of the various parties are quite different and, at least regarding the price, are completely opposed. Financial market traders usually do not worry about having to motivate other traders properly when they trade yen for dollars in a foreign exchange transaction. Consumers do not worry about other parties' motivation when they buy a can of branded soup from a grocery chain. Yet, when a firm seeks to buy the labor services from employees and contractors, it must be very concerned about motivation.

The key difference is in the possibilities for using contracts or reputations to guide behavior in situations where interests differ and where the actions of one party have an impact on the well-being of others. If there is no divergence of interests, then there is no problem, because simple self-interest will lead the parties to act in one another's common best interests. Even when interests diverge, if it is easy to devise and enforce contracts that induce the desired behavior, then there is no real motivation problem. The contract, if well designed, will lead the parties to act in ways that maximize total value creation. Moreover, if explicit contracts cannot be written that adequately guide behavior, reputation mechanisms can sometimes substitute for them and take care of motivation. But if interests differ, and if neither contracts nor reputation considerations are fully effective, then there are significant motivational issues.

In the foreign exchange example, it is clear to both sides exactly what is required to meet the terms of the agreement to trade, and these conditions can be simply included in a contract. Further, it is a relatively straightforward matter to establish whether each side has adhered to the agreement. Thus, courts or other third parties (like arbitration bodies) can enforce these agreements easily. Moreover, if a trader fails to abide by a contract, other traders on the exchange will know and can avoid dealing with the cheater in the future. Commodity trade generally is relatively free from motivational problems, as are dealings where reputations can effectively shape behavior. Pursuit of self-interest does not lead to any remediable inefficiency.

In the soup example, in contrast, there is no contract about the recipe and processes used in making the soup, and until the customer gets it home and tries it, no one knows if it will be to his taste. This might seem an opportunity for the manufacturer to cheat on quality to save cost or to lie about the contents of the can to increase demand. However, most of the actions the manufacturer might take that would have the biggest negative impact on the customer are deterred by regulatory inspections and the possibility of legal action. Meanwhile, the manufacturer's concern with repeat sales discourages its misrepresenting quality in less dangerous ways. Regarding the retailer, there is little the store might do that could negatively affect the consumer and that would be worthwhile, so there is no reason to worry about its behavior. The one exception might be that the store might charge very high prices, but reasonable levels of competition will take care of this too.

Things are different in managed organizations. Decisions and actions affect other parties, interests are typically not fully aligned, contracting possibilities are limited, and reputations are only partially effective. Indeed, these differences actually go a long way to explaining why firms exist!

A central, pervasive instance of such difficulties involves limited observability of behavior and the consequent moral hazard. Individuals' intellectual and physical efforts at their jobs create benefits for the organization as a whole (in lower costs, better sales, reduced risk, and improved reputation), but those efforts usually are not freely observable and precisely measurable in a timely fashion. Because the organization cannot tell exactly what the individual actually did, an enforceable contract cannot be written that would specify what is to be done and what rewards and punishments are to follow from adhering to or violating the contract. The limited observability of actions also undercuts the possibility for reputation concerns to guide behavior. Since others cannot observe the individual's actions, a reputation for behaving well cannot be easily developed.[4] This is the classic context considered in the economic theory of agency. The examples given of the worker deciding how hard to push himself or herself and the manager accepting or rejecting risky projects are examples of this phenomenon, and in fact the basic problem is pervasive.

In such contexts, any formal incentives have to be based on noisy, imprecise indicators of what the agent has done. A prime example is using imprecise measures of behavior, such as intermittent monitoring, as a basis for performance evaluation. Another is basing rewards on outcomes that are only partially determined by the actions in question. As we will discuss below, while such performance pay is increasingly popular, it has its problems.

A related motivational problem is known as free riding. It arises in situations where several individuals can contribute to some outcome but all share the benefits. An example is protection and promotion of a common brand. All the business units using the brand gain when any one of them expends resources to defend or enhance it. Since no unit receives the full benefits that result from its expenditures, each is likely to under-invest. If the actions taken with respect to the brand are hard to monitor, preventing the free riding may be difficult. As well, since the value any unit receives from the brand may be hard for others to determine, it may be difficult to establish an appropriate amount for each to contribute to the brand. This opens the door for misrepresentation aimed at reducing any mandated contributions.

Another example of free riding comes in team-based work where the efforts of many individuals contribute to some final result upon which rewards for the group are based. It is tempting for each person in the team to do less than his share of the total needed for efficiency, because each one incurs all the costs of any extra contributions made and yet gets only a fraction of the incremental benefits generated. Thus, unless the team members can easily monitor one another's contributions, each has an incentive to stop contributing when the additional individual benefits match the additional costs of contributing more. But at this point the total additional benefits accruing to everyone far exceed the costs of a single individual contributing more. Thus, weighing the full benefits against the costs would call for much higher contributions. The resulting inefficiency means there is a motivation problem.

Limited observability of actions is not the only source of motivation problems. In particular, suppose that behavior is directly observed by all the affected parties, so that they all know what has in fact occurred, but that it is not possible to establish the facts for an outside party. Then contracts prescribing (or proscribing) particular actions cannot be enforced by outside third parties, and so they cannot function to motivate efficiently. Another problem arises when the parties fail to specify fully in their initial agreement what should be done in different circumstances. This might occur because the parties did not foresee all the relevant possibilities, or because normal language is not sufficiently precise to distinguish different contingencies unambiguously, or because it was simply judged to be too costly to write such a detailed contract. Then contracts cannot fully specify the desired behavior in every circumstance and so cannot fully resolve motivation problems. Again, linking rewards to observable, verifiable outcomes (rather than behavior) may provide some desirable incentives, but this can be even more problematic than in the earlier case. Reputations may be the only really effective mechanism here.

A further difficulty arises when the actions that are actually taken are based on information that is available only to the person taking the actions. This situation is also widespread: Indeed, the power to make decisions is very often given precisely to those who are best informed and most expert. A divergence of interests in such situations causes difficulties even if the actual actions themselves are fully observable and verifiable by courts or other third parties. The problem is that it may be hard to judge if the actions were really in the best interests of the organization or instead were chosen to advance the interests of the expert. This is the case in the example of the empire-building CEO—there is almost always some story that can be told about how the latest acquisition is strategic and value enhancing, no matter how bad it actually is for shareholders. Once more, outcomes-based rewards (e.g. rewards tied to the stock price) are often a partial solution, but they do not fully solve the problem.

All of these situations fall under the rubric of "agency problems." There is now a very large literature on agency in economics, and it has been applied widely in management studies. Most of this work deals with explicit incentive contacting, and we will review some of the highlights of this work as a background for its application in later chapters.

Simple Agency Theory[5]

The simplest agency model involves a single individual, called the agent, who acts on behalf of another, called the principal. (For clarity, we will treat the principal as female "she," and the agent as male, "he.") Examples include an employee (agent) and employer (principal); a board member and the shareholders; or a contractor, lawyer, or broker and the client. The returns to the agent's actions accrue to the principal except for those personal costs that the agent directly bears. For example, the employee's output goes to the firm, which also absorbs the costs of materials and equipment, but the employee has to bear the costs of the effort he takes. For simplicity we call the action being taken "effort provision," but numerous other interpretations are possible. What is crucial is that, other things being equal, at the margin the agent prefers to provide less of the action taken on the principal's behalf while the principal prefers more. In particular, the agent is assumed to prefer working less than would be efficient from the point of view of maximizing the total benefits produced minus the costs of his action. The agent, in fact, may be willing to exert a nontrivial amount of effort without any explicit incentives, but providing more effort than this imposes costs on him. This creates a conflict of interest that underlies the motivation problem in an agency relationship.

If the agent's choice of effort were observable and verifiable to the courts and if the desired action could be determined and described before the fact, then the two parties could simply contract on the action to be taken. The principal would pay the agent for the effort he provided for her benefit and, in light of the amount needed to compensate him for different levels of effort, she would decide the amount of effort to buy. (We refer to the effort choice that would be made in this context as the "full information" level. Since it would be value maximizing, we also call it the "first-best" level.) If the agent failed to deliver, then he would not be paid. Then he would, in fact, find it worthwhile to act as the principal desired, and there would be no significant motivation problem.

To have a motivation problem in this simplest, barebones model we assume then that the principal cannot directly observe the agent's action. This is a reasonable assumption in many organizational contexts. We also initially assume that some noisy signal of the action is observed and can be contracted upon—otherwise, there is no contractual way to provide any incentives. The measure is assumed to vary with the agent's effort, so observing it provides information about the effort choice, but it also has an element of random variability that cannot be removed. For example, the principal might attempt to monitor behavior but cannot do so with perfect accuracy, observing instead the effort confounded with some random measurement error. This error might simply be that the monitoring is not continual. Then actual behavior is not fully observed, and instead there is an episodic sampling of what was done. Alternatively, some outcome like production volumes, costs, sales revenue, or profit might be observed, but this outcome might be determined both by the agent's action and other factors that are not observed, such as the actions of other parties, or the random performance of a machine, or the state of demand.

The randomness of the performance measure means that the agent may supply relatively low effort but, by luck, the signal on which the reward is based may take on high values anyway. Similarly, the agent might work very hard, and yet the observed performance measure might be low because of the effect of the randomness.[6] Thus, rewards based on the imperfect measures will have an element of randomness that is beyond the agent's (or the principal's) control.

Of course, if the agent bore the full benefits of his actions as well as the costs, he would take the efficient choices. This might seem to suggest that rewards ought to be structured to reflect the full impact of changing the effort choice on the benefits generated, which the agent will then compare to the effect on the costs borne. For example, if the agent were the manager of a firm owned by the principal, selling the firm to him would cause him to bear all the costs and benefits of his actions. He would then certainly face the right incentives. While this solution is sometimes possible and attractive, there are two principal reasons why it might not be feasible or desirable to have the agent bear the full benefits as well as the costs of his actions.

The first reason is that the benefits might be uncertain while the agent is risk-averse, so that receiving an uncertain payment is less attractive to him than getting its expected value for sure. Then having him bear the full—but uncertain—impact of his actions is inefficient because it means that he shoulders all the risk arising from the uncertainty in the benefits, while the risk-absorbing ability of the principal is not used and goes to waste. It would be better to share the variability of returns between the two parties, because this lowers the total cost of the risk being borne. Indeed, if the principal is risk-neutral, then she should ideally bear all the risk, because doing so is costless for her. The problem is that performance varies not just with random luck but also with the agent's choices in ways that cannot be disentangled by the principal because the agent's actions are not observed. Then having the principal absorb some of the variability in returns means that some of the impact of the agent's choice of actions necessarily must also be borne by her. Thus, the agent does not face all the costs and benefits involved in selecting his effort level.

The desirability of risk sharing remains an important factor even when the agent is not being asked to bear all the risk and when the noisy measure being used in contracting is something other than the returns that are generated.

The second reason that the agent may not be able to bear the full marginal returns of his effort choice is that he is financially constrained. For example, perhaps he cannot cover any negative returns that might arise. In this case, selling the firm to the agent either is not possible or, if he has the option of bankruptcy, fails in fact to make him bear the full marginal costs and benefits of his actions. More generally, if there is a minimum payment (perhaps zero, or even negative) the agent must receive in any eventuality, any incentive scheme offered to the agent must involve his always getting at least this amount, no matter how bad the measured performance may be. Thus, it is possible that the agent cannot be made the full residual claimant.

In either case, once the agent cannot be the full residual claimant, the principal's problem is to design an incentive scheme that motivates the agent to provide effort in the desired amount. The intensity of the incentives provided—the extent to which rewards vary with the performance measure, and thus (given how the measure varies with effort) how rewards vary with effort—determines the amount of effort the agent will choose to provide. Making the incentives more intense increases the expected return to the agent from exerting more effort and so he will work harder. Assuming a risk-neutral principal, an optimal scheme simply induces the effort level that maximizes the principal's expected returns net of what must be paid to the agent. Of course, the choice of the incentive scheme must be made in light of the fact that the level of effort actually chosen will be what the scheme motivates the agent to provide—the principal cannot ignore the incentives that the reward scheme gives the agent. Further, the agent must expect to receive enough total compensation to be willing to work for the principal, rather than go elsewhere and pursue the next-best alternative use of his time and talents.

The theoretically ideal design involves a trade-off. The exact nature of the trade-off depends on the reason the agent does not bear all the marginal costs and benefits.

In the limited liability case, providing more intense incentives involves increasing the payment for good results without any offsetting decrease in payments when the performance appears bad (assuming the payment in bad states is already as low as is feasible). Thus, the cost of getting more effort is that expected returns must be passed to the agent, even though his pay is already enough to attract him to the job. In fact, to get the first-best level of effort that the principal would buy from the agent under full observability might require giving the agent an expected payment that exceeds the expected value of the gross returns. This effect may limit the intensity of incentives and result in a lower level of effort provision than would obtain without an observability problem.

In the more widely studied case on which we henceforth focus, risk aversion is key. Giving more intense incentives—for example, increasing the commission rate paid to a salesperson—increases the effort provided because the returns to this effort increase. More intense incentives also make the agent's pay more risky, since a given amount of random variation in the performance measure is now translated into a greater variance in pay. If the principal is risk-neutral[7] but the agent is risk-averse, however, having the agent bear any risk is costly. Even when the principal is not risk-neutral, increasing the intensity of incentives eventually means shifting more risk onto the agent than would be desirable. The principal will have to compensate the agent for the risk the latter is made to bear, and so ultimately she bears these costs.

The principal's problem in determining the desired intensity of incentives then involves trading off the cost of having to compensate the agent, both for exerting extra effort and for bearing more risk, against the benefits generated by the extra effort that is induced by stronger incentives. Generally, the solution is to have the agent face less intense incentives than are needed to induce the full-observability, first-best level of effort, where the risk and the costs it would bring are irrelevant. At the same time, the agent bears more risk than would be efficient absent the need for incentives.

This model is very simple and stylized. Yet, it yields a number of useful predictions and recommendations about the design of incentives. In particular, stronger incentives should be provided when the agent is less risk-averse and when the performance measures more accurately reflect what the agent actually did. The incentives should also be stronger the more valuable it is to the principal to induce higher levels of effort and the more easily the agent can respond to strengthened incentives.[8]

The logic for each of these conclusions is a cost–benefit one. In two of the cases—the dependence of the intensity of incentives on the importance of inducing effort and on the responsiveness of the agent's effort choice to stronger incentives—the logic is very simple. Regarding the first, the greater the benefit of extra effort, the higher is the optimal amount of effort to induce, and thus the more intense should be the incentives. Similarly, the more that effort responds to incentives, and thus the more extra output and value that result from strengthened incentives, the stronger should be the incentives.

These factors may account for the general pattern that incentive intensity increases with the hierarchic level of the agent in most firms. Top executives' decisions arguably have great impact on firm performance, and they have lots of ways in which they can alter their behavior in response to incentives. Meanwhile, less benefit typically flows from increasing the effort of a lower-level person, and such employees have fewer levers they can pull in responding to incentives. In the extreme, paying piece rates to a worker on an assembly line is pointless, because there is no way for the individual worker to increase his output if others on the line do not increase theirs.

The logic underlying the role of the degree of risk aversion is that the cost of the agent's bearing extra risk is lessened when he is less risk-averse. Since the incentive intensity is determined by trading off the costs of his bearing more risk against the benefits from inducing more effort (net of the direct costs of the effort), the reduced marginal cost of risk-bearing leads to increasing the intensity of the incentives. To the extent that attitudes towards risk-taking depend on wealth, we might expect that those with high incomes would be less risk-averse and better able to bear risks. Given that incomes and wealth tend to rise as one moves up the corporate hierarchy, this then might be another reason why more of the pay of top executives is at risk.

The logic for the role of the precision of performance measures is that, when the measures are more accurate and vary less in a purely random fashion, an increase in the intensity of incentives brings less additional uncontrolled risk in the agent's reward, and thus less additional risk-bearing cost. It is then worthwhile to induce more effort via more intense incentives, because the cost of doing so is lower. Thus, in tasks where it is hard to measure performance in an accurate and timely fashion, it is desirable to use little in the way of explicit performance incentives. In contrast, when the link between actions and observed performance is clear and precise, very strong incentives can be given.

It is worth noting that there is actually a complementarity between giving more intense incentives and improving the performance measures. We have already argued that better performance measures should lead to stronger incentives, but things go the other way too. If more intense incentives are desired (e.g. because the value of extra effort has increased), then it is more worthwhile to spend resources to improve the measures on which the incentive payments are based. This is because the value of increasing the precision comes from the reduced costs of risk bearing by the agent, and these costs are directly related to the strength of the incentives being given. So with stronger incentives, the benefits of increasing the accuracy with which performance is measured increase.

A further insight arises from this model. If explicit incentives are to be given at all, they probably should be substantial: It is often better to give no explicit incentives at all rather than weak ones. This is because there may be a discrete fixed cost of using performance pay, even if there are no administrative expenses in using a formal incentive scheme (which, of course, there likely are). If compensation is not dependent on measured results, then the net benefit of a given level of effort provision is simply the net revenues of the firm, less the cost of that level of effort to the worker (for which the firm must compensate him). If incentive pay is used to induce more effort, then the worker faces risk in his pay. This risk has a cost to the worker that is increasing in the personal cost of increasing the provision of effort.[9] If the marginal cost of extra effort is not zero, this term does not disappear as the amount of extra effort that the firm seeks to induce (and, correspondingly, the intensity of incentives) becomes small. Thus, a little bit of incentive pay, although it may induce a little more effort, brings a discrete jump in costs. Only if the incentives are sufficiently strong, and enough extra effort is thereby induced, will these fixed costs be overcome.

In particular, then, if the available measures are very poor, so that only weak incentives might be offered in any case, it may well be better to offer no explicit incentives at all. In this case, other means might be sought to motivate. One we will discuss below is "high commitment" human resource management.

The Choice of Performance Measures

So far we have assumed there was a single measure on which pay could be based. Often, however, there are many possible performance measures that are more or less indicative of how much effort the agent has exerted. For example, both the stock price and accounting returns may carry information about the quality of the job done by the senior managers of the firm, or it may be possible both to monitor a worker's behavior directly and to measure the results he generates. An important issue is which of these multiple indicators should be used in designing performance contracts and how to use them.

The answer from agency theory is that pay should depend on any freely available measure that is "informative" about the agent's effort provision (Holmström 1979). Here "informative" means that taking proper account of the measure allows a more precise inference about the agent's actual choice of effort than is possible without it. Further, if a particular measure is not informative in this sense, then it should not be used.

For example, the profits of an oil company depend not just on how well its people have worked on finding oil, controlling costs, and generating sales but also, crucially, on the crude oil price. Rewarding employees on measured profits implies a lot of randomness in their pay because oil prices may double or triple from one year to the next. Thus, they could have done a miserable job and yet be well rewarded just because oil prices rose. Equally, a superb effort could go unrewarded because oil prices collapsed. This variability has no useful incentive properties and is costly. Instead, it would be better to remove the effect of oil price changes in estimating performance. This was in fact done at BP plc, the global energy firm. It employed "self-help"—essentially the change in performance not attributable to changes in crude oil price changes (and exchange rates)—in performance pay. This amounts to using two measures, actual earnings and the oil price, to give a better indication of what the people in the firm did.

Motivation

Note that this principle points to a need for subtlety in applying the dictum that people should not be held accountable for factors they cannot control. Certainly a measure that is not responsive to the agent's effort should not be used on its own as the only basis for rewards. After all, the point is to induce effort, and paying only on something unrelated to what you are trying to induce accomplishes nothing. But a variable that is correlated with the noise in measured performance may be usefully employed in performance evaluation, even when it is not itself directly tied to and reflective of effort. The reason is that the extra measure can be used to filter out some of the extraneous randomness. This is precisely what BP does by taking out oil price effects.

Another application of this "Informativeness Principle" is to executive compensation. It is common for executives to receive bonuses that are based on accounting earnings and also to have some of their pay tied to the stock price (either explicitly or through grants of stock or options). This makes no sense from the point of view of agency theory unless the accounting numbers carry information that both is not reflected in the stock price and is relevant for inferring how diligently the executives pursued their responsibilities. Under a common assumption about stock market price formation—that the prices reflect all the publicly available information that is relevant for judging the value of the firm—publicly available accounting returns are unlikely to provide additional information beyond the stock price about top executives' behavior. They, thus, should not figure into determining their pay. The stock price should be a sufficient measure. On the other hand, accounting results may be quite informative about the efforts of functional or divisional heads. For example, revenues might carry a lot of additional information about the contributions of the marketing director. Thus, they should be used in his compensation, even if he is also rewarded with stock and options.

Using multiple measures to increase the overall precision in measuring performance may seem complicated, but it need not be. A familiar example here is measuring a sales organization by profitability—that is, revenues and costs—rather than just revenues alone. Doing so, even though the sales people have no control over costs, encourages them to focus their efforts on more profitable sales, rather than on the biggest revenue generators. Rewarding the sales function on profitability is especially important if it controls pricing, because this reward system encourages the sales force to account for costs in pricing decisions.

Another common example is compensating a sales person both on his overall sales and on how he has done relative to the average across the sales staff overall. Accounting for how others have done allows making a better estimate of how hard the particular sales person has actually worked by filtering out the impact of overall market conditions that affect every sales person's results. Reducing the noise in measured performance reduces the randomness in the rewards, allowing stronger incentives to be provided and more effort to be induced. Thus, a rationale for comparative performance evaluation emerges. (Of course, this involves making the pay of one agent depend on something not within the agent's control, namely the others' performance levels.) Similarly, there is some evidence that CEOs' compensation is responsive not just to their own firms' performance but also to how well they have done relative to comparable firms in the same industry (Gibbons and Murphy 1990). This is consistent with the idea of using extra measures to reduce some of the variability in measured performance, and thus to permit more accurate assessments of behavior and more intense incentives.

An extreme form of this comparative performance evaluation occurs in "tournaments," where rewards are based solely on the performance ranking of the different participants, not on how well they performed in any absolute sense (Lazear and Rosen 1981). This system is familiar from golf and tennis contests and team sport leagues, but it also is used in sales contests, where the sales person with the highest volume wins the prize. Promotions are also often effectively a tournament: The best performer wins the prize of a higher salary and status and the opportunity to compete for the next promotion. Tournaments can be very useful when it is hard to specify and measure results in a quantitative way on which pay can be based and yet it is still clear who has done the best job. Gearing rewards to absolute performance is then impossible, but the winner can still be identified and rewarded. In some circumstances, in fact, tournaments may be as effective motivators as explicit performance pay such as piece rates.

All these examples have involved performance measures that are more-or-less freely available because they are generated in the normal course of business or for other purposes. If measures have to be developed and collected, the costs of doing so are likely to involve a large fixed element. This may mean that only some of the potentially available measures will be created and used. Another reason for not using all possible measures is that the resulting system may end up being too complicated for anyone to understand. In this case, it cannot motivate effectively. This possibility would seem to limit the potential effectiveness of schemes that call for large numbers of measures, such as some variants of "Balanced Scorecard" systems.

When choosing among possible costly measures, firms often have to decide whether to measure inputs (behavior) or outputs (results). Which to choose depends on whether the designers know in advance what the appropriate behavior is (Prendergast 2000). If they know what the agent should do, then it is likely that input measures will be effective: Specify what is supposed to be done, check to see if the agent has done it, pay him if he has, and fire him if he has not.[10] There is no need for fancy incentive schemes, and this may explain why performance pay is not more universal. On the other hand, if the designer does not know what ought to be done, then the designer also does not know what behavior to specify and measure. In this case, it is better to measure results and leave it to the agent to figure out how to deliver these results. Note that, to the extent that environmental uncertainty increases the likelihood that the contract designer will not know what behavior is desirable, then the presumptive negative association between uncertainty and incentives may be reversed.

Multi-tasking in Agency Relationships

A richer set of insights arises when we extend the model to recognize that the agent might spend his time on more than one activity that is useful to the principal. In this case, the principal needs both to motivate the overall provision of effort and to shape its allocation among tasks. This becomes a significant problem in two different contexts. One is when the desired activities compete for the agent's time and attention, so that doing more of one increases the cost or difficulty of doing more of the other, while the available performance measures for the two activities are not of comparable accuracy or timeliness (Holmström and Milgrom 1991). In this case it becomes very expensive to offer incentives that will induce the agent to devote significant levels of effort to both activities. The second problem in the multi-tasking context arises when there are not separate measures for the performance on the two tasks, but inducing the agent to do a good job on the one task requires very different incentives than are required for the other task (Athey and Roberts 2001). When any available measures confound the results of the two activities in ways that do not permit disentangling, improving the incentives for one task may worsen those for the other. In either of these contexts where multi-tasking is problematic, the solution to the motivation problem often involves using other aspects of the organization design, especially the design of jobs and the allocation of decision authority.

As an example of the first sort of multi-tasking problem, the two tasks might be providing initiative and cooperation, as discussed in the preceding chapter. The measure on initiative might be individual or business unit performance, which might, in fact, be a reasonably accurate reflection of the effort and thought the agent provided in this direction. Cooperation, however, is likely much harder to measure effectively, since the behavior itself may be hard to observe (especially if it involves refraining from activities that hurt other units) and the results are going to be tied up in the performance of the other units and thus in the efforts their members have exerted. Another example is delivering current performance and developing new business. Performance on the first is relatively easily measured, while information about the quality of effort devoted to the latter is much less certain and slower to emerge. The problem is to induce the agent to devote effort to both in the appropriate amounts.

The agent's choice of how to spend his time—both how much effort to provide in total and how to divide it among tasks—will be governed by the incentives that are provided for the tasks. Suppose first that the activities do not compete for the agent's time and attention—that the costs to the agent of one activity are independent of the level of the other being undertaken. Further, suppose there are separate, independent (but imperfect) performance measures for each sort of effort. Then the choice of the level of one activity to undertake will not affect the cost–reward trade-offs faced in choosing the level of the other. In this case, the incentives for each activity can be set independently to achieve whatever levels of the two sorts of effort are desired.

More often, however, the activities do compete at the margin, if only because time spent on one is not available for the other. Then the agent's working harder on one task raises the costs he experiences in providing more of the second activity. In this case, increasing the rewards to one activity will not only have the obvious direct effect of inducing the agent to devote more time and effort to that

142

activity. It will also lead the agent to reduce his provision of the other activity, because its marginal cost has increased while the returns to providing it have not changed. This means the incentives for the two activities must be designed in a coordinated way.

For example, suppose that all that matters to the agent is the total time and effort spent on the two tasks together, not how much goes into each task separately, and suppose rewards are proportional to performance while expected performance in each task is proportional to the effort exerted on it. Then if the rewards for extra time spent on each task are not identical, the optimal thing for the agent to do is to spend all his time on the better-rewarded task, because this maximizes his returns for any total expenditure of effort. To get attention paid to both tasks, the returns to increasing effort on each must be equal.

The intensities of the incentives for different activities thus tend to be complements: Strengthening the incentives for one activity makes it more attractive to strengthen the incentives for the others. Otherwise, these other activities are ignored. Thus, the incentives offered for multiple tasks should all be intense together, or all relatively muted.

More generally, even when the agent cares about how time is divided among tasks (but doing more of one still increases the costs of doing more of the other), unless the incentives are appropriately balanced, the agent will tend to overemphasize the better-compensated activity and under-supply the other. Indeed, cutting back on the badly paid activity not only frees up time to spend on the better paid one, it reduces the cost to the agent of expanding supply of the well-rewarded activity. In the extreme, the poorly compensated one will just be ignored, even though performance on this dimension would, in fact, be rewarded—just not enough.

Lincoln Electric provides an example of using strong, balanced incentives in a multi-tasking context. Lincoln is famous for its extensive use of individual piece rates to reward production workers, paying them a fixed amount for each item of output on which they complete their assigned tasks. The piece rates provide very strong, direct incentives to produce lots of output. The danger is that, when so strongly motivated to increase quantity, the workers will stint on quality and will be unwilling to help out in various ways that are crucial to the firm but take them away from earning their piece rates. To prevent this, the workers are paid a bonus based on the quality of their work and other factors like the ideas they generate and how cooperative they are. On average, the bonus doubles the employees' already substantial income from the piece rates. Moreover, the bonuses vary dramatically between workers, depending on their assessed performance. These strong, balanced incentives have helped Lincoln achieve unmatched productivity and a reputation for top quality that have led to an outstanding record of decades of business success.

Providing comparably intense incentives for different activities becomes problematic, however, when the available measures of the two tasks differ greatly in their precision or timeliness.

Generally, the more accurately performance in an activity is measured, the less costly it is to provide stronger incentives for the activity in isolation and so to induce higher effort on it. Good measures tend to lead to strong incentives, and poor measures lead to weak ones, because stronger incentives lead to greater increases in risk-bearing costs when the measures are worse.

Suppose then that the quality of the measures on two activities differs significantly, as in the example of controlling costs in current operations and trying to develop ideas for new business opportunities. Realized costs are probably a pretty good measure of cost-control efforts, but the agent might easily work very hard at developing ideas and yet have little to show for it. Or the agent might have come up with some innovative ideas, but assessing their value will take time. In this case, it may be extremely difficult or expensive (in terms of the risk borne, for which the principal must compensate the agent) to give strong incentives for idea generation, even though it is cheap and easy to provide intense incentives for cost control.

We have already seen that this is not be a problem if the activities do not compete at the margin for the agent's time and attention—if doing more of one task does not affect how hard it is for the agent to increase the other. Then, the incentives for each can be set independently. The well-measured one will carry strong incentives and the other task will offer weak ones. The strong incentives will induce lots of effort aimed at the well-rewarded task, and the low returns to effort in the other task mean it will not get very much attention. But still each will be provided at the level the principal sees as appropriate in light of the costs and benefits.

If the tasks do compete at the margin, however, then giving strong incentives for the well-measured one and weak incentives for the other will result in very little or no attention being paid to the latter task, no matter how important it may be to the principal. (Note that the impossibility of observing the agent's choices means the principal's simply directing—or imploring—the agent to do both is not very helpful. The agent is still going to be inclined to make the choices that are good for himself in light of the incentives provided.)

Giving intense incentives for some desirable activities can then be a very bad idea, because these become negative incentives for other activities that cannot be similarly rewarded. The general idea that you get what you measure and pay for has a very precise meaning here.

An example involves merit pay for teachers (Milgrom and Roberts 1992: 230–1). A popular proposal would pay U.S. public school teachers more if their students do better on standardized tests. In contrast, teachers' pay now is usually based on credentials and experience, so the explicit, financial incentives for performance are quite weak (although intrinsic motivation is obviously real and important). Proponents of the proposed reform argue that providing stronger incentives would lead to better performance by teachers and their pupils. In all likelihood it would, in fact, lead teachers to do more of whatever it takes to help their students do well on the tests, particularly if the performance element of pay were substantial. However, it would also likely lead them to spend much less time and effort on things that are not measured on the tests. Indeed, in California, where schools' funding is tied to student performance on standardized tests of mathematics and reading, there are claims that teachers have de-emphasized teaching other subjects, even though their pay is not directly affected by the test results.[11] Some of these other things may be very important. They include not only other academic subjects (which could possibly be included in the testing), but also things that are hard to measure, like helping develop students' characters, teaching ethical behavior, and encouraging good citizenship. Measuring what teachers do on these dimensions in a relatively precise and timely fashion seems very problematic. So merit pay based on test performance is likely to drive these out, although they are provided in the absence of explicit incentives. Even worse, it might lead the least scrupulous teachers to find inappropriate ways to ensure their students succeed, such as getting hold of the test questions in advance. There actually have been some instances of such behavior in New York State, where performance on the state examinations at the end of high school is hugely important.

Thus, if multi-tasking is desired, it may be best to supply relatively *weak* incentives for both activities. Any effective multi-tasking incentive scheme must be balanced, offering similar rewards at the margin for each task, and if some tasks are poorly measured, then making all the incentives relatively strong will entail unacceptable levels of risk for the agent and correspondingly high compensation costs for the principal. The weakness of the incentives then means they will not motivate the agent to exert huge amounts of effort on either task, even the well-measured one to which he could be induced to devote significant effort if it were in isolation. Consequently, the performance on this activity is likely to be much worse than it would be in isolation. Yet, this may be better than getting none of the other activity.[12]

Thus, it may be better to leave teachers' pay largely unrelated to students' measured performance on tests.

Similarly, it is likely a good idea to avoid piece rates in manufacturing when contributions to quality cannot be measured in an accurate, timely fashion. And paying managers for current results can lead them to mortgage the future of the business, especially if they expect to move on to new jobs before the effects of their actions become clear.

The suggestion that performance pay should be avoided for tasks where it might be easily and effectively used certainly runs counter to the message business managers have received in the last decades. Yet, the frustrations so many executives have expressed with the failure to get their people to generate new ideas and growth opportunities indicates that the strong incentives they have created for current performance may sometimes be counterproductive.

An obvious solution here might be to separate the two tasks between two different agents. With no multi-tasking problem, one agent can be given intense incentives and the other more muted ones. Sometimes this approach is feasible, and it may even be the best solution, when the activities call for very different talents or skills or draw on different knowledge.

In other cases dividing responsibilities is very costly. Not only does a second agent need to be paid, but any synergies between the tasks may be lost. For example, sales representatives may have opportunities to learn about customer needs, and thus about new opportunities for product development. It would then be useful to ask them both to sell the current products and to bring such ideas back to the firm. But this creates a multi-tasking problem because the possibilities for measuring performance on the two activities differ so much. A case study of the electronics parts business (Anderson 1985; Anderson and Schmittlein 1984) illustrates the solution. When bringing ideas back is crucial, firms use employees as sales agents, paying them salaries (with little or no bonus for extra sales) and asking them to pay attention both to current sales and to the communication of ideas. This is a scheme with balanced, weak incentives for multi-tasking. When there are fewer opportunities for bringing back ideas, outside sales representatives are used. They are given strong incentives for extra sales (as they must be in order to get them to focus on this firm's products rather than those of other firms they represent) and there is no serious attempt to induce them to develop and share information about customers.

In the extreme, separating the tasks is simply impossible: There is no way to make one worker responsible for the volume produced while holding another responsible for the quality of the output the first one produces. When multi-tasking is unavoidable, it is very valuable to be able to increase the precision of the measures of the agent's performance on the poorly measured task. Lincoln Electric's effort to identify the individuals responsible for the quality of each machine by having them stencil their names on the pieces they produce is illustrative of this imperative.

The second sort of multi-tasking problem involves there not being adequate measures for the different tasks individually. For example, the agents might be the managers of two business units. Each manager needs to exert effort at leading the business unit, and each can also make decisions (about the brand, dealings with shared customers and suppliers, human resource policies, and so on) that may affect the returns to both units. Meanwhile, any available measures confound the results of the effort provision and the decisions. For example, none of the usual accounting measures would permit separating out the specific effects of the manager's effort, of the decisions he took, and of the decisions that the other manager made that affected the first division's costs and sales. Then it is not possible to provide incentives separately for effort and decision-making—any reward scheme will simultaneously affect the incentives for effort provision and for choices. The difficulty is that the sort of incentives that would be used to induce lots of effort may induce poor decision-making, while those that lead to good decisions do not motivate effort provision effectively. Thus, there are trade-offs.

To induce good decision-making on matters that have spillover effects on the other division, the manager's incentives should reflect the performance of both units. This might be realized, for example, by a bonus based on the aggregate profitability of the two. In this way, he will be induced to pay attention to the full impact of his choices. He will also have incentives to work hard to develop the right sort of investment opportunities and the information needed to make good choices. Of course, if his pay is based on overall profitability, the other unit's performance enters positively into his rewards.

On the other hand, to induce effort efficiently, each manager's incentives should be based on narrow measures of his division's performance alone. In particular, the other division's performance should not carry positive weight in determining the manager's compensation. Indeed, if the objective were simply to induce effort, the other division's measured performance might often be expected to have a negative impact on the manager's pay. If the performance of the two divisions is positively correlated because of the impact of common factors like general business conditions, then the Informativeness Principle means that comparative performance evaluation should be used. This means that a manager's performance is viewed less positively when the other division does better, and so the pay actually is negatively related to the other division's returns.

Thus, the incentives that induce good decision-making are bad at inducing effort (because they put too much extraneous risk on the manager). On the other hand, incentives that induce effort effectively lead the manager to ignore the impact of the decisions on other divisions and even to prefer choices that impose costs on other groups.

If the individual managers on their own must make the decisions, then the design of the system simply balances the importance of high effort and good decisions. Getting better decisions means making managers be concerned with the other unit's performance as well as their own. But this implies loading the managers with avoidable risk (from the other division's performance) and the increased costs of the risk lead to giving less intense incentives. In turn, less effort is induced. The optimal scheme balances these gains and losses, with the point of balance determined by the relative importance of effort and decisions. If effort is more important, then incentives will be based primarily on the manager's unit's performance, and he will make decisions that are good for his unit but not necessarily good for the firm overall. If his decisions have a large impact, both on his unit and on the other, then his pay will be mostly on overall performance, and he will not be as highly motivated to work hard for his unit's success.

If it is possible for others to make the decisions for a unit, then new options arise to design the decision-making process as well as the incentive schemes to get better performance on both dimensions. For example, the design might specify that a decision about a project arising in one unit that affects another would be implemented if and only if both units agree to it. As a first approximation, whether a manager will agree depends on what the adoption will do to his pay, which in turn can depend either just on the manager's own unit's measured performance or on both units' results. Since under any well-designed incentives, each manager's pay increases in the manager's own unit's performance, any project that is accepted under these rules will improve the measured performance of both units and presumably that of the firm overall. However, units will tend to reject projects that hurt them, even if they increase overall value. Further, if comparative performance evaluation is used, then the fraction of projects accepted will be small. This is because projects that help one unit's performance are bad from the other's point of view. Thus, projects will be accepted only if they give comparably positive returns to each unit. As a consequence, this system is problematic if projects tend to have their main impact on the division in which they emerge (so that, under comparative performance evaluation, the other division will not like them) but do have direct effects on other units (so that they get to veto projects).

In this context, a better design would be that if both units agree, then the project is implemented, but if they disagree, then the decision is referred to a third party. Other things being equal, this party should be given incentives that ensure good decisions, while the unit managers get incentives that motivate them to work hard. They will then accept projects that improve the measured performance of both units (and thus of the firm as a whole, if these are the only affected units). Meanwhile, projects that are worthwhile overall but harmful to one unit will be referred to the third party, who will accept them. This referral process is presumably costly, which is why it is worthwhile to let the affected units decide if they agree.

This latter process is in fact quite similar to the "concurrence" system that was used at IBM (Vance, Bhambri, and Wilson 1980). Under this arrangement, business units had to obtain the sign-off of any other affected units before they could implement projects. If concurrence was withheld, then the implementation decision would be passed to the units' direct hierarchic superiors. If they could not agree, it would pass further up until a common superior with authority over both units was reached and made the decision. This process could go as far as the executive committee, and it occasionally did.

Other designs encompassing incentive contracts and decision processes can be optimal in other contexts. The key is that multi-tasking causes problems and that the solution may involve multiple aspects of organization design.

Group Performance Pay

Many management experts have argued against individual performance pay on a variety of grounds. A major one is that it allegedly destroys cooperation and teamwork. This effect may indeed be real, as the logic of multi-tasking makes clear, and it is especially likely if performance is judged on a relative basis. In fact, it may be easier to subvert a colleague's performance than to improve one's own.

Of course, to the extent that the group can be thought of as acting in concert, the preceding theory can be applied to motivating a group using rewards based on their collective performance. A very direct example is the practice in California of paying teams of tree-fruit pickers by the total number of boxes they fill. The problem is that there may be free riding, because the results of extra effort by any group member are shared across the whole group. The resultant shirking may be effectively limited, however, by mutual monitoring within the group, especially if the group is not too large. This is an argument for keeping groups small for performance measurement and reward purposes. It is also necessary that a group norm of working hard be established and enforced by the group on its members. Of course, a norm of group-wide shirking might emerge instead. For example, Roy's classic study of a machine shop (Roy 1952) documented how workers physically punished colleagues who exerted too much effort and threatened to undermine the norm of featherbedding. Managing this element of culture is then a crucial task for management.

These free-rider issues are especially relevant to the common practice of paying rewards based on overall corporate performance, whether through bonuses, profit sharing, stock grants, or option awards. In a typical large firm with tens of thousands of employees, the free-rider problem would seem especially intense. Suppose an employee's efforts would create an additional million dollars in earnings. Then this might lead, generously, to an extra hundred thousand into the bonus pool. At most a few thousand of this is likely to trickle down to the employee responsible. More likely, he would get much less than this. Thus, from a purely financial point of view, the employee will rationally undertake the extra effort only if the costs are less than the extra bonus he can expect. Yet, the value of the extra effort to the organization is many, many times this amount—a million dollars. Effort is rationally under-provided because the benefits are shared but the employee bears all the costs. The situation is even worse with stock-based pay.[13] The employee's share of the extra value created by his actions is just the employee's fraction of the ownership of the outstanding stock. This is almost surely a trivially small number.

Stock-based pay thus seems remarkably inefficient as a direct motivation tool. Yet it is common, and not just at senior executive levels. While there are certainly other reasons for giving ownership claims to employees, such as encouraging them to invest in firm specific human capital (Roberts and Van den Steen 2001), it just does not seem a sensible way to motivate effort.

A plausible explanation for its prevalence lies in its supporting norms of hard work and mutual monitoring. If stock ownership somehow changes employees' mindsets, making them "think like owners," then it could be an effective motivational tool. This is especially likely if the firm combines this with a series of other measures in what is often called a "high commitment" work system (see below).

Manipulation of Performance Measures

A second complaint against performance pay is that, too often, the available measures are manipulable—the agent can find ways to increase measured performance that are easier than doing what is wanted. Then higher measured performance may be achieved by lowering the actual value created for the organization. The examples here are all too numerous. Paul Oyer (1998) has documented how paying bonuses for meeting annual performance targets leads managers to accelerate or delay sales in the last quarter of the year in order to make the numbers while not "wasting" sales that exceed the target. This increases the agents' pay, but cannot help the firm. At H. J. Heinz & Co, division managers were required to post steadily increasing results every year in order to earn bonuses. They manipulated the accounts to achieve their targets (Horngren 1999: 937–8). As the capital markets have come to demand steady earnings growth, such practices have become appallingly widespread. In two of the more egregious recent examples, industrial giants Enron and Worldcom each collapsed into bankruptcy after the exposure of the manipulations that they employed to hide their true performance and hold up their stock prices. Enron's trickery was sophisticated, misrepresenting the true balance sheet situation and profitability via asset transfers to nominally unrelated entities that in fact were controlled by Enron executives. Restating the firm's earnings to undo the chicanery reduced them by two-thirds from their reported levels. Worldcom's approach was simpler. It inflated its earnings by blatantly recording billions of dollars worth of current costs as capital expenditures and by treating non-recurring receipts as if they were revenue that could be expected to be ongoing. These deceits were easier ways for the executives to bolster the value of their stock holdings than actually generating the returns honestly.

These examples involve misleading corporate superiors and/or shareholders, but customers can be the target victims as well. Sears Roebuck in 1992 sought to motivate the mechanics in its auto repair business by setting targets for the amount of work they did. The mechanics responded by telling customers that they needed steering and suspension repairs that were in fact unnecessary. Customers could not easily verify the need for the repairs themselves, and many paid for the unnecessary work. When the fraud was uncovered, Sears not only paid large fines, it lost much of the precious trust it had once enjoyed among its customers.

In some of these instances, the problem is that the incentives are poorly designed. Giving a fixed bonus if and only if a target is met invites the agent to meet the target and no more. This then can lead to the problems of manipulating the timing of sales and of doctoring internal accounts.

In other examples, monitoring some elements of behavior directly would have helped control the manipulation. Sears' incentive scheme led to a major shift in the sort of work being done, with the extra business being concentrated in repairs the need for which it is easy to misrepresent. If Sears' managers had monitored the mix, they could have caught the cheating. The top executives at

Enron and Worldcom claimed ignorance of the accounting manipulations. If they were indeed ignorant, they certainly had not done a very diligent job of monitoring.

Making pay less responsive to the manipulable measure is also an appropriate response (Baker 2000): If the people at Enron had not had such huge amounts tied up in the company's stock and options, perhaps they would not have been so eager to push up the stock price.

Another important way to limit the incentives for manipulation is to avoid formulaic reward schemes, replacing them with more subjective evaluations and basing rewards on these. In fact, subjective evaluations and subjectively determined pay represent an important alternative to direct performance pay in providing incentives.

Subjective Evaluations

The basic theory of agency assumes that enforceable contracts can be written on the observed performance measures, even though the actual desired behavior is not directly contractible. In many instances, however, there may be information about performance that is available but not easily used in explicit contracts because it is too complex and too difficult to describe, or too hard to verify by third parties who might enforce the contract. Most subjective evaluations are of this form. Yet, such information obviously might be useful for motivation if rewards—whether pay, or promotions, or something less tangible but still valued—can be tied to it.

The problem comes with the firm's incentives actually to carry through on its promises to pay the appropriate rewards when they have been earned. There are at least two sorts of difficulties.

First, once the job has been done, the principal may gain by reneging on the promised rewards. The most obvious problem involves refusing to pay, claiming falsely that performance was not satisfactory. The lack of an explicit contract means that the cheated agent cannot go to court to enforce the agreement. But if the principal's promises are not credible to the agent (as they certainly will not be once the first reneging has occurred), they will not induce effort in the first place. Indeed, even without the principal having yet cheated, if agents understand her incentives they will be unlikely to trust her to pay them honestly and so will not work hard.

In a related vein, perceived arbitrariness and ambiguity in evaluations can undermine incentives. If the basis for the subjective evaluation is unclear to the agent, then he cannot respond by altering his behavior in the desired ways. Bias and favoritism too can be a problem. If employees believe that the rewards will flow to the favored, not to the deserving, the promised rewards will not induce the desired behavior.

It is also possible that the principal may be too forgiving, paying rewards that were not really earned. This may seem unlikely when the principal is acting on her own account, but it is certainly an issue when the principal is also an agent and is not well motivated. For example, the compensation committee of a board of directors may reward the CEO handsomely despite the firm's miserable performance because they feel more allegiance to the CEO than to the shareholders. They get away with this because free riding and informational asymmetries mean the shareholders do not and cannot monitor the Board effectively.

The second major difficulty with subjective performance evaluation is that it may be subject to influence activities. Without a clearly articulated, mutually understood, unambiguous basis for evaluating performance, the agent has every reason to try to affect the principal's judgments and decisions. The agent can marshal arguments and evidence that, in fact, he did a great job, and there is some reasonable expectation that this may sway decisions. Moreover, if the evaluation involves any comparative aspects, then the agent also has incentives to try to make others look bad. The danger is that the whole system becomes politicized, and the rewards are ultimately given for success in special pleading, self-promotion, and sabotage, and not for doing one's job. The perversity of such incentives is clear.

The solution to many of these difficulties lies in the principal's reputation (Baker, Gibbons, and Murphy 1994). If the principal has a history of not acting opportunistically, keeping its non-contractual promises, and not being swayed by influence activities, then agents may extrapolate this past behavior into the future. They may then be motivated by the principal's promises. They expect her to keep her promises, because not doing so would hurt her reputation and thus her ability to induce others to behave as she wants in the future. In effect, her reputation becomes an asset that generates value by affecting the behavior of both the principal and the agent.

Reputations

Reputations can arise in many contexts and the same general principles apply across them all. In particular, managers (agents) may be motivated to work hard and generate good performance by their concern with their reputations in the labor market (Holmström 1982*a*; Gibbons and Murphy 1992). Even when there is no explicit pay for performance, doing well increases their market value and this may affect their pay in the future. However, we will develop the analysis by continuing with the principal–agent framework and the principal's use of her reputation in supporting motivation via non-contractual rewards.

If the reputation mechanism is to be effective, then in each interaction the returns from maintaining an unsullied reputation must exceed the gain from violating trust and reneging on promises. The value of an intact reputation comes from its leading others to trust the principal's promises and so be willing to act as she would want— working diligently and cleverly in the current context. This means there must be future opportunities for her to use her reputation, that the future gains from using an intact reputation to affect behavior are significant relative to the immediate gain from reneging, and that the principal does not discount these future returns too heavily.

Frequently repeated dealings, either with the current agent or with others, give the basis for future use of the reputation. This means that each time the parties interact the principal must anticipate additional opportunities to gain from the reputation. Consequently, there has to be at least some probability of the stream of dealings extending indefinitely, and short time horizons are a major problem for reputation formation and use. Meanwhile, increasing the number and frequency of interactions helps support good behavior by increasing the returns to maintaining the reputation.

For there to be significant future gains from the reputation, the agents who will deal with the principal in the future also must be able to observe and recognize cheating whenever it occurs, even if they are not directly affected. Then they must be willing and able to punish the cheating by behaving differently than they would have if the promises had been kept. All this puts limits on the possibility of using reputation. When performance is hard to describe, the measurements are subjective, and any promises are necessarily vague, knowing whether the implicit contract has been breached is problematic. Did my performance merit better treatment and more reward? Did yours? And will agents be willing to punish the principal when she apparently has cheated? Punishment cannot be too costly for the punisher, or it will not be invoked voluntarily. Here a sense of fair play, a desire to see justice done, or a psychological need for taking retribution can be helpful, because they lower the costs of punishing transgressors. They thus deter cheating.

Even large gains to inducing good behavior in the future by maintaining a reputation for fair dealing and keeping promises will not be enough to motivate the principal if she discounts future returns very heavily. Even the most honorable principal, if faced with imminent bankruptcy, is likely to find that the immediate gains from reneging on promised but non-contractual rewards are just too tempting. The principal recognizes that her reputation may be shot and that this will mean that any future dealings may be more difficult. Still, if the options are keeping agreements and going broke or reneging and surviving, the choice is clear.

While it seems clear that reputations in fact play a huge role in reward systems within firms, some of the most striking evidence on their use comes from trade in economies where the institutions of contract law are not well established. John McMillan and Christopher Woodruff (1999*a*, *b*) studied emerging private business in Vietnam. Businesses there cannot count on courts to enforce contracts. Consequently, they rely on reputations heavily. People in the same business meet regularly to discuss which customers have refused to pay them, so that all may avoid future dealings with the cheats. This raises the cost of cheating in a particular deal, because all sellers punish the cheater, not just one. It thus supports better behavior. As well, large amounts of effort go into screening potential customers before taking the risk of supplying them. Once a successful relationship has been established between trading partners, the asset will be used repeatedly, even to the extent of their increasing the scope of business activities so as to be able to trade more with one another. This leverages the scarce asset, trust. Moreover, it also supports more cooperative behavior in each transaction, because more is at stake across the many dealings.

The value of reputation and the importance of the reputation-bearer's being long-lived (so that it always has more opportunities to use the asset) suggest an advantage of organizing a permanent firm rather than leaving transactions to be market dealings between individuals (Kreps 1990). A corporation is, in principle, immortal. Further, it will have many more opportunities than any individual to use any reputation it develops. Thus, it may be an effective mechanism for supporting efficient dealings.

PARC and Motivation

Formal agency theory has tended to emphasize contractual responses to motivation. Yet, these are only some of the means that are available for motivating. In fact, all the aspects of organization can be employed, alone or in concert, as can managerial vision and strategy. We will illustrate with a number of examples.

Managerial vision is a clear conception of a desirable future state of the world and the business. For example, Nokia's vision in the early 1990s was that "Voice will go wireless." Mobile phones would become ubiquitous, making it a very attractive business for Nokia. Steve Jobs and Steve Wozniak of Apple had a vision that the personal computer would be similarly ubiquitous. Having a leader whose vision is very clear and certain can be highly motivating for employees, inducing more effort and guiding its allocation, because they are sure of what will be rewarded (Rotemberg and Saloner 2000; Van den Steen 2002). Strategy can serve a similar function (Rotemberg and Saloner 1994). If there is clarity about what the firm will do and what it will not, well-placed effort is more likely to be rewarded and, thus, to be provided.

Turning to the organization, first the people dimension can be used. Whom the firm attracts and selects as employees can have a tremendous effect on their motivation. Clearly, it should seek to attract people who are interested or challenged by the work being done. This is intuitively clear—if people like their work, there is less of a problem motivating them. More formally, this sort of matching reduces the divergence of interests that underlies the motivation problem. Also, it is clearly advantageous to match people with the rewards that can be offered. For example, if it is desirable to provide intense incentives but performance measures are not very precise or results are hard to forecast, then it is important that the people put in these jobs not be too risk-averse. If only non-monetary incentives can be offered, then get people who value the rewards that are possible.

In this context, it is important to recognize that the formal rewards systems offered will cause potential employees to self-select. Thus, an element of the organizational routine affects the people dimension of the organization. For example, Safelite Auto Glass, which is in the business of replacing broken car windshields in the field, instituted a piece rate to replace the hourly wages it had previously paid installers. Productivity increased by 44 percent within the year following the change. Half the gain was attributable to the motivation effect of the piece rate's leading installers to work harder and faster. The remaining 22 percent increase was due to selection effects. People who were willing to work hard were differentially attracted to Safelite, where their efforts would be rewarded, and turnover among the most productive workers fell dramatically (Lazear 2000).

The importance of having a good fit between the people and the other elements of the organization became evident when Lincoln Electric made a number of foreign acquisitions in the early 1990s (Bartlett and O'Connell 1998). Lincoln Electric's pay system offers exceptional monetary rewards for production workers who are willing and able to work very hard. In its home base of Cleveland, the bargain is well understood, and self-selection is effective. Employee turnover is well below average, Lincoln's people willingly work large amounts of overtime when it is available, and the company actually had to make a rule that production workers could not be on the factory floor more than a half hour before the start of their shifts because they were so anxious to get to work and start making money. The company discovered to its chagrin that the employees in a number of the acquired foreign operations had very different tastes than those in the Cleveland plant. They did not respond well to the piece rates, they were reluctant to work overtime, and they showed, for Lincoln employees, an unusual taste for taking time off. The acquisitions failed, leading Lincoln to suffer its first losses in a century of doing business.

Organizational architecture can also be used to affect motivation. For example, creating small business units can have strong effects via a number of different mechanisms. First, it facilitates measuring performance more precisely and so supports giving stronger incentives. In this regard, Asea Brown Boveri, the Swiss–Swedish engineering company, went to the extreme. In the early 1990s it had over 1,300 separate business units, each a separate company with its own balance sheet. These in turn were broken down into 5,000 profit centers, each of which averaged about thirty-five employees and was concerned with a very narrow product range in a single geographic market. Managers in these units were compensated on their units' performance, which was carefully tracked through the company's ABACUS reporting system. A second effect of creating such small units is that it lets people see the impact of their efforts more clearly, which is itself directly motivating, whether or not pay is tied to performance. People tend to put more into tasks where they perceive they can make a difference and where the results they generate are clear to them. This enhancement of intrinsic motivation may be especially important when direct performance pay is not easily employed. As well, organizing in small units reduces the extent of free riding, because the credit for extra results is shared more narrowly.

The basis on which organizational units are defined can also affect motivation. Most simply, the basis for organizing shapes perceptions of what is important. For example, people in a functional organization are likely to focus on excellence in their respective functions. The fact that jobs are defined functionally signals that functional excellence is important to those who designed the firm. The close, frequent contact that naturally occurs with immediate colleagues, all of whom are in the same function, reinforces the tendency to see excellence in that function as centrally important. As well, since evaluations are done by others in the same function, rewards are more likely to flow to those who demonstrate functional excellence. In contrast, organizing around customer groups or production facilities will turn people's attention in the corresponding direction.

The recent popularity of the "front-and-back" model for organization reflects the impact of architecture on motivation. In this model, production and product development are organized functionally as the "back-end" of the firm, while "front-end," market-facing units deal with customers. The idea is to get functional excellence while preserving a customer-oriented focus. Correspondingly, the two types of units are measured and rewarded differently. The challenge then is to achieve effective coordination between front and back. In this regard, Tenaris, a global supplier of pipe for the petroleum and auto industries, has a sophisticated supply management system linking its four customer-defined front-end business units operating in twenty countries and the eight manufacturing plants around the world that are the back-end of its organization.

The effect of organizational architecture on motivation and behavior also underlies the decision by Stanford University's Graduate School of Business not to subdivide its faculty into academic departments, although many other leading business schools do have a departmental structure. Instead the Stanford professors are organized into multiple, overlapping groups for different purposes—MBA teaching, doctoral student supervision, faculty recruiting—and the membership of these groups changes over time. This system is managerially complicated, and it would certainly be simpler to organize along departmental lines. The reason it is used is that the School wants to foster cross-disciplinary interactions in teaching and research, and it fears that departmental lines would get in the way of collaboration across fields.

The external boundaries of the firm can also be used to effect motivation, particularly in a multi-tasking context. For example, it may be important that managers of a business both drive current performance and invest to support future growth. It is easy to measure current performance but probably harder to tell if investments for the future are appropriate. Then if the business is a unit within a larger enterprise, the future may be under-emphasized. (This is especially likely if the managers can expect to move on to new jobs before the results of any investments become evident.) It may then be better to spin-off the unit and give the managers a large ownership stake in it, so that they have the more balanced incentives that come from the stock price. Of course, the market will not be likely to do a perfect job of evaluating investments either, but investors do have very strong incentives to measure performance on this dimension—their personal net worth is on the line. Thus, their evaluations are likely to be pretty good and they will certainly enjoy an integrity that internal measures often lack.

Whether someone should be an employee, using tools provided by the firm, or an outside contractor owning his own tools may also be responsive to motivational concerns (Milgrom and Roberts 1992: 231–2). It is desirable that someone using tools at work both produces output and maintains the tools. It may be fairly easy to measure or accurately infer the effort the worker devotes to production, but telling whether the tools are being properly cared for is more difficult—determining the actual depreciation on capital goods is notoriously hard. Thus, there is a precise measure for one activity and only an imprecise measure for the other. Yet, balanced incentives are clearly needed. Balanced weak incentives come from making the person an employee, paying in a manner that is largely independent of output, and having the employer own the tools. To a first approximation, because the worker is paid the same no matter how he spends his time, he will be willing to allocate his effort between production and maintenance as the firm requests. If, on the other hand, the worker owns the tools—as an independent contractor—he bears all the costs and benefits of the effort he devotes to maintenance. Then the worker needs to be given comparably strong incentives for producing output. Providing strong balanced incentives may most easily be done outside the employment relationship. Strikingly, contractors much more often face explicit performance incentives than do employees doing similar sorts of work. Which of the two solutions is best then depends on the ability of the worker to finance the purchase of the tools, his ability to bear risk, and how important it is to induce high levels of effort.

Another way that the boundaries of the firm may affect motivation is through outsourcing. Moving supply to an outside contractor can reduce influence activities within the organization, since there is no longer a common boss over the buyer and seller.

The allocation of decision authority can affect incentives as well. Empowering managers may induce them to do a better job of gathering information and making choices because they expect that their actions will have consequences that they control (Milgrom and Roberts 1988b, 1990a; Aghion and Tirole 1997). If, instead, their decisions are frequently overruled, this reduces their motivation. The cost of this empowerment is that the decisions that are made are those that are best for the manager, not necessarily the firm as a whole, unless the reward systems or other mechanisms have brought about alignment of interests.

Finally, the financial and ownership structure adopted for the firm can affect motivation in many ways. The publicly traded corporation gives limited liability to shareholder-owners and allows them to diversify their holdings, facilitating more risk-taking. Among the risks that are more easily borne are those of entrusting the actual operations of the business to others, including professional managers. The downside is that the same provisions reduce the incentives for owners to monitor. In contrast, members of a partnership have very intense incentives to monitor decision-making in their firms. The management buyouts that became popular in the 1980s meant that agents became principals, and the effect in many cases was to improve performance radically. Having a single large shareholder rather than dispersed ownership affects the incentives for owners to monitor directors and managers and so may affect agents' behavior. Buying back shares causes a given number of shares held by the executives to become a more intense incentive scheme, because the executives now get a bigger fraction of any changes in the value of the firm.

Processes and routines can also be used to reduce agency problems. An important example is improving the performance measures. This can be done by investing in the measurement system to reduce the divergence between the measured performance and what the agent actually did, by developing measures that are less manipulable, or by adding additional measures that carry extra information. In terms of the theory sketched above, any of these allows providing stronger incentives.

For example, developing even imperfect indicators of actual behavior rather than just relying on results can be very useful, especially when results are uncertain or come only after some long lag. Casino operators spend large amounts to monitor employees' and customers' behavior directly rather than relying on any sort of outcome-based rewards and punishments to thwart cheating. Venture capitalists gear continued funding of start-ups to the passing of "milestones," largely because financial data are not very informative. Information systems can play an important role by increasing the accuracy and timeliness of performance measurement and permitting more effective linking of rewards to performance.

As noted earlier, redefining jobs to reduce the need to multi-task when measures are not of comparable accuracy can also allow giving stronger incentives. More generally, job design can be an important effect on motivation.

Culture can also be a factor in dealing with motivation problems. Norms about how hard one works, what sort of risks one takes, and, generally, about what sorts of behavior are appropriate differ tremendously across companies and even among units within them. These norms are enforced by social pressure and the desire to conform. To the extent that managers can foster a culture that emphasizes performance, motivational problems are diminished. Two examples illustrate this.

BP, having disaggregated its exploration and production stream into small business units, connected these units together in peer groups, each of which involved about ten business units that faced similar technical and commercial challenges. Members of a peer group were encouraged to call upon one another for assistance in dealing with such problems. The groups also met frequently, without any headquarters personnel present.

Over time, strong personal networks (and friendships) developed across business unit boundaries, and strong norms developed about sharing best practice and responding to requests for help. Remarkable levels of cross-unit cooperation resulted, despite the fact that the performance management system did not track or explicitly reward such behavior.

The sharing of best practice was a crucial element in BP's successful drive to improve its costs and volumes. Initially the pay of business unit managers was tied to the cost and volume performance of their individual units. As a strong, shared belief in the importance of cost and volume performance developed and permeated the organization, and as norms developed that units managers would deliver the performance they had promised, the explicit linkage of business unit leaders' pay and their units' performance was reduced and then eliminated. The values had been sufficiently internalized that no explicit incentives were needed to motivate managers to deliver performance, and the compensation system could be directed to motivating other elements of behavior.

Culture was also crucial to motivation at Nokia Corporation, the Finnish mobile telephone manufacturer. Nokia nearly failed in the early 1990s. The new top management team who assumed control at that time helped create a culture where everyone was dedicated to making the company succeed. The culture encouraged individual initiative, hard work, and judicious risk-taking in a technologically turbulent environment where it was crucial that lower- and middle-level people acted quickly and decisively on the basis of the information they alone had. Successes were celebrated, and failures were not punished. Even when problems in managing logistics led to a 50 percent drop in the stock price in 1995, no one was fired. An atmosphere of mutual trust was established among employees and between them and top management. Fear, so often a central fact of corporate life, was banished. People were simply expected to do their best and were trusted to act in the best interests of the company. They responded by doing just that.

Nokia became one of the most successful corporations of the 1990s, at one point becoming Europe's most valuable company, and its success continued even after the bursting of the bubble in the telecommunications industry. It consistently introduced great new products while achieving lower costs than its competitors, in large part through highly disciplined operations. Yet, all this was done in a context where pay was not high relative to the employees' outside options—a top executive described Nokia's people as "happily badly paid"—and where rewards were tied to group or overall corporate performance.

The model of "high commitment human resource management systems" presents a general example of using several different elements of PARC to achieve motivation. As outlined by the leading text in the field (Baron and Kreps 1999: 190), key elements of such systems include guaranteed employment (except after egregious misbehavior); egalitarian values and norms; self-managed teams for organizing production; attempts to make work interesting and fulfilling; premium compensation, perhaps involving team, unit, or firm-wide (but not individual) performance pay; rigorous pre-employment screening and extensive socialization and training of employees; transparency of information within the firm and open communication channels between employees and managers; a strong culture focused on an overarching goal such as the organization's vision; and a strong emphasis on employees' symbolic and financial "ownership" of the firm. The basic deal is that people work hard and cleverly, in the interests of the firm, in return for good pay, empowerment, trust, and interesting, fulfilling work. They do so first without any obvious, explicit formal incentives because they identify their interests and those of the firm more closely than in the set-up assumed in the agency models. Beyond that, mutual monitoring and social pressure among employees enforce the desired behaviors. The screening, socialization, and identification with the vision help ensure that the enforcement mechanisms are at work.[14]

Such systems are especially attractive when it is difficult to measure performance accurately, and thus to provide incentives through more direct reward systems. There are costs to establishing a high commitment system, and many of these costs are fixed and sunk. Pay is above the minimum necessary to attract and retain workers, screening and training are costly, creating an atmosphere of trust is not easy or automatic, and getting the workers and managers to buy into the system may be difficult. It is worthwhile if it results in sufficiently higher levels of effort than an explicit performance pay system generates. This will tend to be the case when effort is important but performance measures are bad.

The trick in such systems is to ensure that the standards do not degrade, so that effort is low but the costs remain high. Perhaps the surest way for this to happen is for the workers to lose trust in management because it appears either to have violated the terms of the deal or to not trust the workers. This example points to an apparent contradiction with the use of measures and rewards. Closely monitoring behavior and explicitly rewarding it, particularly financially, may undermine trust. The near-universal norm of reciprocity can lead to workers' performing at quite high levels if they perceive that they are trusted and that the firm is treating them well. The norm, however, may not survive if the workers are closely monitored and if the firm introduces explicit incentive pay. Aspects of culture and explicit performance incentives may be substitutes, at least over certain ranges. In this case, if the culture supports high levels of effort provision, it may be wise not to use explicit incentive pay. Certainly, a small amount of incentive pay supported by the measurement systems it requires will not be worth-while if it undercuts the culture of trust and the norm of reciprocity.

More generally, it is important to consider the interaction of different mechanisms in affecting motivation. While some elements of organization design may be complementary in motivating people, others may conflict and undercut one another. Performance-based rewards are more effective if performance is measured better. Creating small business units works better if their managers are genuinely empowered. On the other hand, overly close monitoring of behavior against mandated processes and procedures may destroy the motivating effects of empowerment. We will return to the problems of designing motivation systems in the remaining chapters, where we consider more specific objectives that the designer is attempting to realize.

Notes

1. For surveys of this subject, see Gibbons (1997), Gibbons and Waldman (1999), and Prendergast (1999).

2. While motivation problems can be manifested at the group level, we focus our discussion on the problems of motivating individuals because these are logically prior and because most of the arguments are more directly made in this context.

3. See Avery, Chevalier, and Schaefer (1998) for an analysis of CEOs' motivations for making acquisitions.

4. This is not to say that reputational concerns cannot help here. However, the fact that behavior is unobserved will mean some unavoidable inefficiency.

5. The basic reference for simple agency theory is Holmström (1979). See also Hart and Holmström (1987) for a survey and Milgrom and Roberts (1992: chapters 5 and 7) for an elementary formal development.

6. The simplest case is one where the agent's effort is either high ("working hard") or low ("being lazy") and the probabilities of different outcomes are shifted by the effort choice. In fact, most of the insights obtained in more general formulations arise in this context (Hart and Holmström 1987). Another central case is one where the agent's preferences show constant absolute risk-aversion with respect to his money income less the cost of effort (so there are no income effects), performance varies directly with the effort choice, the additive noise term in the performance measure is normally distributed, and the contract is linear (Holmström and Milgrom 1991; see also Milgrom and Roberts 1992: chapter 7). This set-up gives very rich predictions/explanations and our discussion is largely based on this case.

Motivation

7. The assumption of risk-neutrality for the principal is a reasonable approximation when, for example, we think about the compensation of an employee by a large firm owned by shareholders who are able to diversify their portfolios and thus are largely indifferent to the variation in the firm's returns that one person's pay represents.

8. The optimal strength of the incentives (in the linear case described in note 6) is directly proportional to the expected marginal benefit to the principal of extra effort and inversely proportional to a term that is equal to one plus the product of three terms: The variance of the measurement error, the agent's risk-aversion parameter, and an inverse measure of how the agent's effort choice responds to increased incentives. The claimed results follow from this relationship. For details, see Milgrom and Roberts (1992: chapter 7).

9. The dependence is actually on the variability of pay, which depends on the intensity of incentives. But the agent's optimal effort choice will cause the marginal cost of effort to be equated to the marginal incentive intensity, so that the risk cost can be expressed in terms of the marginal cost of effort.

10. Unless the monitoring is certain to catch any misbehavior, the amount paid will necessarily be above the level of the employee's best outside option, so that being fired is costly and the threat of termination is a real incentive. The extra pay is called an "efficiency wage" because paying more than the employee's opportunity cost increases effort and efficiency.

11. San Jose *Mercury News*, October 2, 2000.

12. It is useful to consider the extreme case where the agent's cost of effort depends only on the total amount that the agent provides, not on its allocation among tasks, the

marginal cost of effort is increasing linearly in the effort level, and pay is a linear function of the measured performance on each activity. If multi-tasking is induced, the intensity of incentives must be the same for both activities. In this case, the optimal linear payment scheme inducing multi-tasking gives strictly *weaker* incentives than would be provided for either task in isolation. Thus, the total effort is strictly lower under multi-tasking than if effort is induced on just one activity, even the poorly measured one.

13. The practice of paying for individual or small-group performance with shares of company stock is not subject to this criticism, which is aimed at situations where employees are given stock in amounts that are independent of their current performance with the idea that holding these shares will motivate effort.

14. One interpretation of these systems is they involve an efficiency wage (see note 10 in this chapter) and the workers supply lots of effort because if they collectively do not, the firm will revert to more standard Human Resource Management systems that are less favorable to the workers.

5

Organizing for Performance

In this chapter we seek to apply the concepts and theories developed in earlier chapters to examine how firms can organize themselves to increase their performance against their current strategies. The key idea is to design the organization to provide as focused, intense incentives as possible within the constraints implied by the corporate form and the interdependencies that it both creates and is meant to control. Doing so necessitates a variety of choices of architecture and routines, supported by cultural changes, that together can be called *disaggregation*. The key architectural elements involve redrawing the horizontal and vertical boundaries of the firm to increase strategic focus; creating relatively small subunits within the organization in which significant decision rights are lodged; and decreasing the number of layers of management and the extent of central staff. Routines and processes are altered to hold the subunits accountable for delivering performance while linking them together by various means to manage the interdependencies among them. Finally, cultural norms are developed that facilitate the pursuit and realization of improved performance.[1]

In fact, some firms have long employed organizational designs that involve many of the features of the loosely coupled, disaggregated model. Johnson & Johnson, the pharmaceutical, medical equipment, and consumer products company, is a prime example (Pearson and Hurstak 1992). Johnson & Johnson is composed of over 150 separate companies that each serve different markets. The fiercely independent companies carry out their own product development, production, marketing, and sales, paying dividends to the parent. The highly decentralized design generates intense incentives in the companies to create new products and increase sales. Meanwhile, a strongly shared set of values and norms helps ensure that behavior is aligned with overall performance.

In the last decade, however, many more firms have adopted this design model in response to increased needs to improve performance. Falling barriers to international trade and investment and the increased ease of long-distance communication and transportation have allowed firms to enter new foreign markets. This has increased competition in product and service markets around the world, making improved efficiency necessary for success and even survival. At the same time, capital markets are arguably becoming more demanding, putting increased pressure on firms to perform. The increased acceptance of creating shareholder value as the prime obligation of management, the greater activism of institutional investors, and, in some parts of Europe, the emergence of hostile takeover bids all contribute to this. Finally, the increased linkage of top executives' compensation to performance, which has gone furthest in the United States but has occurred elsewhere too, means that the incentives to improve performance are much stronger than in the past.

BP plc, the integrated oil and natural gas company formerly known as British Petroleum, exemplifies use of the disaggregated model to improve performance. Although we have discussed aspects of BP's organization at a number of points already, a more systematic treatment is worthwhile.

In recent years, BP has reported some of the highest profits ever recorded by any corporation—over $14 billion in 2000. While high prices for crude oil certainly contributed to BP's outstanding financial results in this period, the company's extremely cost-efficient operations were crucial to its underlying performance, which was strong throughout the last part of the 1990s and into this century. Indeed, BP was widely recognized in the energy industry for its effectiveness in finding hydrocarbon deposits and its efficiency in bringing these into production and extracting the crude oil and natural gas. This operational excellence was actually maintained and improved in quite difficult circumstances that could have resulted in major disruptions in the workings of the firm: Between 1998 and 2000, the company absorbed two other major integrated oil companies, Amoco and Arco, that together were almost as large as BP itself, as well as a lubricants company, Burmah Castrol, a retail joint venture it had in Europe with Mobil, and Veba's German gasoline retailing operations.

Strategic and organizational changes implemented over the preceding decade under three successive CEOs formed the basis for BP's success. A dozen years earlier, BP had been a politicized, top-heavy bureaucracy

Organizing for Performance

organized through a cumbersome matrix structure. The company was still spread across numerous distinct lines of business, the result of its not having yet completely undone the conglomerate diversification in which it (along with the other major oil companies) had indulged in the 1970s. Financial proposals required fifteen different signatures before they could be accepted; head-office staff filled a thirty-two storey building; and meetings of eighty-six different committees absorbed the top executives' days. Performance was in decline, the company was heavily indebted, and in 1992 it reached a financial crisis that almost resulted in its bankruptcy.

The changes that would eventually transform BP began with its divesting unrelated lines of business. This process, begun in the 1980s, was completed by the early 1990s. The company was then focused on three basic businesses or streams: Upstream oil and gas exploration and production; downstream petroleum refining and marketing; and petrochemicals. These lines of business were obviously related, as upstream's products are the basic inputs to the other two streams' production. In fact, however, they could be and were run quite separately in a largely decoupled fashion. Well-functioning world markets allowed efficient purchase and sale of crude oil, so the company did not need to rely on internal transactions.

The organizational changes began under CEO Robert Horton, who took over in 1989. His "Project 1990" sought to improve the speed and effectiveness of managerial decision-making. Horton transferred authority for many decisions from the corporate center to the business streams. In the process, layers of management were eliminated and headquarters employment was reduced by over 80 percent.

Employees were encouraged to take responsibility and exercise initiative, and values of caring, trust, openness, teamwork, and cooperation were espoused. At the same time, as economic difficulties mounted, capital budgets were slashed and employment was cut deeply.

Horton's abrasive personal style and the dissonance between the proclaimed values and the reality of job cuts alienated employees, while performance continued to deteriorate in the context of the general economic slowdown of the early 1990s. In 1992 Horton was replaced as CEO by David Simon, who had been Chief Operating Officer. Simon was more popular among the BP employees, but he continued Horton's aggressive rationalization agenda. Employment fell from more than 97,000 in 1992 to just over 50,000 in 1995. Some of this was associated with divestitures and asset sales, but a significant amount of it represented reductions in employment in ongoing operations. Performance improved radically. The company moved from a loss of $811 million in 1992 to a profit of $2.4 billion two years later, while debt levels fell by $4 billion.

The biggest changes during this period occurred within the upstream, exploration and production business, BP Exploration (BPX). There, John Browne, who would succeed Simon as BP Group CEO in 1995, undertook a fundamental organizational redesign. The model, which BPX called an "asset federation," typified disaggregated design. It later was applied across the company as a whole.

Browne began by refocusing the upstream strategy on finding and exploiting large hydrocarbon deposits where the technical difficulties and attendant risks meant that BP's expertise and size gave it a relative advantage over smaller firms. (In this period, smaller exploration and production companies—labeled "petropreneurs"—were often more successful than the large integrated oil companies.) This led to disposal of a number of smaller holdings, purchases of other fields that complemented existing ones, and the redirection of exploration towards areas that were more likely to have really major deposits. This meant that each of the company's oil or gas fields was of some substantial size. In the late 1980s these fields were concentrated in the North Slope of Alaska and the North Sea, whence BP had drawn most of its production since the 1970s. However, focusing on major opportunities meant that in the future BPX's exploration activities would be focused on new areas where technical or political difficulties had prevented earlier development. Thus, BPX's operations would become increasingly dispersed around the globe and would be increasingly in developing and transition economies.

The next move was organizational. BPX had been structured through a collection of geographically defined Regional Operating Companies (ROCs), which had staffs of technical and business people overseeing the actual operations. The heads of the ROCs and of the functions joined Browne in a Global Management Group that ran the stream. Performance data were normally aggregated to the level of the ROCs, and the managers of the actual fields had very limited discretion and very little control over the resources used in their units. Browne, however, began to push performance evaluation discussions down to the level of the individual fields. This led to a conscious experiment in organizational design, with the managers of a number of fields being given authority to decide how to run their operations and how to meet performance targets that were negotiated directly with top management of BPX. When this change resulted in increased outputs and reduced costs, the model was applied throughout BPX, beginning in the crisis year of 1992.

All the exploration and production operations were divided into some forty separate business units, called assets, each of which consisted of a major oil or gas field or a group of co-located fields. Each was headed by an asset manager (later called a business unit leader). The ROCs were eliminated, with senior management of the stream being pared down to Browne and two others. As the BPX Executive Committee (ExCo), they together directly oversaw the assets, with no intermediate layers of managers. The technical and functional staffs were also largely dispersed to the assets.

The asset managers were given charters that set bounds on their activities (e.g. limiting their drilling to their own sites). They also signed explicit, individual performance contracts with the ExCo, agreeing to deliver specified levels of performance in terms of production volumes, costs, and capital expenditure. Within their charter bounds and the limits of general corporate policy, the asset managers were then empowered to figure out how to achieve their promised performance. They could decide on outsourcing and choose suppliers, do their own hiring, and determine where and how to drill.

The performance of individual assets was not aggregated below the level of the stream itself and was fully transparent to Browne and the ExCo members. They tracked performance closely, especially through rigorous Quarterly Performance Reviews. Through conversations in these meetings, Browne coached the asset managers, helping them develop their managerial skills and inculcating the values and norms he sought to spread through BPX.

The performance contracting was not limited to the asset managers. Instead, the promises made in the performance contracts at the asset level became the basis for performance contracts for all the individuals within the asset. All employees' compensation was tied to their assets' performance and to the overall performance of the stream. This increased the variability of pay and the intensity of incentives significantly.

The asset managers found the new system very liberating, but the leanness at the top meant they could not rely on stream headquarters to advise and support them when technical or business difficulties arose. To respond to this need, the assets were aligned into four peer groups that (after some experimentation) were defined on the basis of the life-stage of the assets. One group consisted of actual exploration activities, including obtaining rights to develop fields; the second included assets that were being developed and brought into production; the assets in the third group were in full, plateau production; and the fourth included assets that were approaching the end of their economic viability and were in decline. The key point was that assets within a group, although geographically dispersed, were likely to face similar technical and commercial problems.

The asset managers were encouraged to rely on the peer group colleagues for support. Indeed, the peer groups were designed to facilitate mutual assistance among their member assets and to promote the sharing of best practice. To this end, the system of peer assists was established under which an asset facing a problem could call on people from other assets to come and help solve the problem. As well, numerous other "federal groups" came into being, linking people with common interests and challenges across the different assets.

The peer groups were also given another role early on, called peer challenge. Under it, peer group members were expected to challenge one another on the targets that they negotiated individually with the ExCo. This process allowed the asset managers' collective expert knowledge to be brought to bear in establishing targets. Later, the peer groups each took collective responsibility for meeting the performance targets of the member assets and for allocating capital among them.

At the same time, increasing reliance was put on outsourcing. This included significant elements of the human resource management and accounting functions and extended even to activities previously seen as critical, including the generation of seismic data on potential new fields (only the interpretation of the data was kept in-house). Strikingly, the logic of the performance contracts was sometimes extended to outside suppliers, whose payments were made a function of their performance. A triumph for this approach was the Andrew field in the North Sea, which had previously been believed to be too expensive to bring into production. By sharing cost savings with its contractors, BP was able to develop the field at a fraction of the original cost estimates and in much less time than had been believed necessary.

This organizational model led to BP's remarkable successes. New fields were found and developed, many in areas that were previously thought to be technically too difficult to be economically feasible. The cost of developing fields was reduced substantially and kept being squeezed, and the productive life of assets was extended long beyond what had been believed possible.

After Browne became CEO of British Petroleum in 1995, this model was applied across the whole of the company. The appropriate definition of assets was less obvious in the other streams than it had been in BPX, and establishing the right performance measures also presented some challenges. Still, the system of discrete business units, peer groups and peer assists, small Executive Committees for each stream, performance contracts, and peer challenge was instituted. Performance management began with a performance contract between CEO Browne and the Board, which then cascaded down through contracts for the Managing Directors who led each stream through to the Business Unit Leaders and then on to the individual employees. In addition, a set of Regional Presidents was established to provide assurance that company policies were being met with regard to issues that tended to cross stream boundaries and were best handled on a national or regional basis, such as safety and environmental matters or legal and regulatory affairs.

These changes in the architecture and routines eventually led to fundamental cultural changes. BP's people developed a deep, intrinsic dedication to delivering ever-improving performance. Strong norms emerged of mutual trust, of admitting early when one faced difficulties ("no surprises") and seeking assistance when needed, of responding positively to requests for help, of keeping promises about performance. These had powerful effects, generating a remarkable amount of cooperation while still inducing great initiative.

This model has been adjusted since, but in its basic logic persisted through the 1990s. It proved especially valuable during the absorption of Amoco and Arco, where the newly acquired assets were quickly integrated into the BP system with the support of the peer groups.

In the wake of BP's success, many firms have sought explicitly to emulate its organizational design. Others have adopted similar organizational designs on their own. There is, of course, no one best way to organize that all firms should adopt. The best organization design depends on the strategy being pursued, the market and non-market context, and the administrative heritage of the organization. Nonetheless, real gains in performance can often be achieved by adopting designs that adhere to the basic logic underlying BP's disaggregated model. These include a tendency towards focusing the activities of the firm to a select set; creating business units with clear scope of responsibility and clear accountability; giving strong incentives for unit performance; linking units horizontally rather than requiring all communication to pass up and down through the hierarchy; flattening the hierarchy and increasing spans of control; outsourcing; improved information, measurement and communication systems; and, ultimately, the creation of a culture that is oriented to delivering performance.

These design elements are complementary and so the significance and impact of each can be understood only by recognizing the interactions among them all. However, it is worth first looking at each in isolation.

Vertical Scope

An important element of designing the organization for greater performance is to focus the firm on just those activities where it can create the most value. For many firms, this has involved vertical disintegration, turning over to others the provision of goods and services that the firm formerly provided for itself.

A striking manifestation of this process of outsourcing and vertical disintegration is a set of firms exemplified by Nike (Brady and de Verdier 1998; Whang and de Verdier 1998) and Benetton (Stevenson, Martinez, and Jarillo 1989) that have adopted the role of "vertical architect" or "value chain organizer." This role involves the lead firm's organizing and managing a value chain—in sports shoes and, more recently, apparel and sports equipment at Nike, and in fashion wear for Benetton—but actually owning few of the assets involved and carrying out few of the activities that are needed to create value. Nike, for example, outsources all its production, but does the product design, marketing, and distribution to (independent) retailers. Benetton actually outsources the basic design work and most of the manufacturing for its products. It also relies on retail outlets that are independently owned, although selling only Benetton products, and it deals with these retailers through agents who are not Benetton employees. The outlets are, however, linked to Benetton's information systems to track sales. Benetton takes care of creating the patterns from the designers' drawings, dyes the clothing, handles the logistics of distribution, and runs the advertising and marketing for the brand. In both cases, the lead firm manages a complex set of relations

191

with other value chain participants and coordinates activity among them.

This model has been extensively adopted in the electronics industries. For example, in the personal computer industry, many of the leading firms outsource almost all manufacturing to such electronic manufacturing services (EMS) companies as Solectron and Flextronic. Both of these EMS companies do tens of billions of dollars of business a year, but they have no products of their own. Further, the computer firms are also beginning to outsource logistics, order fulfillment, and post-sales service, and even the design and manufacture of their low-end products.

There are, of course, numerous very good reasons why a firm should prefer to purchase goods and services rather than provide them in-house.[2] Fundamentally, unless the firm has some special competence in carrying out the supply activity, others are likely able to do the job better and more cheaply. This could be because they specialize in this task and, through learning, become more proficient at it; or because they enjoy economies of scale in supplying multiple customers which the buying company cannot itself realize; or because their focus reduces organizational complexity relative to the integrated alternative and thus results in lower costs of management. Greater focus also reduces measurement and attribution problems, facilitating the provision of stronger incentives to employees. Moreover, relying on competition to set prices may be much better than attempting to determine internal transfer prices. Outside supply is also attractive because it is probably easier to induce competition among external suppliers than it is when the suppliers are inside the buyer's firm. In particular, replacing an unsatisfactory outside supplier is much easier than getting rid of an internal supplier that is not performing well.

On the other hand, a variety of reasons have been offered to justify vertical integration. Some of these stand up to rigorous analysis; others do not. For example, the transaction cost and property rights schools of economists accentuate the protection of specific assets against hold-up. Owning the assets associated with providing the good or service and supplying it in-house may provide better protection for such assets and thus stronger investment incentives. Other reasons to integrate have to do with the protection of intellectual property or, more generally, the difficulties of operating efficient markets for information. Relying on internal provision may protect sensitive knowledge from misappropriation by suppliers. Because interests may be more aligned within the firm than across firm boundaries, internal provision may also facilitate the transfer of valuable information between the supplier and customer.

The provision of appropriately balanced incentives for multiple activities can also drive firm boundaries. The example discussed in Chapter 3 of the choice between an outside distributor and an employee sales force is illustrative. If it is important that sales people also serve as an information conduit from customers back to product development, then keep sales inside the firm. It will be difficult to motivate an outside distributor to undertake this activity, which is hard to measure and thus to reward, while also providing incentives for sales that are sufficiently strong that the distributor will focus on the firm's business rather than that of other firms it might represent.

Instead, the firm should employ its own internal sales force. It would then give the sales people incentives that are balanced (to induce both sorts of activity) but relatively muted (since strong incentives for the ill-measured activity are likely to be too random and costly) and simply tell them they cannot sell other firms' products. In a related case, integrating forward into retail sales may facilitate the provision of customer education about use of the product. An independent seller, unless it has an exclusive territory, may be reluctant to provide this costly service. It fears the customer will come to it for the information but then actually buy from a lower-priced competitor that free-rides on the first seller's educational activities.

Yet another reason to favor internal procurement may be to lessen the incentives for opportunistic slacking on quality (although in fact it seems that many managers view internal suppliers' quality as more problematic than outsiders'). Finally, to the extent that being in the same firm, with the managers of both activities reporting to a single boss and with the employees all belonging to a single company, facilitates coordination, then integration is favored.

To the extent that outsourcing involves trading off lower costs of production against increased transactions costs (from hold-up, information leakage, or whatever), globalization, improved information and communication technologies, and more flexible manufacturing systems would favor a shift to more outsourcing. The Internet facilitates finding new suppliers, improved communications makes dealing with them easier, and lower transport costs and reduced trade barriers allow working with more distant suppliers. Thus, the costs available through outsourcing should be lower, and this favors doing more of it. More flexible manufacturing systems, such as computer numeric controlled machines, also favor increased outsourcing by reducing the threat of hold-up: The supplier's flexible equipment can be reassigned to other uses if the buyer tries a hold-up, and the flexibility of competing suppliers means that the buyer can find others with which to deal if the supplier tries to grab more than its share. Thus, standard theories of the make–buy choice would predict increased outsourcing in the current context.

All of these theories, however, have largely focused on one-off dealings between discrete parties who do not act as if they expect to transact again and who do not worry about the effect of their behavior in this transaction on their reputations. They can then be assumed to maximize their immediate returns in the current transaction.[3] In such a context, it is relatively easy to justify integration, because of the fear of excessively sharp dealing when transacting with outside parties.

The distinguishing feature of much of the outsourcing that companies have been adopting recently, however, is precisely that the supplier–buyer interaction is structured as an ongoing relationship, partnership, or alliance. The long-term nature of the relation radically changes the incentives that can be provided, whether these are to make investments, respect intellectual property, maintain hard-to-monitor quality, or whatever. They thereby greatly increase the attractiveness of outsourcing compared to a situation where the outside dealings are simple, one-off, arm's length ones. Repeated dealings allow for much more cooperation. Meanwhile, moving the supply relation from being a long-term one within the firm to another long-term one that crosses firm boundaries permits gaining many of the advantages that were always inherent in outside supply. The opportunities for inducing initiative are also increased.

In terms of the cooperation–initiative trade-off, organizing through a long-term relationship is an organizational innovation that shifts the frontier of feasible combinations to allow achieving much more cooperation than one-off market dealings but much more initiative than internal supply. Points like R are now available that were not before (Figure 9).

The leading Japanese automobile manufacturers—especially Toyota—were among the first to develop fully the model for this sort of long-term supplier relations.[4] In part the Japanese firms chose to outsource extensively in response to government policies that favored dealings with smaller firms. In part too, the permanent employment

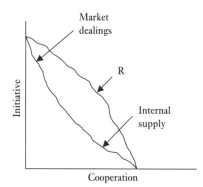

Figure 9. Long-term relations expand the set of attainable behaviors

policies adopted by the major Japanese firms may have favored using outside suppliers to maintain flexibility. Still, the model proved very effective: Its use has been credited with a significant portion of the cost and quality advantages the Japanese auto firms enjoyed over their U.S. rivals in the 1970s and 1980s (Womack, Jones, and Roos 1990). Since then, other auto companies have adopted this model, and it has spread widely to other industries.

In such an ongoing relationship, the relative focus for each party is supposed to shift away from attempting to appropriate value (at the possible cost of reducing the total value created) and towards creating value, with the presumption that the extra value will be shared appropriately. The basic logic of the relation is that incentives for cooperative, value-enhancing current behavior are provided by the promise that good behavior will result in continued future cooperation and sharing of the resultant returns, while misbehavior will result in future punishments, up to and including the termination of the relationship. The parties in effect enter a "relational contract"—a shared understanding that they will cooperate and divide the resulting gains. The exact behavior that will be needed in every eventuality cannot reasonably be described in a formal contract and verified by the courts, so the relational contract must be self-enforcing. The enforcement mechanism is the future behavioral responses of the parties to current good or bad behavior.[5] To make this logic work, a number of conditions must be met. These flow from the fundamental incentive problem and the nature of its solution.

The fundamental issue is that, at various points in time, either of the parties may see opportunities to increase its current returns by behavior that hurts the other party but that cannot be effectively deterred through normal, court-enforced contracts. For example, the supplier might not expend as much effort as would be efficient at controlling costs or maintaining hard-to-observe quality. Similarly, the buyer might refuse to absorb its share of the costs that the supplier has incurred to serve the buyer's needs, even though the understanding between the parties was that the buyer would compensate the seller. Or the buyer might make unreasonable demands for speedier delivery and threaten not to pay unless the seller acquiesces. If cooperation is to be maintained in the face of such temptations, then giving in to temptation today must bring consequences in the future that are sufficiently unpleasant that today's gains are more than offset by tomorrow's losses.

In effect, each party must always anticipate that resisting temptation will result in continued cooperation while succumbing will elicit punishment—a response from the other party that is worse for the tempted party than ongoing cooperation. Further, the difference in the present value of the two possible streams of future returns must exceed the magnitude of the immediate gain realized by giving in to the temptation. When this is so, the overall return to cheating is negative and so misbehavior is deterred.

Thus, a first requirement for a successful partnership is that there must be an opportunity to create value by cooperation, over and above what would be available under either self-supply by the buyer or normal, short-term market transactions. This immediately means that there is likely to be little reason for adopting a relationship-based model if there are numerous external suppliers who are always ready to meet the buyer's needs efficiently. This would often seem to be the case when procuring standardized commodities. It also applies even when the purchased item is not standardized but producing it does not involve extensive specialized investments in knowledge or physical capital.

The long-term outsourcing arrangement must then ensure that this gain is shared between the parties so that each is in fact better off in the relationship than out of it.

Further, for the threat of punishment to be effective, it must be that the injured party can retaliate and do things that are relatively unpleasant for the transgressor. Ending the relationship, thereby depriving the cheater of the future profits it would have earned, is often the strongest punishment available. An alternative might be reverting to the short-run, non-cooperative mode of market dealing. Moreover, these options must be sufficiently attractive for the punishing party that it will prefer to adopt them than to continue to deal with the transgressor. Since conjectured punishments that would hurt the punisher too much will not likely be imposed, they cannot deter misbehavior.

Note that the larger the gains from cooperation over alternative arrangements and the worse the punishments that can be imposed, the easier it will be to induce cooperation. So if the parties are really committed to the relationship and do not fear that a change in circumstances might make them both want to end it, they may actually gain by worsening their outside options and making themselves more dependent on one another. For example, the seller might close its marketing group so that it is in a worse position if the relationship ended, or the buyer might allow its capabilities in manufacturing the item in question to erode. Of course, this is a double-edged sword—it helps as long as the relationship continues, but can be very harmful if it dissolves.

Further, it is important that the participants place enough weight on their future dealings. This is facilitated if the dealings are more frequent and if the parties do not heavily discount future returns. Clearly too, it is important that the relationship be expected to continue more or less indefinitely, or else, as the end approaches, there is not enough future in which to give rewards and punishments to deter giving in to temptation, and cooperation will tend to break down.

Finally, it is better if it is clear whether a party actually has transgressed, so that punishment is meted out if and only if it is warranted. Otherwise, cheating may not be punished, and so cannot be as effectively deterred, or punishments may be imposed when they are not deserved, limiting the extent of realized cooperation and mutual gain (Abreu, Pearce, and Stacchetti 1990).

Features of the way that leading firms actually arrange their long-term supplier relations are responsive to these requirements.

First, long-term relations are not used for acquiring all products. When the product or service is standardized, when numerous suppliers are available, and when delivery and quality are not problematic, then simple arm's length dealings are used. This is because there is no real basis for creating value through a partnership over and above what is possible in regular market arrangements. Also, some activities are systematically kept within the firm rather than outsourced to a partner. In the auto business these typically include at least product development and assembly, although there have been recent experiments in turning assembly over to partners. Almost all firms do the career management aspects of the human resource function and the management of their financial resources themselves. Arguably, both the knowledge needed to carry out these activities and that gained in doing them are so crucial to the firm that there is no value in having another undertake them.

Second, significant attention is given to selecting partners and establishing the basic understandings with them. For example, in selecting suppliers for Toyota's first wholly owned assembly operation in the United States, Toyota's purchasing staff spent months meeting with each of the suppliers it considered, and more time with the ones it actually chose, visiting their facilities, encouraging them to visit Toyota's, teaching the Toyota Production System, and establishing common expectations (Milgrom and Roberts 1993). This was true even of firms that were already supplying NUMMI, the joint venture with GM in California that Toyota managed. This intense and extended interaction was not aimed at developing and negotiating any detailed, explicit contract. Indeed, the actual contracts with the suppliers were short and very simple, essentially committing the partners to work together to resolve problems as they arose. Rather, it was first a screening process, as Toyota sought to identify suppliers with whom the most value could be created and who would be cooperative partners. Then it was a matter of establishing the relationship and the shared understandings that it entailed.

Once the relationship is established, the gains from cooperation between the auto company and the supplier are in fact shared, with both parties getting more than they would in their next-best alternatives. Prices are negotiated. Toyota then helps its suppliers improve their efficiency, even assigning personnel to the suppliers' factories to serve as consultants, and cost improvements do not immediately result in offsetting price reductions. Thus, both parties get some benefit from the cost improvements.

The parties also pay attention to the punishments that can be inflicted for bad behavior. The most direct, extreme form of punishment is to sever the relationship. This is obviously easier for the buyer—and thus a more credible threatened punishment—if there are other qualified suppliers to which it can turn. Toyota in fact maintains a "two-supplier" policy: While any particular part or component for a specific model of vehicle will have a single supplier for the life of the model (roughly four years), there will normally be another firm supplying similar inputs for other models. For example, one firm might supply headlight systems for the Camry, but another would supply them for the Corolla. If necessary, Toyota will take on this second-source role itself. For example, Toyota has long relied very heavily on Denso for automobile electrical components and systems. As electronics came to become more and more important in cars, Denso developed major capabilities in the area, and Toyota began to be uncomfortably dependent on this one supplier. It then chose to develop significant internal capabilities in electronics. It thus is at least conceptually possible to cease dealing with Denso, thereby providing a severe but plausible punishment threat (Helper, MacDuffie, and Sabel 1998).

The two-supplier policy in fact permits giving more nuanced incentives than simply the threat of termination.

Toyota keeps careful track of its suppliers' performance in cutting costs, improving quality, coming up with ideas, and behaving cooperatively. Suppliers are rated using this information, and when models are redesigned, higher-rated suppliers get more business. This induces some competition between the suppliers, and this competitive pressure is a source of the advantage of outsourcing over (typically monopolized) internal supply. Meanwhile, compared to arm's length, short-run dealings, the stronger incentives that can be provided for mutually advantageous, value-creating behavior in an ongoing relationship also favor this approach.

There are costs to the two-supplier policy. Two relationships must be managed, rather than just one, and this takes time. There may be some loss of possible economies of scale. More subtly, there is less value being created between Toyota and any one of its partners than there would be if it were a sole-supplier relationship. This, in turn, may limit the extent to which the promise of future cooperation and value sharing can induce good current behavior. There is, thus, a trade-off here: Having only one supplier means that more value may be created if cooperation is maintained, but having multiple suppliers may, by increasing the range and credibility of punishments, make a higher level of cooperation more likely to be achieved.

A major difficulty in managing a system based on implicit threats and promises rather than formal contracts is in knowing whether the parties have in fact adhered to the terms. It might seem that unforeseen events would be problematic in this regard, because what is appropriate behavior may not be obvious. The parties might then individually choose to act in ways that each perceives to be perfectly appropriate but that the other finds non-cooperative and objectionable. This ambiguity should be a real problem, however, only if the parties cannot consult one another and negotiate successfully what is to be done. While these negotiations might well be difficult, a bigger problem arises with informational asymmetries, whether of the hidden action or hidden knowledge type.

If the parties' actions are not directly observable to one another, then it is possible that misbehavior will not be detected or that it will be inferred when in fact it did not take place. For example, suppose realized quality is not entirely under the control of the supplier. Then it may be tempted to cut back on its quality control in hopes of not being caught, or, if caught, of managing to make the poor quality seem accidental. Moreover, even if the supplier is scrupulous about attempting to achieve the desired quality, accidental failures may look to the purchasing partner like evidence that the supplier has cheated. In terms of the hidden information problem, if the costs and benefits to each party from various courses of action are not reasonably clear to the other party, then what is in fact the optimal thing to do is also unclear. This, too, can make cooperation hard to achieve. For example, if the supplier's costs vary over time in ways the buyer cannot confirm, then requests for price adjustments can lead to very contentious bargaining because it is unclear if they are justified.

The extensive information sharing that marks Toyota's dealings with its suppliers helps minimize these asymmetries and the resulting problems. Even after the relationship is well established, Toyota purchasing department engineers are frequent visitors to the supplier plants, and suppliers are often at the Toyota facilities. Toyota has extensive knowledge of the production processes at its suppliers and, correspondingly, of their capabilities and costs. Meanwhile, it shares its production scheduling plans with the suppliers and keeps these updated.

If there is a weakness in the system of supplier relationships that Toyota has created, it is that Toyota may be in too strong a position relative to the suppliers. They are very dependent on Toyota, especially in Japan, where suppliers to Toyota rarely also supply the other leading automakers. It would seem that Toyota could, if it chose, squeeze its suppliers, demanding unreasonable concessions and expropriating the returns they expected when they made investments to serve it. A supplier that had been mistreated like this would not have a lot of recourse, and so such misbehavior on Toyota's part might seem tempting. Then the threat of mistreatment—not to mention the actual experience of it—might lead the suppliers to behave less cooperatively or to expend resources trying to protect themselves, either of which is value destroying. Yet, it does not seem to occur.

Suppliers want to work with Toyota—in an eleven-year period, only three of the 176 members of *kyohokai*, the association of Toyota's Japanese suppliers, left the group (Asanuma 1989), while other firms (including General Motors' parts operation, now spun off as Delphi) have been anxious to become Toyota suppliers. Moreover, Toyota's suppliers in Japan regularly make heavy investments that are completely specific to Toyota, apparently undeterred by fear of hold-up. They typically do the actual design work to create products to Toyota's specifications, and they own the dies that are used to make products to Toyota's specific needs. (In contrast, the norm in the American industry, where short-term contractual relationships with outside suppliers prevailed until recently, was that the auto company did any specialized design work, and if an outside supplier needed special dies to make a product, the auto company would own these. These practices eliminated the threat of hold-up of the supplier.) As well, there is econometric evidence that, as is asserted by the industry, Toyota and the other Japanese auto companies actually do share returns with their suppliers (Kawasaki and McMillan 1987; Asanuma and Kikutani 1991). Finally, the fact that Toyota purchasing engineers are welcomed into the supplier plants and supplier personnel are often in the Toyota facilities indicates a fundamental trust.

Presumably, Toyota is sufficiently concerned with its reputation that it does not act opportunistically. One factor that may support this is that the suppliers are in contact with one another—indeed, Toyota itself encouraged the leading suppliers to its Georgtown, Kentucky, plant to form a formal association. This effectively means that any mistreatment of a single supplier will be known to all. If Toyota's taking unfair advantage of one supplier would lead all of them to withhold full cooperation, this would significantly temper any incentives Toyota might have for opportunism relative to what they would be if any punishments were from just the individual firm it had exploited. Further, the low interest rates at which Toyota has been able to borrow mean that future returns are not likely discounted heavily, so its reputation with partners looms large. This fits, of course, with the general long-term orientation for which the firm is known.

The importance of future returns' not being heavily discounted means that maintaining a cooperative relationship is easier when interest rates and, more generally, the cost of capital are low. Thus, two weak firms are unlikely to create a strong, productive alliance, even if their capabilities and resources are very complementary. Future returns are not sufficiently salient to offset current temptations and induce full cooperation. And when a previously strong firm gets in trouble, its partners need to be very wary. A partner facing a cash crisis is apt to behave in a very short-run oriented way, even if it would be completely trustworthy in more normal times. When immediate survival is at stake, longer-term considerations are just not very salient. Two examples from the auto industry illustrate the difficulties.

General Motors in the late 1980s and early 1990s had made some moves towards establishing the sort of long-term relations with a select group of suppliers that we have been describing. It sought to engage them, to get them to share cost information that they would normally have kept completely confidential, and to work cooperatively to create value. Then GM got in financial trouble—it ultimately registered a loss of $23 billion in 1992. Part of the response was to use the cost information gained from suppliers to force large price cuts. This breach of trust soured relations with the suppliers for years afterward. Yet, it was completely rational in the context of the crisis: Some GM executives credited the money squeezed from the suppliers with saving the company from bankruptcy.

In such circumstances, it probably was in the interests of the many suppliers to help General Motors, voluntarily adjusting the terms of the bargain to give the troubled partner a temporarily bigger share. This would not only have helped GM through its difficulties, it would also have improved its incentives and might have helped maintain cooperation. The problem would have been to coordinate all this and overcome the free-rider problem among the suppliers that each would like the others to help GM while it kept to the original terms of the deal. This may be less of an issue when the numbers are smaller.

The second example illustrates the possibility of offering to help a partner in trouble, but it also shows the dangers of being dependent on such a partner (Burt 2002). The case involves the hold-up of Ford's Land Rover subsidiary. UPF-Thompson, a small British firm that was the sole supplier of the chassis for Land Rover's Discovery model, went into receivership in December 2001. KPMG, the accounting firm, was appointed to run the company while exploring a possible sale. Anxious to keep its supplier operating, Ford offered to increase the price it paid for the chassis by 20 percent and to make an additional "goodwill payment" of £4 million. KPMG rejected this offer, demanding that Ford make an up-front payment to UPF of £35 million and also increase the price by substantially more than Ford had offered. The total demand was estimated to amount to £61 million, although Land Rover had been spending only £16 million a year on the Discovery's chassis. The KPMG partner in charge stated that his firm was merely fulfilling its legal obligation to get the most from the assets of UPF: "Land Rover's reliance on the company is an asset and we need to obtain the best value on the asset." Ford officials were furious, and before obtaining an injunction requiring UPF to continue delivery, Ford was reported to have been considering ceasing production of the Discovery rather than submit to the hold-up attempt.[6]

Even when there is nothing as dramatic as a bankruptcy to disturb arrangements, long-term relationships generally need to adjust over time. It is not sufficient to set the original terms of the understanding and then let it run, appealing to the original contract when issues arise. At a minimum, as volumes depart from those that were forecast, prices may need to be adjusted to ensure an equitable division of the returns and thus maintain both parties' interest in the relationship. Moreover, as technology, markets, competitors, customers, and the partners themselves change, the opportunities for cooperation will change, as will the parties' outside options. All these affect the extent of cooperation that can be maintained in the relationship, the divisions of the returns that are acceptable, and even the appropriate mix of activities for the parties to undertake. It thus becomes crucial to the survival and success of the relationship that the parties be willing to adjust its terms.

The complex relationship among Xerox, Fuji Photo Film, and Fuji Xerox, a joint venture of the first two companies, provides an outstanding example of such adaptation. Fuji Xerox was established in 1962 and continues successfully today, one of the longest-surviving international partnerships or alliances (Gomes-Casseres and McQuade 1991). The roles of the parties, the activities undertaken by each of them, the ownership structure of the joint venture, the nature and direction of payments between the parties, even the identity of the parties to the partnership have all changed over the years in a flexible, adaptive fashion that has been crucial to the success of the arrangement.

Fuji Xerox was originally intended simply as a vehicle to sell Xerox's revolutionary plain paper copiers in Japan.

It was in fact a creation of Rank Xerox, itself a joint venture of Xerox and a British firm that had been set up to market Xerox products outside the United States at a time when the fledgling Xerox Corporation lacked resources to exploit its technology worldwide. A Japanese partner was sought to facilitate entry into the Japanese market, and Fuji Photo Film was chosen, the only firm among those interested that was not in the electronics business. Xerox was to provide the product, exported from America, and Fuji Photo would staff the sales organization and provide market knowledge. Government regulations mandated, however, that the joint venture had to do manufacturing as well as sales. Thus, Fuji Xerox was given a role in manufacturing (largely assembly of knock-down kits from America), which it then outsourced to its parent, Fuji Photo.

The initial formal contract between Rank Xerox and Fuji Photo Film specified payments from Fuji Xerox to Xerox for use of the latter's technology. It also provided for protection of Xerox's intellectual property—Fuji Photo Film had no right to use any Xerox technology about which it might learn through the joint venture. In fact, Xerox insisted on adhering strictly to this condition, refusing at one point even to consider ideas that Fuji Photo Film developed for new uses of the Xerox technology. At this point, Fuji Photo Film effectively became little more than a financial partner in the arrangement, passing manufacturing back to Fuji Xerox, but not withdrawing its money from the partnership or the people it had sent.

This realignment of Fuji Photo Film's role was just the first of many changes in the basic structure of the partnership. A few years later Xerox increased its owner-ship share in Rank Xerox to greater than 50 percent. As a consequence, Fuji Xerox came under direct control from Xerox headquarters rather than through the inter-mediary of Rank Xerox. In the early 1990s, Xerox and Fuji Xerox set up a further joint venture, Xerox International Partners, to market Fuji Xerox's laser print-ers in the United States. As well, responsibility for selling Xerox products in the Asia–Pacific region was shifted from Rank Xerox to Fuji Xerox. In the late 1990s, Xerox bought full ownership of the Rank Xerox joint venture, so Fuji Xerox was now a 50–50 joint venture of Xerox and Fuji Photo Film. Most recently, with Xerox facing finan-cial difficulties, Fuji Photo Film bought half of Xerox's interest in the joint venture.

That Fuji Xerox had laser printers to sell in the United States was a reflection of other fundamental changes that had occurred in the relationship over time. From the out-set, Xerox had always been focused on developing and selling larger, faster copying machines aimed at corpora-tions that used them in central copying facilities. The dif-ficulties of reproducing documents written in Japanese *kanji* meant, however, that a larger part of the demand in the Japanese market was for smaller machines that could be put in every office. When Xerox refused to develop such machines, Fuji Xerox found money in its budget to develop them itself, in direct contravention of Xerox policy. The Fuji Xerox machines proved to be of high quality and sold well, and eventually they were accepted by Xerox. In fact, Fuji Xerox came to provide all the lower volume copiers sold by the Xerox group through-out the world. This evolving role for Fuji Xerox was recognized by repeated renegotiation of the contractual payments between Xerox and Fuji Xerox.

Perhaps the greatest adjustment occurred in the flow of knowledge between Xerox and Fuji Xerox. Xerox won acclaim in the early 1990s as the first American company to have gained back market share after losing a dominant position to Japanese competitors. Fuji Xerox played a huge role in this. Initially most learning flowed from the Xerox's technology to Fuji Xerox. Once Xerox lost the protection of its key patents in an antitrust action, however, it faced a wave of entry. The parent company focused on the threat from such established American giants as Eastman Kodak and IBM, but the Japanese entrants to the industry were Fuji Xerox's concern. The Japanese in fact proved the greater threat to the Xerox group as they came to dominate the lower end of the U.S. market and then to start making inroads into higher-volume copier segments. Fuji Xerox had already learned the techniques of designing and manufacturing products at low cost and with exceptionally high quality that became the competitive advantage of Japanese manufacturers, including those like Canon and Ricoh that entered the copier business. Once Xerox finally awoke to the true nature of the competitive threat (after what it labeled a "lost decade"), it was able to import Fuji Xerox methods of management and production, as well as Fuji Xerox products, to reverse its decline. Thus, the parent learned from the organizational child, as the flow of expertise reversed from its original direction.

These adjustments, involving the explicit contractual terms and the implicit relational contract, were key to the survival and success of the joint venture.

While evolution of any long-term relationship is inevitable, the parties need to careful about taking actions that would force adjustment in the partnership, because these can be destabilizing even when their intent was not to force changes in the terms. Choices that either partner makes that alter the returns that the partnership can generate can affect the possibility for continued cooperation. They could also undercut cooperation by causing the partner to become concerned about its ability to protect itself against misbehavior. For example, developing an in-house capability in an area that has been the partner's responsibility reduces the difference in value between the what the partners can achieve by cooperation and what the firm can achieve on its own, making cooperation less valuable. It also may make the partner worry that it will be replaced, which may deter it from committing future resources to the partnership.

In a related vein, making the parties more dependent on one another or increasing the difficulty of severing the relationship generally tends to make cooperation easier to achieve. It was this effect that led telecommunications giants AT&T and BT to avoid specifying up-front the terms for dissolution of their Concert joint venture, which was to serve the telecommunications needs of the two companies' multinational business clients. But if there is some danger that external events, like regulatory changes or demand shifts, could eliminate the basis for cooperation, then there is a substantial cost to such measures. When demand for Concert's services proved less than anticipated and the difficulties of integrating the two parents' businesses more substantial, the lack of agreed terms for dissolution proved very costly.

Despite such difficulties, the innovation of managing supply through long-term relations has spread and plays a major role in explaining the increased outsourcing of the last decade.

Horizontal Scope

In the 1960s and 1970s, conglomerates—companies involved in multiple, unrelated lines of business—were in fashion. In the 1980s they fell from favor, and much of the merger and acquisitions activity of that decade in the United States essentially involved unwinding complex combinations of distinct businesses created in the preceding decades.

The stock market appears to have believed in conglomerates in the 1960s and 1970s, when they were first put together, for unrelated acquisitions were rewarded by increases in market valuations that made the combined entity more valuable than the pieces going into it (Matsusaka 1993). Later, demergers were also rewarded (Comment and Jarrell 1995), and scholars identified a "conglomerate discount" (Montgomery and Wernerfeldt 1988; Lang and Stultz 1994), with the market apparently valuing firms in multiple lines of business at less than the sum of the values the component businesses would have as stand-alone operations. While the extent to which the market actually does apply such a discount is now a topic of some debate, it is clear that focus is much more in favor than it once was. It would seem that even the wave of merger and acquisition activity that occurred in the late 1990s did not lead to firms having as broad scopes as twenty years ago, at least in the major English-speaking economies. Meanwhile, there are some signs that continental European firms are starting to reduce their scope. Novartis and ICI are prime examples: Both have disposed of lines of business and become more focused. Earlier, Daimler Benz had done the same.

Why should putting two distinct businesses under common ownership and management affect the value they create? Or, equally, why should breaking them up into separate businesses affect their value? What is the impact of corporate strategy?

In an earlier era, the claim was made that combining businesses under common ownership served a risk-reduction purpose: The diversified firm was like a diversified portfolio, with the aggregate being less risky than any one of the pieces. Of course, this diversification is of no particular value to shareholders, since they could hold both firms' shares on their own and achieve the same result. In fact, since the combination forces all shareholders to hold the claims on the two earnings streams in fixed proportions, the merged entity actually restricts shareholders' portfolio choices (although prominent asset pricing theories would suggest this latter factor may be unimportant).

Note that there are at least two points that might counter this powerful argument against the idea that diversification creates value by reducing risk. First, if shareholders cannot easily diversify on their own, then there may be a risk-reduction value to having diversified firms. This may, in fact, rationalize diversification in some contexts. An example is family-owned firms, especially in countries with poorly developed capital markets. The family cannot easily diversify through the financial markets and does so instead by entering numerous lines of business. Second, while stockholders can diversify their financial portfolios, the managers and employees of the firm are not able to diversify their employment. If diversification allows for cross-subsidization of businesses doing badly by ones that are doing well, and if this in turn reduces the likelihood of pay cuts and layoffs, then the risk faced by the employees is reduced. This has value, some of which might accrue to the shareholders if the lessened risk allows reducing average total compensation.

A diversified firm might also have advantages if it were able to allocate resources between businesses more effectively than the market can. Williamson (1975) suggested that capital allocation might be done better within firms than across firm boundaries. Possibly the information asymmetries that confront the internal capital allocation process are less troublesome than those in market dealings. For example, the manager of each unit might privately know something about the value of extra capital allocated to it. If the managers of different businesses are in the same firm, it may be easier to align their interests with efficient allocation between the businesses than would be possible in a market. Then each may be more inclined to reveal the relevant information, thereby permitting better capital allocation.

Similarly, if sensitive or subjective information about people and jobs flows more easily within a firm than across firm boundaries, it may be possible that the allocation of human capital is more efficient within the firm. Even though, in comparison to the market, having fewer people to match with fewer jobs reduces the possibilities

216

for a great fit between the person and the job, the quality of the average match may be better because of the improved information. Certainly there is some reason to expect that there are such advantages in communication within the firm, because shared experiences and shared language make communication more effective. A diversified firm may also be better positioned than the market to offer managers a rich set of experiences in different businesses, and thus may have some advantages in developing human capital. This argument has been made in the case of General Electric, the most successful of the surviving conglomerates.

Diversification might also make sense if the firm has capabilities or non-marketed resources that are not fully being utilized in its current line of business, yet further expansion of that business is not attractive. An argument made in the 1960s by Harold Geneen, head of ITT, perhaps the archetypal conglomerate of the day, was that his firm had access to superior executives who together could manage assets and businesses better than others could. ITT's expansion was then justified by the possibility of letting its superior team of managers work with a larger set of resources to create greater value. Expansion in any single line of business was presumably restricted by the strict antitrust enforcement policies of the day, and so ITT became a conglomerate.[7] More recently, Virgin's expansion of its scope, from airlines and trains through music and bridal stores to soft drinks, may possibly be rationalized by regarding the Virgin brand as such an incompletely utilized resource.

In a related vein, externalities among businesses might also favor integrating the businesses inside a single firm. Absent efficient Coasian bargaining or complete contracting, coordinating across businesses to handle the externalities will require cooperation in the sense used in Chapter 3—behavior that supports others' welfare. Inducing cooperation may be easier inside the firm than between separate organizations because the firm can offer more muted but better balanced incentives than those that come from dealings between distinct, autonomous parties. Thus, for example, if customer lists can be shared or if a common brand gainfully used by different businesses, or, more generally, if investments will affect multiple businesses, then integration may have advantages. The Walt Disney Company's expansion from its base in animated films to television shows, theme parks, retail stores, cruise lines, and more, can be seen in this light. In each case, the characters and general brand characteristics (wholesome, family-oriented fun) were leveraged to gain advantage in the new activity. This was more easily accomplished within a single firm because the brand created externalities among the businesses and these needed to be coordinated.

Complementarities can be a basis for interdependence between potentially separate businesses that can favor their integration. The rationale offered by Sony Corporation for its acquisition of Columbia Pictures and CBS Records between 1987 and 1989 was based on the complementarity between "software" or content—films, TV shows, recorded music—and "hardware"—Sony's consumer electronics products that turned content into entertainment (Avery, Roberts, and Zemsky 1993). Managing a company combining consumer electronics and recorded entertainment has been problematic for

Sony. However, at the time of the acquisitions Sony had had a string of experiences that convinced its executives that the key to success for new consumer electronics products might well be the ability to provide content that could be played on them. The film and recording companies had historically resisted every new delivery technology that had emerged: Television would destroy the movie business; audio cassettes would destroy the record business by permitting copying; home video cassette recorders would destroy television and the movies, again by permitting copying; the compact disk would just be another costly medium that would bring no extra demand for recorded music. In fact, each innovation eventually created huge new profits for the content providers. Meanwhile, Sony perceived that the CD had succeeded only because Sony and Philips, the co-developers of the technology, each controlled recording companies and required them to issue recordings in the new format. Further, some within Sony believed that Sony's Betamax might have won the standards war for videocassette recorders against JVC's VHS standard if Sony had controlled recorded video entertainment that it could have issued only in its format. Anticipating that it would continue to develop new delivery systems for entertainment (including the then much-heralded High Definition TV), Sony bought control of the two content providers, hoping thereby to ensure the success of its future consumer electronics products. Strikingly, Sony's strategy was soon copied by its archrival, Matsushita, which also bought a studio and record company.

The Sony experience points to some of the drawbacks of integrating diverse businesses within a single firm. In fact, it appears that the hoped-for synergies never emerged. None of the products Sony has developed in the intervening years seem to have benefited significantly from its ownership of the entertainment businesses, although perhaps there has been some spillover between video games and the studio. There may yet be some value to emerge from the combination if digitalization leads to convergence of various industries including consumer electronics and entertainment, as some now anticipate. Yet, the eventual returns would have to be immense to offset the initial multibillion-dollar outlay and the subsequent losses that Sony experienced and that led to a $3.4 billion write-off on the acquisition.

The first problem was that the Sony leadership had little experience with or understanding of the new businesses. They knew something of the recorded music business from having had a joint venture with CBS Records in Japan, but Hollywood was unknown territory. Almost of necessity, they were forced to rely on managers hired into the corporation from the entertainment industry. The ones they chose appear to have acted in a very opportunistic, self-interested way, assuring their Sony bosses that the extravagances they enjoyed and the failures they generated were the norm in the business. Perhaps the geographic distance and the gaps in corporate and national cultures, compounded by choices Sony made to give the studio executives remarkable freedom and minimal oversight, made the difficulties uniquely severe in this case. Yet, the general point remains that broadening the scope of a firm's activities can make the top executives' task of evaluating and controlling the individual businesses harder and invites managerial moral hazard.

At the same time, Sony's top executives were diverted from their previous single-minded focus on the consumer electronics area. It may be only coincidence, but in the period after the acquisitions Sony experienced an unaccustomed lack of success with a number of new products—high definition television failed to take off, digital audio tape never caught on, the Minidisk® was a failure. Perhaps if the leadership had not been distracted by the new businesses and if the amount of attention they could give to the traditional business had not been correspondingly limited, these failures might have been avoided or mitigated. Further, if the entertainment businesses had not been losing money there might have been more resources to support investment in consumer electronics.

Having the disparate businesses in the same company also created tensions between the groups. For example, Sony's head of consumer electronics in the United States complained publicly about announcements affecting his business coming from the entertainment side. He eventually left Sony, but that surely did not eliminate the problem. Top executives had to deal with these rivalries and conflicts. Generally, heterogeneity invites corporate politics and influence activities, with all the attendant costs.

Another problem comes in organizational design. Different businesses, with different technologies, markets, and strategies, would on their own typically adopt different organizational designs—different sorts of people, different architectures, different managerial processes and routines, and different cultures. Putting the businesses in a single firm means that either the firm must deal with the complexity and difficulties of comparison that maintaining organizational differentiation

221

implies, or else the organizational designs must be made more common, so that they are no longer optimized for the individual businesses. Either choice is costly.

Sony opted to maintain as much differentiation as possible. The result was complexity, increased influence activities, and loss of control. It is perhaps more common to insist that standard operating procedures be applied across the company, precisely to avoid these problems and increase comparability. Then the cost is likely to be diminished performance from having an organizational design that does not fit any of the individual businesses' needs well.

A prominent example is Tenneco's takeover of Houston Oil and Minerals (Williamson 1985: 158). Houston was in the business of finding and developing hydrocarbon deposits. Tenneco was a conglomerate with some activities in oil and gas exploration. Houston was known for the very intense incentives it offered to its exploration personnel, including giving them an interest in any petroleum deposits they found. The spirit of the company was very entrepreneurial and its people were highly motivated and very skilled, and Houston was extremely successful at finding gas and oil. At the time of the acquisition, Tenneco vowed to run Houston separately from its other operations to maintain its entrepreneurial spirit, which it hoped would spread to the acquiring company. Within months, however, Tenneco had imposed uniform corporate processes and compensation systems on Houston. An executive explained that common processes and procedures were imperative. The bulk of the talent that had made Houston so successful then left the firm. Eventually what was left of the Houston unit was rolled up into the existing operations. Other examples of the same sort abound.

Sony sought to limit influence activities and the problem of complexity by its hands-off management approach. It did not assign any Japanese executives to Hollywood and oversaw the entertainment businesses from an office in New York rather than from Tokyo headquarters. This contributed, however, to the difficulties in control and in allocating resources effectively between the groups.

Allocating capital between businesses is an especially important potential source of inefficiency in the diversified firm. As noted, one of the early justifications of the conglomerates was the possibility that internal capital allocation might actually be better than the market would achieve. More recently the billions of investment dollars lost by the dotcom start-ups and the collapse of the bubble in technology and telecommunications stocks have revived the belief that the market may do a far-from-perfect job in allocating capital. So it seems possible that internal capital allocation processes might well do a better job. On the other hand, there are also reasons to suspect that internal capital budgeting may be grossly inefficient and that separating businesses into distinct firms may thus create value.

The risk-reduction for managers and employees cited earlier as a possible advantage of multibusiness firms means, *a fortiori*, that capital is not automatically being invested where it has its highest-value use. While there may be gains in terms of the insurance offered to employees, there is a cost in using capital in low-valued uses. Further, this cross-subsidization has an additional cost that incentives are muted from what they would be in a stand-alone operation. If losses in one unit are made up by resources generated in others, then the threat of bankruptcy and job loss becomes less motivating. Thus, the internal allocation of capital becomes subject to a much more complex calculus.

Moreover, even if bankruptcy and job losses are not an issue, having multiple businesses in a single company may result in inefficient capital allocation because of influence activities or the desire to limit these. For example, in the 1980s Nokia Corporation undertook a number of acquisitions to shift from its traditional focus on low-growth commodity businesses (wood pulp, rubber goods, cables) to electronics. However, to maintain morale in the old-line businesses, they too were allowed to make acquisitions of their own. This expenditure came at a high cost—the debt Nokia took on for these acquisitions nearly bankrupted it in the early 1990s—and the costs would certainly have been avoided if the old-line businesses had not been part of the firm. (They were, in fact, shed after the crisis in the early 1990s, when Nokia chose to focus on telecommunications.)

The methods available to compete for capital differ depending on whether it is allocated by the market or through an administrative process. This means that the resulting outcomes may differ. In particular, the opportunities to deprecate or sabotage others' projects are much more extensive inside organizations. It is clear that this sort of behavior can be costly in many ways.

An extensive empirical literature has developed on the efficiency or inefficiency of diversification. The earliest work documented an apparent "diversification discount."

The U.S. stock markets valued diversified firms at a lower multiple of the replacement cost of their assets than more focused firms (Montgomery and Wernerfeld 1988). The market also apparently valued diversified firms a lower amount than it would have given to the sum of their constituent parts (Lang and Stultz 1994). Later work replicated this last result, showed it also held in the United Kingdom and Japan, and traced it to inefficient internal capital allocation processes (Berger and Ofek 1995; Shin and Stultz 1997; Scharfstein 1998; Lins and Servaes 1999; Scharfstein and Stein 2000).

The technique used in many of these studies was to match each diversified firm with a collection of single-segment, stand-alone firms that, in aggregate, replicated its range of businesses. Then the stock market performance and investment choices of the actual firms and the constructed matches were compared. Doing so revealed that the diversified firms apparently invested less in strong divisions with good prospects than did the focused companies in these same lines of business and, correspondingly, overinvested in the weak ones. These distortions were typically traced to the impact of influence activities, which led to cross-subsidization of losers by winners. Two possible mechanisms could have been at work. The influence activities may have been successful in twisting choices, with businesses with limited opportunities getting more resources than they should for efficiency (Meyer, Milgrom, and Roberts 1992; Rajan, Servaes, and Zingales 2000; Scharfstein and Stein 2000). The other possibility is that the firms deliberately adopted evaluation and decision processes that distorted capital investment in order to limit influence and reduce the attendant costs, for example, dividing resources more evenly than they would for efficiency (Milgrom and Roberts 1990c).

The finding of a conglomerate discount has had a major impact—management consultants refer to it in advising their clients to "stick to their knitting," limiting their companies' scope to a narrow range of businesses. Many executives now believe there is a prima facie case that diversification will reduce value, and there is indeed substantial evidence that the market rewards increases in corporate focus (Comment and Jarrell 1995; Berger and Ofek 1996). Yet, much of U.S. employment remains in diversified firms, and almost as many firms increased their diversification in the first half of the 1990s as reduced it (Villalonga 2002b). This presents two puzzles—why would executives pursue apparently value-destroying activities, and how could they get away with it?

Very recently, empirical scholars have questioned the presumed inefficiency of internal capital allocation and even the existence of the diversification discount. The problem is that there may be biases in the process researchers use in selecting groups of single-business firms against which to compare the investment choices made by the diversified firms and their market valuation. Measurement error may also be a factor, and together these—rather than any real relative inefficiency or resulting discount—may account for the statistical findings.

For example, Judith Chevalier (2002) examined the investment behavior of businesses in the 1990s that later merged with one another. These firms showed the same patterns of apparent over- and underinvestment when independent of each other as they did after combining. Thus, she concludes that the apparent distortions cannot be attributable to cross-subsidization. Belen Villalonga (2002*a*, *b*), looking at the same period, found that the apparent distortions that were found when using standard methods to select the single-business firms to match with the diversified ones disappeared when she used more sophisticated methods. So, perhaps, there is no significant amount of inefficient cross-subsidization.

Further, Chevalier and Villalonga both found (as did Campa and Kedia (2002), who looked at a longer time period) that diversifying acquisitions in the 1990s were actually met with positive stock market reactions—the market perceived them to be value-enhancing. This is in line with other studies that have consistently found positive stock market returns to the acquired firm and essentially zero return to the acquiring one, implying that the market perceives that value is created in aggregate in the mergers. It also fits with a large number of studies that suggest that diversified firms are more profitable in accounting terms. However, it is in some conflict with other studies that have shown somewhat negative returns to diversifying combinations (offset by positive returns to combinations that involve more closely related businesses). Moreover, firms that diversified in the 1990s actually traded at a statistically significant discount *before* they diversified. Thus, if there is any causal linkage at all between poor performance and diversification, it appears that low performance leads to diversification, not the other way around.

Finally, there is the conundrum of General Electric—one of the most diversified of businesses and, throughout the last half of the twentieth century, consistently one of the best performing.

What then to make of all this? How can both acquisitions that increase diversification and those that increase focus be good? There is an obvious answer. If executives are actually making choices that increase value, then changes in scope, whether they increase or decrease focus, should bring a positive response from the market. Some firms sometimes can increase value by exiting businesses, focusing on what they do best and reducing the costs of complexity and influence. Others can gain by increasing the range of businesses, especially if the new business can take advantage of underutilized capabilities or resources or if they have significant externalities with existing businesses that cannot effectively be handled contractually. When such moves are made, value is also increased.

There has, however, been a strong suspicion among management scholars and economists that diversification is often a value-destroying manifestation of moral hazard by executives. If executives enjoy heading bigger companies and if the opportunities for growth in existing lines of business are limited, then the obvious choice is to grow by increasing scope. This would seem to have been at work in some cases, particularly in the oil industry in the 1970s. High oil prices brought huge cash flows, while nationalization of the oil industries in Africa and the Middle East limited the multinational oil companies' opportunities to invest in the industry. Rather than give the money back to shareholders, the oil companies diversified. Some of these investments were plausible, even if they proved unsuccessful. For example, several oil companies went into coal mining on the basis that it was another energy business based on extraction of subterranean hydrocarbons. Other moves seem completely bizarre: One oil company bought a circus and another went into fish farming!

Certainly there are cases where executive empire building has occurred. Further, the executives pursuing it may have been behaving quite rationally from a personal point of view. Leaders of bigger firms make more and have more prestige, although it is unclear that acquiring other firms leads to higher pay. In any case, those who do acquisitions tend to get invited to serve on the boards of other firms (Avery, Chevalier, and Schaefer 1998). Until the scandals around corporate malfeasance erupted in 2001–2, board memberships were plums. Yet, it seems incorrect to assume that current diversification is primarily a matter of empire building. Indeed, if it were, the stock market should react negatively, and it does not.

The reason to reject a general presumption that diversification is simply empire building is that, at least in the United States, executives of large firms now typically have significant stock and option holdings that should make them very sensitive to the value of the firms they lead. Moreover, although changes in state laws have largely removed the threat of hostile takeovers that arguably drove much of the value-enhancing de-diversification in the 1980s, corporate boards seem to have become much more diligent and demanding monitors of their executives, and some institutional investors have become quite active in pushing for performance. So it would seem that executives would have little incentive or opportunity to indulge any taste they might have for empire building if it is at any significant cost in performance.

Thus, we return to the logic that changes in scope are presumptively aimed at creating greater value. In this context, we would expect increased diversification to be part of a strategy that emphasizes growth. Decreased scope, on the other hand, would be consistent with a strategy that emphasizes increasing value by focusing on delivering performance in current businesses. One might then expect to see increased focus being adopted in conjunction with other changes in organization that are designed to improve current performance.

Further, if environmental changes allow new opportunities for growth in a firm's core businesses, it might be expected to focus on these and to leave other lines of business that it had entered when they were the only avenues for expansion. Thus, we might expect to see decreased scope even among some firms that are focused on growth. Globalization is one such change: Lowering barriers to trade and investment and increased ease of communicating, traveling, and shipping across borders mean that companies have new opportunities to expand internationally and can grow by increasing their geography without increasing the scope of products or services they offer. Deregulation and changes in antitrust policies have had the same effects in particular instances.

Internal Organization and Performance

While much economics research has addressed the vertical and horizontal boundaries of the firm and given a basis for analyzing and evaluating the changes that we observe there, much less has dealt with the internal organization of the firm and its impact on performance. Thus, our discussion here must be much more speculative. Nevertheless, economic logic can shed some light on the sort of changes that are occurring and their possible causes and effects.

The popular perception is that the technological and competitive environment of business is changing more rapidly than in the past, and business people assert that many of the changes they are making in their organizations are responses to this acceleration. The logic they offer is similar to that we suggested in the case of the eighteenth-century Canadian fur trade. Recall that the Northwest Company overcame the Hudson Bay Company's huge cost advantage by creating an organization that empowered those close to the relevant information to make key strategic and operational decisions, motivated them via more intense financial incentives and ownership to make the right decisions and to exert remarkable efforts, and created mechanisms to ensure that information was shared and that the decisions of the many individuals were aligned. This worked spectacularly well in the newly competitive environment and led to the near collapse of the HBC, with its more traditional, hierarchic command and control systems that had worked so well for more than a century while the HBC had been a monopoly.

The changes implemented at BP and in other loosely coupled, disaggregated organizations share many of the same features. A number are particularly germane:

- establishing clarity about strategy and about corporate policies;
- creating discrete organizational units that are smaller than previously favored;

- giving these units' leaders increased operational and strategic authority, and holding them strictly accountable for results;
- reducing the number of layers in the hierarchy in a process of delayering;
- reducing the number of central staff positions;
- increasing incentives for performance at the unit and individual levels, perhaps accompanied by increased rewards tied to overall performance;
- increasing the resources devoted to management training and development;
- promoting horizontal linkages and communication among managers and staff, rather than requiring all communication to move up and down through the hierarchy;
- improving information systems that facilitate both the measurement of performance and communication across units and up and down the hierarchy.

These moves are linked by a rich web of complementary relationships, so the impact of adopting any one is increased by doing the others as well. Thus, we tend to see all being done together. Indeed, firms that adopt only some of them not only fail to achieve the substantial performance improvements experienced by those adopting all; they may even suffer performance degradations.

Creating discrete, focused operating units and giving their leaders substantial decision rights over their activities should have a number of direct effects that each improve performance. The first is to improve the incentives for people in the unit to work hard on their unit's performance and think cleverly about their responsibilities—to show initiative. This can come about in several ways.

First, knowing that you really have the responsibility and authority to make decisions can be motivating in itself. If the decision is surely yours to take, or even if your boss is just less likely to overrule you, you will care more about the decision and probably invest more in developing the information needed to decide well (Aghion and Tirole 1997). Further, if hierarchic superiors have given up decision power, then your incentives to spend time and effort on influencing their decisions, rather than on getting your job done, are reduced (Milgrom and Roberts 1988b, 1990a). This can lead you to pay much more attention to your unit's performance.

Delayering augments these incentive effects of creating small, empowered units. Delayering typically means that spans of control—the number of people reporting to any single manager—will increase, in particular for those directly above any level that has been removed. This may effect a commitment by such managers not to intervene in the lower-level decision-making, particularly if the number of staff personnel has been cut, because they will not have the time and resources. This, in turn, increases the motivating effect of reallocating decision rights. Moreover, if decision rights and authority are reallocated away from middle managers, there is less need for these managers and so getting rid of them is more attractive. Thus, delayering and the creation of small, empowered organizational units are complementary in affecting incentives for initiative.

The second way that creating smaller units affects motivation is by making clearer the relationship between individuals' choices and actions and the performance of their unit. This can support both increased intrinsic motivation and the provision of more intense formal incentives. If the organization is structured so that performance can be tracked and measured only for large subunits, the link between what an individual does and the results of these actions is very ambiguous. In a smaller unit, the linkage likely is clearer. This can increase intrinsic motivation because you can see how your actions make a difference.

At the same time, measuring results for smaller units probably improves the accuracy of performance measurement, reducing the randomness in any system linking behavior and rewards, since results are no longer buried in an amalgam with the effects of other people's and units' actions. This, in turn, allows giving more intense formal incentives at the unit level without imposing too much risk. Thus, these features of the design are also complementary, and creating empowered units makes it more attractive to increase incentives. This is so both for explicit financial rewards tied to performance and for less formal rewards ranging from enhanced prospects of promotion to well directed praise.

Moreover, measuring performance for a smaller group makes providing explicit incentives to the group more effective by reducing the free-rider problem. This problem arises because the returns to any improvements are effectively shared among those whose performance is measured together (Holmström 1982b). When credit is shared less widely, the incentives are stronger. Finally, social norms to encourage performance-enhancing behavior may also be more effective in smaller groups.

Increased incentive intensity, in turn, is complementary with improving the measurement of performance: If stronger incentives are indicated, then the benefits of improving performance measures increase. This can be achieved both by defining smaller, focused performance units and by improved information systems. At the same time, as the quality of measurement increases, the attractiveness of increasing incentive intensity goes up. So falling costs of measuring performance lead to more intense incentives. Clarity about strategy, so that it is clear what constitutes good performance and what needs to be measured, thus leads to giving stronger incentives. Finally, improved measurement supports broadened spans of control. Thus more of the common features are linked.

A second effect on performance of creating small, empowered units is to increase the likely speed of adaptation to new information, at least to the extent that the information is first available to those in the operating units rather than higher-ups in the organization. Information about customer needs, supplier and competitor behavior, and production conditions and opportunities should be most readily available to frontline personnel, who are in direct contact with the sources of this information. (In contrast, information about emerging political and regulatory issues, social trends, financial market conditions, and corporate policies is arguably more likely to be available first at the corporate center.) Empowering those with the information to act upon it clearly speeds action, provided those with the decision rights are motivated to make the decisions. There is no need to wait while the information is communicated up, absorbed, and analyzed, and then the decisions sent back down. Further, because aspects of the relevant information may be difficult to communicate and, in any case, communication tends to result in garbling, the decisions are likely to be based on more accurate information when they are made close to the source.

Increasing the speed of decisions is more valuable the more rapid the environment is changing. There is certainly a popular perception among business people that the world is changing at an unprecedented and yet ever-accelerating rate. This then favors moving decision-making to the front lines.

One cost of empowering small, frontline units is that quality of decision-making may worsen. In the traditional hierarchic organization, a variety of decisions were made by the middle managers whose jobs are eliminated in delayering. In particular, decisions affecting several units but not the whole organization, such as the allocation of capital or customers between two divisions or whether one unit can undertake a project that will harm another, would naturally have been made by an experienced manager who oversaw both units and who was responsible for the results of both. Responsibility for such decisions now moves, either down to lower-level people or up to the top. Either can potentially be problematic.

If the decisions are moved down, the decision-makers may not have the information needed to account for spillover effects on other units or the organization as a whole. They also may not be properly motivated to account for these effects. Further, to the extent that the newly empowered frontline managers have less relevant experience than the displaced middle managers, the quality of decision-making may slip. On the other hand, if the decision power moves up, then motivation is presumably not a problem—top executives will want to advance the performance of the overall organization. As well, since the top management is no further from the front lines than were the now-gone middle managers, the amount and quality of information to which they can gain access is not likely worse. This is especially true if information, measurement, and reporting systems have been strengthened, as is normally part of the set of organizational changes. Instead, the difficulty is that executive overload—too much to do and too many decisions to be made—may lead either to hasty, bad decisions or to costly delays. There is also a danger that the results of top-level interventions will be applied on a blanket basis, undercutting the loose coupling and the enhanced incentives that are important elements of the model. This means that, in fact, the bulk of the decisions formerly made in the middle must move down. Thus measures to improve decision-making by front-line managers are complementary with delayering.

If the problem is that front-line managers do not understand the full implications of their decisions, one solution is to provide the relevant information. This is increasingly easy with improved communication and information systems, investment in which then makes the reallocation of decision authority more effective. Linking managers of different units directly so that they can inform one another about spillovers may be especially valuable, so this practice is also complementary with the others in the package. Much of this may occur through information technology, but face-to-face, personal contact is important, especially at the start when relationships are being established. Being clear about strategy and about overall corporate policy will also help, because it will set bounds on decisions and will focus attention on key issues.

If the poor decisions come from misaligned incentives, the obvious answer is to provide the appropriate incentives. This might come from reducing the extent to which performance pay is linked to the individual unit performance and paying more on overall firm performance, although this may limit initiative and have negative implications for unit performance. Establishing strong norms with regard to decision-making in the context of spillovers will also be useful if they lead managers to account more fully for the effects of their decisions on others. BP's tying pay in part to overall corporate performance in part had this aim. Even more, its creating the peer groups worked to increase cooperation, because unit managers had to work with and rely upon the other managers who experienced many of the spillovers from their decisions.

On the other hand, Johnson & Johnson's decentralized structure had great difficulties inducing cooperation among the thirteen J&J companies selling to hospitals in the 1980s. The company sought to introduce a shared service model for logistics and billing that would consolidate orders and shipments to the hospitals for the J&J companies. This was competitively important for many of the companies, which were losing market share, and would have generated important savings and increased convenience for the customers. The values of the company then should have induced cooperative acceptance of the change, because these accentuated that the first duty was to the customer. However, the strongest businesses with the best products, which were competitive even when the customers were not well served, were unwilling to give up any of their independence.

If limited capabilities are the source of the problem, then the first question is whether the center would do any better. After all, it lacks the relevant information and must depend on the line managers for it. Even so, the solution may be in increasing the capability of the line through investments in managerial development and the provision of staff in the units. BP has, in fact, invested heavily in management development.

A second difficulty that can arise with creating small, focused, empowered units is that the organization may have trouble responding to challenges and opportunities that are most naturally addressed on some basis other than the "natural" linkage patterns derived from the primary dimensions of performance. At BPX, where the focus was largely on increasing volumes and controlling costs, the linkages among units connected ones facing similar technical problems in achieving low costs and high volumes. Thus, units that were located in the same geographical area would not be linked together directly. But, for example, regulatory and environmental issues might be better approached on a national or regional basis.

The natural response to these problems is to create matrix forms. These can vary in how explicit and formal they are. ABB's matrix of geography and product, with every line manager reporting to two bosses, was at the one extreme. General Motors employs a "basket-weave" model. The primary dimension of organization is by product and region, but senior executives take cross-unit responsibility for processes such as quality and manufacturing. BP tried having a Regions and Policies group that was nominally to be on a par with the business streams, but would only have an assurance role. The business units, linked in their peer groups, would still report to the stream Executive Committees, but the Regions and Policies staff would be in contact with them on matters that did not fit well into the business focus of the main structure. This was not fully successful, however. As the mergers and moves into new business areas increased greatly the complexity of the company's business and its geographic spread by the late 1990s, it began to adjust its design to handle regional issues better by giving additional, explicit regional responsibilities to senior managers overseeing the business units.

The Whole System

The complementarities described among the features of internal organization in fact extend to the horizontal and vertical scope of the firm. Clarity about strategy and the meaning of performance is easier when the firm is more focused. A narrower scope also means that there is less room for the interdependencies among units that can be problematic for the disaggregated model, although the logic of partnering means that outsourcing does not relieve the need to handle interdependencies effectively. Further, a small top executive team makes a narrower scope more attractive, as the overload problem is lessened. So all the pieces fit together.

The implications of these arguments have in fact been tested. Andrew Pettigrew and colleagues (Ruigrok *et al.* 1999; Whittington *et al.* 1999) studied 448 European companies in the period 1992–6 to examine the linkage between their performance and the extent to which they adopted elements of this model (the researchers focused on ten elements involving changing the boundaries of the firm, its internal architecture, and its processes). They found a number of statistically significant positive correlations among the practices adopted in the best-performing companies in their set: Adopting one of the features (such as greater horizontal linkages) was associated with adopting others (such as higher IT investments). Strikingly, the worst-performing companies often showed the reverse patterns, so that weak firms that had increased horizontal linkages were likely to be investing less in IT.

These observed patterns are in line with the argument above, with the existence of complementarities among the features of the design, and with the new model having positive performance effects. These results held up in a full econometric estimation of the determinants of performance. Adopting a coherent collection of the measures was shown to have a strongly positive effect on performance, even though individual elements adopted on their own often hurt performance.

The researchers also found that most companies in their sample had begun to move to the new model, adopting at least some of the collection of features. However, only a tiny percentage (about one in twenty in the sample) had gone all the way, adopting the full model by changing their structures, processes, and boundaries in fundamental ways. Those that had done so experienced much higher profitability than firms that had not moved at all towards the new model. Strikingly, those firms that adopted only one or two of the three elements actually did substantially worse than those that had not moved towards it at all.

Thus, the changes that are being adopted, when seen and acted upon holistically, make excellent business sense. Together they improve performance substantially, while mix and match does not work.

Notes

1. For a detailed examination of the range of changes and a survey of the evidence that they are occurring, see Whittington *et al.* (1999). See also Lichtenberg (1992) on focus, McMillan (1995) on outsourcing, Rajan and Wulf (2002) for evidence on delayering, and Nagar (2002) on delegation and incentive pay.

2. See Milgrom and Roberts (1992: 552–61) for a general discussion of the issues involved. See also McMillan (1995) and Holmström and Roberts (1998).

3. Baker, Gibbons, and Murphy (2001), Levin (2003), and Doornik (2001) are recent exceptions.

4. The norm in the Japanese auto industry has been for only some 30 percent of the total cost of the vehicle to be incurred by the final manufacturer, with the rest being done by outside suppliers. In contrast, General Motors in the 1980s did 70 percent in-house, sourcing much less from outsiders. See McMillan (1995) and Milgrom and Roberts (1993) for more details and references.

5. The basic logic is very similar to that developed in the discussion of reputations in the agency context in Chapter 4.

6. In fact, Ford had earlier stopped selling its Explorer sports utility vehicle in Europe after Arthur Andersen, the receiver for another insolvent British supplier, had demanded a 60 percent price increase, with the threat to stop delivery of cylinder heads for the Explorer. In that case the British High Court had ruled that Andersen had acted properly in exploiting the customer's vulnerability, since the receiver's responsibility was to raise money to repay creditors.

7. Geneen also directly appealed to the risk-reduction argument.

6

Organizing for Growth and Innovation

Delivering current performance may please shareholders, but they are even happier if the firm is not just profitable, but if its profits and profitability are actually increasing. Moreover, the members of the firm are apt to like growth too. Work is more fun in a growing company. Growth means more opportunities for new, exciting assignments and promotions, and unpleasant conflict is lessened, because there can be more for everyone from the ever-bigger pie that is being divided. Yet realizing growth without undercutting current performance and destroying value can be very problematic.

As long as the potential of the firm's original business is not exhausted, then delivering current performance and achieving growth can be completely compatible. That is not to say that growth is necessarily easy. Size brings complexity, and organizational designs that were adequate in a small firm may fail to scale up successfully in a larger one. But there is no inherent conflict in extending the basic strategic model as the business expands.

There are limits to such organic growth, however. Management scholars have argued that most industries go through a life cycle, from founding through a period of rapid growth to maturity, when the industry essentially grows with the overall economy, and then perhaps to ultimate decline.[1] While no single firm necessarily follows through this whole cycle, because some enter late and others exit before the industry dies, the dynamics of the industry set the context for the growth of individual firms. When the industry is growing fast, attracting new customers, there is lots of room for individual firms to grow rapidly too. Thus, some auto companies and the industry as a whole grew very fast in the early twentieth century, while firms in the software, semiconductor, computer, and telecommunications industries grew at tremendous rates in the later part of the century.

At some point, however, market growth must slow. It may still be possible for a few firms to keep growing fast by attracting customers from competitors, but this is likely to be increasingly difficult. Another possibility is to expand into new geographic markets, but there are often real limits to this approach. Leading a process of industry consolidation by absorbing competitors can also bring continued growth for some time. But there are obvious limits to this source of growth as well: Even if further consolidation would be economically possible, antitrust is likely to prove a barrier.

Thus, if the firm is to continue to grow at substantial rates, it must ultimately be by developing business opportunities beyond its original scope. Moreover, if demand for a firm's original products declines, then developing new options can be crucial to its very survival.

Acquisitions are one way to get into new businesses: Buy products, divisions, or companies already in these fields. The other option is for the firm to create and develop new opportunities on its own. Acquisitions readily lead to higher sale numbers and higher total profits, but the implications for value creation and profitability are less clearly positive. Innovating, on the other hand, is an inherently uncertain process. Moreover, the organizational designs that support it are very different from those that support delivery of current performance. This means that sustaining growth at rates exceeding the rate of growth of the economy is a difficult process—one that few firms manage successfully for very long. Meanwhile, huge amounts of value may be destroyed in pursuing unattainable growth ambitions.

This chapter is about organizing for growth. We will first discuss briefly the acquisition option. Then we turn to our main focus, the problem of organizing for innovation while continuing to deliver performance in the existing businesses.

Buying Growth

Acquisitions can certainly lead companies into new businesses and new growth opportunities. General Electric has undertaken hundreds of acquisitions. In recent years many of these were by the company's GE Capital financial services group, which in the process became a hugely diverse concern in its own right whose growth was a major element of the parent's. Acquisitions have also been used by some companies to maintain the flow of new products needed to compete and grow in high tech businesses. Most prominently, Cisco Systems bought scores of smaller companies to obtain the technologies and people it needed to keep innovating in its business in routers, switches and other network equipment, and software. Acquisitions have even been used to transform companies completely. Westinghouse Electric, the venerable American manufacturing concern, in 1997 transmogrified itself into a media company called CBS, owning the CBS television network, cable channels, and radio and television stations. It did this largely by buying the media businesses and selling off its original manufacturing operations. Similarly, Mannesmann in 1990 epitomized German heavy industry, producing coal, iron and steel, pipes, industrial machinery, and automotive equipment. Nine years later it was a pure-play mobile telecommunications provider. Beginning in 1990 with a license to start a wireless communications network in Germany, Mannesmann grew to become a major player in the industry by acquiring wireless companies in other European countries. In 1999 the company exited all its industrial businesses, completing its transformation. (Strikingly, both Mannesmann and CBS have since been absorbed by other companies, the former by Vodafone and the latter by Viacom.)

The big problem with acquisition-based growth strategies is generating value for the acquiring company's shareholders through the process. Profitless growth is not worthwhile, because just being bigger has no real value. In general, it seems very hard for firms to benefit their owners by buying other firms. The difficulties are twofold. First is to avoid having all the potential value creation flow to the shareholders of the acquired firm. The second is to realize the potential gains once the transaction is completed.

A consistent finding from a number of studies is that, when measured by stock-market reactions, mergers and acquisitions on average do create value, but most or all of it accrues to the target firms' owners. The general pattern is that the stock price of the acquired firm shows significant positive "abnormal returns" (its price rises relative to what would have been predicted from general market movements), reflecting investors' perception that the target's shareholders usually do very well, receiving a significant premium for their shares. On the other hand, the stock price of the acquiring firm tends to be unaffected on average, or to fall somewhat.[2] So, on net, investors perceive that there is value created in the average deal, but that little or none of it accrues to the acquiring firm.

This distribution of the surplus is what one would expect if there is active competition to acquire companies and potential targets are in short supply relative to the number of interested buyers. Of course, it is not inevitable that sellers should be on the short side of the market, but it appears that they systematically are. Perhaps this is reflective of the desirability to executives of growing and keeping one's job over being acquired and possibly terminated. It may also reflect the targets' actively seeking additional suitors once the possibility of being acquired arises. Indeed, the directors of the target arguably have a duty to their shareholders to try to get an auction going in which the price of their firm will be bid up by competition.

Even if competition for targets is not overly intense, an informational problem may help explain the distribution of the benefits from acquisitions. It is known in the literature on competitive bidding as "the winner's curse." The basic idea is that, in auctions where the value to the different bidders of the thing being sold has a common element, unless the bidders are sophisticated there will be a tendency for the winner to end up paying more than the item is actually worth. Target acquisitions may have this feature.

What a company is worth to any other company may be expressed as some common amount that it is worth to any possible acquirer, which reflects the underlying value of the business, plus an idiosyncratic component that reflects the particularities of the fit between the target and the individual bidder. No bidder likely knows either of these two elements with certainty. Instead, they must be estimated. If bidders with higher estimated values tend to bid more aggressively, then the winner will tend to be the firm that estimates the sum to be largest. But even if each firm's estimate of the value is unbiased, the largest of the estimates of the common component is systematically likely to be an overestimate of the actual amount. Unless the bidder takes account of the fact that, when it is the winning bidder, it has the highest estimate of the value of the target (which means that it is likely an overestimate), it will tend to bid too aggressively and pay too much.

Sophisticated bidders may learn to avoid the winner's curse by adjusting their bids downwards. For example, the oil companies have been aware of the problem for many years and presumably have learned to deal with it in their bidding for oil leases. Whether companies bidding to acquire others have learned to overcome the winner's curse is less certain.

Even if the winner's curse is avoided, the fact of competition for targets means that growth by acquisition can be value-enhancing for the buyer only if the target is worth discernibly more to the acquirer than to others. In an auction of the sort that often occurs in competing to acquire a company, the price will tend to reflect the highest valuation of the target among the losing bidders. Unless this is quite a bit lower than the winner's valuation, all the gains will flow to the acquired firm's shareholders.

What makes a target worth more to one firm than another? First, we need to distinguish whether we are thinking about the value to the executives of the acquirer or the value to the shareholders. If the executives are building empires, or if they are afflicted with hubris and overestimate their abilities to create value in running the target, these valuations may clearly differ. But as we argued in the previous chapter, the rise of activist investors and the increased reliance on executive compensation that is tied in one way or another to the stock price means that this form of managerial moral hazard is perhaps less of a problem than it may have been in the past. Then the answer depends on two things: The potential for creating extra value by having the assets of the two companies under common direction, and the actual ability to realize that extra value.

The potential for value creation in a business combination depends on there being complementarities between the two firms that cannot be realized except through unified management and governance. In particular, if the gains can be realized without combining the two firms—say, by an alliance, partnership, or contractual arrangement—then putting the two firms together cannot be worthwhile.

The requisite complementarity could come from assets that are underutilized in one of the concerns and that can be used in both. Many of the "synergies" that are often claimed in mergers and acquisitions are of this sort: Having just one accounting or human resource department would allow savings if there are any scale economies or indivisibilities and if the efficiencies these offer cannot be realized by, for example, outsourcing these functions. Importantly, the relevant underused assets may be intangible ones, like knowledge. For example, it is arguable that much of the value created in BP's acquisitions of Amoco and Arco in the late 1990s came from applying BP's superior management systems to the American firms' human and physical assets. An attractive market position that can be leveraged to include the new business might also be the source of the gains. Cisco Systems could make money buying technology companies because of its unmatched position as a provider of network equipment to large businesses and the reputation it had with its customers. These meant it could get more from the technologies it bought than could another bidder. The complementarity gains may also come from each firm having assets that are made more valuable by being used together. So if one has capabilities in manufacturing and another in marketing, then possibly the combined firm can do better than the sum of the parts.

The existence of complementarities that are economically significant is plausible when the target and acquirer are in related businesses. For example, Newell Company has grown to be a major force in the home products business by buying other companies in the general field, including Rubbermaid, to expand its product line (Barnett and Reddy 1995). Newell adds value by applying its unique management systems and by leveraging its relations with retailers. Such complementarities would seem less likely, however, when the acquisition is meant to take the buyer into new businesses. Thus, achieving real value-creating growth in this fashion is apt to be difficult.

Moreover, even if there are potential complementarities in bringing two existing businesses together, actually realizing them can be a major organizational challenge. Postmerger integration is notoriously difficult. It is easy to understand why.

There are basically three models for organizing after a merger or acquisition. One is to keep the two organizations as separate as possible. This was the path initially followed by Sony after buying Columbia Pictures. This approach largely gives up on realizing any significant complementarities, but it permits each part to have an organizational design that fits its business. It may be appropriate if the objective is to get into a new business, perhaps to leave the old business behind as Mannesmann and Westinghouse/CBS did. However, it is hard to see how any value is going to be created in the process, and any premium that was paid for the target will be difficult to recoup.

The other two approaches actually seek integration. One picks one of the two organization's models (typically the acquirer's) and attempts to institute it across the board, with the target being reorganized and absorbed. This was done in the BP–Amoco merger, where the BP organization design prevailed and the Amoco assets were brought under the BP business unit model. The third approach seeks to find the best in both organizational designs and to combine them to create something quite different. This is a common pattern, especially when comparably sized firms are involved in a "merger of equals." The integration process following Hewlett-Packard's acquisition of Compaq is a prominent example.

Imposing the organization of one of the firms has the great advantage of minimizing the confusion and disruption that is involved in organizational change. It also contributes to rapid integration. There is a clear model, and the new people simply have to adapt. Of course, the inclusion of a new group of people in the organization will necessarily change it, and their adoption of the selected model's culture may be a slow and unsure process. This approach may work very well when the two companies are in the same business, as in an industry consolidation like BP led. It is also the approach used by Cisco Systems in acquisitions of much smaller firms for technology and human resources. Indeed, Cisco screens potential targets with respect to the people and culture elements of their organizations to ensure that they will easily fit into Cisco (O'Reilly 1998). However, if the objective is to bring in a really new set of business opportunities, imposing the acquiring firm's model is likely to be very inefficient, because it is unlikely to be well adapted to coordinating and motivating people to carry out the activities of the new business. At the extreme, it risks driving away the people who came with the acquisition, and thus possibly losing the capabilities that were the reason for the deal in the first place. The example of Tenneco and Houston Oil and Minerals cited earlier illustrates this danger.

The first danger in the "best of each" approach is that choices will be delayed and performance will consequently suffer for an extended period. What is the better way needs to be determined, and this may not be immediately evident. Moreover, the choice can be an occasion for immense politicking and resultant influence costs, as each side competes to have the way it knows be chosen. Indeed, sometimes choices may never be made. Some twenty years after the merger that created Japan's Dai-ichi Kango Bank, there were still separate Human Resource departments in the bank to deal with the people who had come from each of the original companies. HP may actually have benefited from the delay in carrying out its merger occasioned by shareholder opposition, because it gave extra time for the design issues to be settled before the actual combination occurred.

The second problem is that, to the extent that the original designs involved coherent systems, the selection of the apparently best-performing features of each may not yield a coherent design. As we argued in Chapter 2, mix and match is often a recipe for disaster in the design problem.

The conclusion from all this is that trying to grow profitably through acquisitions is difficult, and that creating value by getting into new businesses by this route may be especially problematic. Thus, we turn to the problem of promoting innovation within established firms while maintaining performance in the original business.

Innovation in Established Firms: Exploring and Exploiting

Organizing to support the generation of new ideas is not hard. Research universities provide the model. Get bright, curious people together, give them time and resources and minimal direction, let them communicate with other smart people who will both share thoughts and subject ideas to rigorous examination, and make sure that the people whose ideas are judged best are rewarded in a way they value (not necessarily with lots of money!). The old Bell Laboratories of the American Telephone and Telegraph Company operated this way, and it generated several Nobel prizes for the fundamental work done there, including inventing the transistor and finding evidence of the Big Bang. Xerox's Palo Alto Research Center was similarly designed and similarly productive: Object-oriented programming, local area networks, and many of the key features of the personal computer were all developed there. Of course, neither parent company made any money from these great ideas—perhaps they were organized a little too much like universities!

Thus, the problem is not just to create ideas, but also to turn them into successful businesses. Many established firms struggle painfully to find new business opportunities, and others never seriously try. Meanwhile, there are other firms that are constantly creating not just new products, but whole new product categories. Yet, many of these firms that are so proficient at innovation struggle to deliver day-to-day performance. They can invent things and create novel businesses, but they seem unable to run them with real efficiency. Firms that manage to be both innovative and efficient are rare. Our first concern will be to discover why this is so. We then discuss emerging research that suggests how to encourage the innovation needed for growth without giving up too much in current performance.

James March (1991) has distinguished the two tasks that are involved in firms creating new businesses and then running them successfully. One is to *exploit* effectively the opportunities inherent in the current situation—the basic business model the firm has adopted, the market segments it addresses, the products or services it offers, and the technology it employs. The other is to *explore* for and develop new opportunities. Exploration and exploitation are quite different tasks, calling on different organizational capabilities and typically requiring differing organizational designs to effect them.

The essence of exploitation is achieving maximal performance in delivering on the current strategy. As described in the Chapter 5, consummate exploitation requires complete focus on the current agenda, with all energy aimed at effective, timely execution. Consequently, exploitation involves organizational designs—people, architecture, routines, and culture—that facilitate focus and execution. Incentives are likely to be strong and based whenever possible on quantitative measures of operational performance, costs, revenues, and profitability. Control of processes is tight in order to reduce uncertainty and manage risk. Meeting current customers' recognized needs is accentuated. Slack—resources not devoted to delivering on the strategy—is ruthlessly eliminated.

Lincoln Electric has done a superb job of exploitation. Over many decades it has consistently and very effectively pursued its aim of reducing the cost of the arc welding equipment and supplies it makes, allowing it to reduce prices to customers and dominate its markets. As described earlier, everything in its organizational design is geared to encouraging workers to increase the productivity with which they carry out their assigned tasks. This runs from Lincoln's famous piece rates and its remarkable bonus pay scheme through to the way jobs are designed and on to the ownership structure. Every bit of cost is relentlessly squeezed. Even what might appear to be waste turns out to be a required element of the strategy for realizing efficiency. For example, Lincoln's unusually high levels of work-in-process inventory are needed to allow individual pacing of the work, which is crucial to the effectiveness of piece rates and the incentives they generate to work hard and be smart about how to do one's job better. Similarly, the high level of employee earnings—they are at least twice the average for manufacturing workers in Lincoln's home region—could not be reduced without undermining the trust and long-term loyalty of the workforce and without damaging the incentives for initiative (from the piece rates) and cooperation (from the bonus).

Exploitation is not just a matter of static efficiency in a narrow sense. Indeed, it can involve large amounts of innovation. Lincoln could not have achieved its record of ever-increasing output per hour without developing and implementing innumerable process innovations over the years. Similarly, BP Exploration, a superb exploiter, has made numerous major innovations in finding and extracting oil, including developing the ability to drill horizontally and in very deep ocean water. Moreover, firms in technologically very dynamic industries have operated as effective exploiters. For example, through the 1990s Intel exploited the opportunities in the X86/Pentium microprocessor architecture with remarkably single-minded determination. Getting maximal yields in manufacturing for each new generation of the chips was always a key priority, so that costs could be minimized and price could be reduced. The development process for new chips was highly regularized and disciplined. The focus on the microprocessor business was complete—so much so that the desert creosote plant, which extrudes a poison that kills any other plant that invades its space, became an accepted metaphor describing the effect of the microprocessor business on any initiatives that might divert attention away from it (Burgelman 2002).

Although exploiters do innovate, radical innovations are not the product of exploitation, but rather of exploration. Both exploitation and exploration involve searching for improvement. But exploitative search is largely conducted in the course of normal business, looking for improvements in the context of the current agenda and model or for fairly limited extensions of them. Exploration involves search over broader domains, looking for new opportunities outside the current paradigm. It necessarily involves much greater uncertainty, both as to whether anything will be found and then whether it is actually better. It fundamentally depends on slack—that resources be allocated to uses that contribute little or nothing to executing on current strategy. Think of "New, Improved" Tide® detergent versus the digital compact disk. Proctor & Gamble's tinkering with one of their established products in a way that intensive consumer research tells them will meet expressed customer needs is search in an exploiter mode. Sony's and Philips's creating a new delivery system for entertainment whose advantages the potential customers could not imagine is much more exploratory search.

A few companies have adopted a thoroughgoing exploratory orientation. The purest explorers focus completely on generating ideas, leaving it to others to select among them as to which might be worth trying to develop into businesses and then to create and run these businesses. This is how research universities operate, deriving some revenue from licencing their technologies, but few commercial organizations can afford this approach. Still, some come close. Rather than ever trying to build and run businesses themselves, they sell the ideas they generate or spin them off into freestanding companies. IdeaLab is an example. Although IdeaLab has run into difficulties with the collapse of the dotcom bubble, its original business model was to create Internet businesses from the ideas of its founder, Bill Gross, and company researchers. CEOs for the new businesses were recruited from outside, and IdeaLab functioned largely in the now familiar role of incubator, a role it helped create. It provided the initial idea, capital, office space, business services, specialized skills, and advice, and it later assisted in connecting to venture capitalists. The businesses became independent companies, with IdeaLab retaining a substantial ownership in each. As of 1998, there were over thirty independent companies that had come out of this process.

Few companies are content to be pure explorers or incubators, and yet they still focus heavily on exploration. One of the most notable is 3M, especially in the period through the 1960s (Bartlett and Mohammed 1995). This company has a huge array of products, from the wet-use sandpaper it developed a century ago, through the reflective signs used worldwide on freeways, to Scotch brand adhesive tape, and medical supplies. Its forte has been developing new, breakthrough products. This requires imagination, thinking "outside the box," a willingness to take significant risks and to accept failures (and even celebrate, rather than punish, ones that had a chance), openness to the new and untried, and finally the slack resources to generate and develop ideas that may initially seem very far from successful product offerings. 3M put together its organization to make all this possible.

Multiple R&D groups were established, and there was little attempt to coordinate and rationalize activity across them. Direct communication among groups was strongly encouraged, however, and became the norm. Thus, a thousand flowers were let bloom, and multiple approaches to a problem could co-exist, compete, and cross-fertilize one another. 3M also gave its people unusual freedom and autonomy in deciding how and on what to work. To protect this freedom, it actually mandated that technical people should be able to devote 15 percent of their time to "bootleg" projects of their own choice, rather than working on the ones to which they were officially assigned. The ubiquitous Post-It® note came out of such efforts. Moreover, those who resisted directives from senior managers to abandon projects and instead carried them through to success were heroes in the organization. Even the CEO told stories lauding such rebels who had directly disobeyed him when he had tried to kill their pet projects.

At a corporate level, objectives were set for the share of revenues coming from new products. Performance measurement for subgroups or individuals, however, tended to involve subjective evaluations or milestones achieved, not the financial numbers generated. Rewards had large non-monetary elements, especially personal autonomy and professional recognition, and a separate scientific and engineering career path was created so technical people could advance without having to move into management. The sales people were charged as much with being a communication link between customers and the labs as with selling products, and their pay was arranged accordingly.

On the more mundane side of business, the motto was "make a little, sell a little." 3M did not attempt to impose the sort of discipline that was needed to compete in mass markets on the basis of cost. Rather, it pursued niche markets, abandoning these when competition from imitators proved too intense.

Both 3M and Lincoln are extreme types, and such specialization is rare. The reasons are clear. An explorer is very vulnerable to fast-follower competition that operates more efficiently and can undercut the originator of the product, stealing the market before the costs of development can be recouped. Indeed, 3M in the 1990s faced increasingly tough competition of this form, leading it to spin off its videotape and computer diskette businesses. More generally, the 3M model generates lots of ideas, but does not rigorously select among them, and so costs are inflated by the resources sunk over extended periods on ideas that will never become products. Meanwhile, long-run survival as a pure exploiter requires more than being very good at executing on the strategy. In addition, the strategy must remain viable. This means that there cannot be major shifts in demand and that superior new technologies do not undercut the firm's competitive advantage. This latter danger has threatened Lincoln in the last decade as new competitors have introduced welding equipment using new, lighter materials and new electronic controls. The competitors have also moved to supply customers on much shorter lead times than Lincoln can guarantee because its policy against layoffs constrains its hiring in busy periods. Thus, firms need to mix elements of explorer and exploiter if they want to innovate and grow profitably on an ongoing basis.

Even in the simplest case—a company that comes into being to create, develop, and sell just a single product and that is content to go out of business if and when the demand dries up—the firm must move between exploring and exploiting as it develops. The early stages of the firm's life require it to operate in explorer mode, but then it must shift to become an exploiter if it is to prosper. This in itself may be problematic. Venture capitalists insist on having the right to appoint the CEOs of their portfolio companies, and they make frequent use of this power to replace companies' founders (Hellmann 1998). They do this presumably in part because the characteristics needed to come up with the original business idea and prove its value are not the same as those required to develop the idea into a functioning business or to run the business effectively once it is established. Organizationally there may be problems as well. The people who were attracted to the firm in the freewheeling early days of exploration may not fit in the disciplined, focused exploiter context. The communication patterns and decision processes that were appropriate in the small start-up may need to be replaced by more formalized, bureaucratic ones as the firm grows. The culture of working together to create something must be replaced by one of taking responsibility for executing assigned tasks. All this can be disruptive. However, once our single-product firm makes it to the stage of exploitation, it can focus on that one mode of operation until it ultimately ceases to exist when the product cycle ends. As the Lincoln and Hudson Bay Company examples make clear, this can be a long time— Lincoln has been in the arc welding equipment business since 1895, and the HBC was still buying furs and selling manufactured goods three centuries after its founding.

To move beyond this model, where growth prospects are tied so completely to the single product's market, firms must develop multiple business opportunities, and to continue to grow and survive they must do this on an ongoing basis. Thus, at any time they must have a portfolio of activities going on within the firm: Searching for new opportunities, selecting from among identified opportunities, building new businesses, running existing ones, exiting others—all may need to be done at once. In particular, they must explore and exploit at once. This puts the companies right in the middle of the multi-tasking problem of exploring and exploiting simultaneously. Striking and maintaining an appropriate balance between exploration and exploitation can be hard. Moreover, the better you are at one, the harder it is to do the other well.

The first difficulty with multi-tasking is the motivational problem that was discussed in detail in Chapter 4. The difficulty is in inducing employees to allocate their time, effort, and attention appropriately among different tasks when these differ significantly in the timeliness and accuracy of the available performance measures, as is the case with exploration and exploitation.

If two tasks compete with one another for employees' time and attention, the incentives offered for each must be of comparable intensity, or else the employees will tend to overemphasize the well-compensated one and undersupply the other. In the extreme, the employees will just ignore the less well-rewarded one completely, because that is the way to earn the highest rewards from any given level of total effort. Providing comparably intense incentives for different activities becomes problematic, however, when the available measures of the two tasks differ greatly in their precision or timeliness.

Generally, the better the performance measures on an activity, the less costly it is to provide stronger incentives for the activity in isolation and so to induce higher effort. A major reason for this is that the poor measures mean the employee faces large amounts of uncontrollable risk in her rewards, which will vary not just with her choices, but also with the randomness in the measures. This uncertainty is costly to a risk-averse person, and the cost rises as the incentives become more intense, causing the amount of uncertainty in the rewards to scale up. Since the agent must be compensated for bearing this risk, good measures tend to lead to strong incentives and poor measures to weak ones.

When the quality of the measures on two activities differs significantly, it may thus be extremely difficult or expensive to give strong incentives for the ill-measured activity, even though it is easy to provide intense incentives for the other. Thus, providing strong, balanced incentives for both can be problematic. Consequently, if both tasks are desired, it may thus be necessary to supply relatively weak—but balanced—incentives for both. (Indeed, theory suggests that the optimal incentives to induce multi-tasking may be even weaker than those that would be given for the poorly measured activity in isolation.) The weakness of the incentives then means the agent will not devote much effort to either task, even the well-measured one to which she could be induced to devote significant effort if it were in isolation.

Exploratory activity is typically hard to measure in any precise and timely way. The appropriate behaviors are hard to specify in advance, the connection between the employee's efforts and the results that are achieved is subject to real randomness and may be poorly understood, and the actual value of the results may not become clear for a long time. Exploitation, on the other hand, is much more easily measured. Sometimes the tasks are so well understood that the desired behavior can be specified in advance and controlled directly. More generally, the connection between effort and results is likely to be much clearer and less noisy, and the measures of performance—operational and financial results—are readily available. Moreover, the tough, disciplined mindset appropriate to generating current performance is likely rather different from the more open, experimental one that might go with generating new ideas in previously unexplored fields.

Consequently, if current performance is desired, quite strong incentives can be given and significant effort induced at a reasonable cost. On the other hand, if only innovation is desired, it too can be induced, although making the incentives very intense can be quite costly. Getting both sorts of activity from employees can be a problem, however. This is especially true in a context where one of the two modes of operation has been the primary focus, and the company now wants to do both.

In many firms in the last decade, the focus has been on cost control, and appropriately intense incentives have been provided for this one activity. Suppose one of these firms decides it wants to encourage growth, and for this it sees that it needs to induce more innovation from employees. Yet, it is loath to give up the performance it has been enjoying in cost control. What can it do?

Note first that simply adding some incentives for innovation to the employees' existing reward package is unlikely to have any effect. Until the incentives for attempting innovation are comparably intense to those for cost control, the employees will rationally ignore them, because diverting thought and effort towards innovation will lower their expected rewards. It may also increase the variability of the rewards and thus the risk they face. This may help account for the often-heard complaint from executives that, despite their being eager to welcome growth-promoting ideas, their people just seem to lack the imagination to come up with anything. The fact is, for all the talk, the inducements offered just do not justify diverting attention away from what is really rewarded towards risky and poorly compensated activities.

As the incentives for innovation are increased, at some point they may become sufficiently intense that they do induce the employees to allocate some attention in this direction. But because the two activities compete for their time, unless the incentives for cost control are also increased, the effort and expected performance in this activity will fall. This is a second sense in which multitasking is problematic—inducing one sort of behavior increases the cost of getting the other. Moreover, the now-intense incentives are tied to noisy, imperfect measures. This means the employees' rewards vary significantly with the randomness in the measured performance and only partially with their own efforts. This variability is costly to risk-averse employees. The cost might be expressed in terms of discomfort with the lack of control they experience. Their rewards vary immensely, but not with their efforts! Then either expected total compensation must be increased, which is directly costly to the firm, or else the employees may quit.

Both these alternatives are actually taken in organizations. Many start-ups in the 1990s used stock options to give very intense incentives for exploratory activity. Even given the probability that the options would prove worthless, the expected returns on them—and thus the expected total compensation offered to employees—was likely much higher than they could expect elsewhere (or, at least, the employees who chose to join such firms perceived this to be the case). This high expected monetary value was needed to offset the risk that the employees faced. The "solution" of losing people is adopted implicitly when firms do not give adequate returns to offset the risks they attempt to load on employees when they ask them to undertake risky projects. The employees face the risks to their incomes and career prospects that accompany failure but get little of the returns that success generates. Many just refuse the offer, either by quitting or, more subtly, by diverting attention to lower risk activities. In either case the firm in fact fails to get the innovation it claimed to want.

These factors help explain the problems that some firms have experienced in trying to become more innovative. For example, despite very large investments in R&D, Proctor & Gamble, the U.S. consumer products firm, regularly failed through the 1990s to develop and successfully introduce really new, innovative products. Late in the decade it decided to reorganize to speed new product development and introduction. In the process, however, it lost control of costs, revenues did not climb as quickly as they had (let alone as fast as had been hoped), earnings fell, and the stock price collapsed. All this led to the CEO's replacement in June 2000, after less than two years on the job.

Related problems arise if an explorer tries to push for greater operational efficiency. The natural way to do this is to try to introduce a little more focus and discipline and to try to weed out some of the slack. For example, management may start measuring operational performance and talking about the need to control costs. Such moves may have little effect, because the incentives are unbalanced. This is obviously unfortunate. More serious is the possibility that the measures will work, but that in the process they destroy innovation.

In an organization that is giving relatively intense incentives for exploration, as through stock options in a start-up, introducing limited incentives for current performance may have little effect, because the main rewards are still for the innovative activity. Moreover, it is likely that the people who were attracted to the firm when it offered such rewards will not have a great taste for the perceived drudgery of exploitation, and they will be inclined to ignore calls for it, even if these come with some explicit rewards. After all, they came to the company to work on cool things and to get a chance at the big prize; responding to calls for boring cost control is not what they want to do.

The situation is different in more established explorers, like 3M, where the incentives have probably been more muted. People have likely been motivated primarily by pride in their work and the intrinsic pleasure of it, and they likely value the freedom that they enjoy. The natural means to increase efficiency, such as tighter controls, more disciplined resource allocation, and more explicit rewards tied to outcomes, are likely to have a significant effect. In particular, they may shift attention radically. In effect, the failures that must be common in really exploratory activity now become very costly to those involved. This can reduce risk-taking immensely and severely curtail innovation. Moreover, the problem of mismatch between what attracted the current people to the firm and what it now offers them is likely to be at least as intense as in the start-up.

The last several chief executives at 3M have sought to increase efficiency while not destroying the innovative engine that was their company. Thus, while they instituted more stringent reviews of research projects and speeded up dropping unpromising ones, they also increased research budgets significantly. However, they were undertaking a tough balancing act, and there have been suggestions that the effects on innovation were negative.

Job Design for Multi-tasking

One obvious solution to the multi-tasking problem may be to divide the jobs, with some employees exploring and some exploiting. Then each has a simple agenda, and neither faces any conflict between tasks. There may be drawbacks, however, if it would otherwise be advantageous to have one person or group undertake both activities. For example, the probability of a successful innovation may depend on knowledge of the current technology or markets that can best be gained from working in the area.

Other motivational problems arise when a business unit seeks to pursue multiple goals and assigns different groups within the unit to each activity. These problems have to do with internal competition within the unit and influence activities. The problems are likely to be especially severe if growth and innovation are added to the agenda of a unit that has been focused on current performance.

If a single unit is expected both to push performance on current products and services and to develop new ones, the teams assigned to each task are likely to be in competition over resources. Funds can go into developing new products or making and marketing current ones. Talented people can be assigned to one group or the other. The attention of the unit leaders can be allocated to supporting the growth team or the performance team. The next promotion can go to a member of one team or of the other. This internal competition is apt to be costly and divisive under the best of circumstances. Each side will be tempted not just to argue the merits of its own case, but also to denigrate the other. Each may become more focused on the internal competition than on the external competitors and customers. Resources earned from the efforts of the team handling the current offerings are spent on the pet development projects of the other team, generating jealousy and discontent. When the products being developed would themselves compete with the current offerings, the competition can become really intense and destructive. The results can be inadequate attention being given to either task, compounded with severe morale problems.

Moreover, it really is not possible to eliminate the multi-tasking problem by assigning exploration to one group and exploitation to another. If the firm is going to both explore and exploit, someone will have to multi-task.

At a minimum, the head of the organizational unit who is responsible for motivating its members to do the different tasks must face multiple objectives. So even if each of the people in the unit is given a simple task, the head must face balanced incentives if she is to be induced to motivate the units' people to undertake both sorts of activity in the appropriate amounts.

If the unit leader's rewards could be structured so that they depended on the full returns generated by the unit over time, then from the point of view of inducing multi-tasking it would be equivalent to the leader's making decisions on her own account. There would then be little problem in motivating the manager's multi-tasking (although there might be trouble motivating those below her). In reality, however, business unit managers rarely face such incentives. Their rewards are typically tied to overall corporate performance, to unit accounting returns, and perhaps to some subjective measures or the passing of various milestones. Tying results to corporate performance, even if it is measured in stock prices, buries the impact on rewards of any results generated by the individual unit itself and creates a free-rider problem. Accounting measures are a poor proxy for the value created, let alone for the effort and imagination that has been employed, especially in a context where innovation is being pursued. Indeed, current accounting profits are likely to be hurt by innovative search. Subjective measures and milestones may provide more effective incentives for innovation than do the accounting numbers, but using them to provide very intense incentives is certainly problematic. Big rewards tied to subjective evaluations are an invitation to politicking and their administration can easily seem capricious, biased, and unfair. Consequently, motivating unit managers to pursue a balanced agenda of both performance and growth is tough.

On the other hand, top executives may be appropriately motivated to make the right choices between exploration and exploitation. At least in the United States, typically a large fraction of their substantial compensation is tied to the firm's stock price. To the extent that the stock price recognizes both the short- and long-run prospects of the firm, executives do have strong, balanced incentives. Thus, it might seem that an easy solution to the multi-tasking problem is to have only the top executives responsible for both exploration and exploitation. Then individual business units and functions can focus on simple agendas of performance or growth.

Typically, this would involve creating different units to pursue projects outside the normal scope of the existing businesses.[3] The existing units focus on exploitation of current opportunities, while the new units explore for new ones and build them into businesses. Creating a separate exploratory unit also facilitates application of processes and measures that are appropriate to a new business and may help ensure that it gets the needed managerial attention. However, it does not eliminate the conflicts between those charged with delivering performance in current businesses and those seeking to build new ones. Instead, the battleground shifts to the corporate level, and the resultant influence costs may be even greater.

To protect the new business from the "creosote plant" effect of the existing ones, some companies try to separate them radically via the "skunk works" model. The term referred initially to teams working on top-secret defense projects at Lockheed. To maintain secrecy, the teams were isolated from the rest of the organization. The model has since been adapted and widely adopted. IBM developed its first PC using a new ad hoc unit that was located far from other IBM facilities and whose existence and mandate were kept a secret from other parts of the firm. The idea was to protect the project from the dominant culture of the mainframe computer business, then IBM's core. Similarly, General Motors created its Saturn Division to be "a new kind of car company" producing "a new kind of car." To protect it and allow it to develop new ways of working and of relating to suppliers and employees, Saturn was located far from GM's Detroit home base. The question with the skunk works model is whether the new unit can ever be integrated back in successfully. IBM succeeded, but GM has struggled with Saturn. The new unit will still meet resistance and possibly jealousy, and to the extent it is organized differently from the rest of the company, there is complexity and the opportunity for influence costs.

There are other difficulties, moreover, with passing responsibility for multi-tasking to the top levels of the firm. Most obviously, the top executives may be far removed from having first-hand knowledge on which to base allocation decisions. This is true under the best of circumstances in large firms, and when the decisions involve such matters as the returns to different lines of exploration, it is even more likely to obtain. Thus, the decisions will necessarily be based on second-hand knowledge and on hunches and gut-feel. This can obviously result in less than ideal decisions. Moreover, the information that the executives will have for decision-making will be very asymmetric. Exploration will have a difficult time quantifying the costs and benefits that might flow from giving it resources, while the exploitation groups will be able to document their cases well. This may tend to bias decisions in favor of the established, performance-oriented businesses.

To compensate, executives may try to adopt a bias towards the exploratory, but this too can cause problems. When a project gets the CEO's early support, it will tend to get resources that it might not objectively deserve. For example, Intel spent hundreds of millions on a camera product to permit video-conferencing using personal computers (Burgelman 2002). CEO Andy Grove's belief in the product kept resources flowing to it despite signs that it would be a failure in the market (which it was). Similarly, Apple's Newton personal digital assistant was the pet project of CEO John Sculley. Although the product was good in concept (as Palm later showed), the failure of the Newton itself might have been forecast, and huge amounts of resources saved, but for the CEO's promoting it. Even absent such problems, the top executives' time is limited, and this may result in delays in decisions, overload, and frustration for all concerned.

An orthogonal approach to the problem of multi-tasking is to try to change the fundamental trade-offs involved, largely by working on the people and cultural elements of organizational design. The idea is to try to bring greater alignment between the interests of the firm and its employees so that the agency and incentive problems that underlie the multi-tasking problem as we have discussed it are lessened or even eliminated (Day *et al.* 2002). The general term used for this approach is "high commitment" human resource management. As argued in Chapter 4, if only very weak explicit performance rewards are possible, then it may be especially desirable to incur the costs of adopting high commitment HRM because it may lead to higher levels of effort (and a better allocation of it among tasks) than can be induced by the weak explicit rewards. The hallmarks of this system are trust, transparency, empowerment, egalitarianism, job enrichment, teamwork, the absence of explicit individual monitoring and performance pay, and employees' identifying their interests and those of the firm and accepting its vision wholeheartedly.

Nokia Corporation has used many of these organizational levers with some success in achieving both innovation and remarkable efficiency in operations. In 1992 Nokia was a failing Finnish conglomerate whose products ranged from rubber boots through wood pulp to television sets. The collapse of the Soviet Union had sent the Finnish economy into severe depression, the rest of Europe was experiencing a sharp recession, and both the company and the Finnish banks that were its leading shareholders were in serious financial difficulties. In this crisis it offered to sell its small mobile phone business to Ericsson, but the Swedish company was not interested. By 2000, Nokia had Europe's highest market capitalization and the fifth most valuable brand in the world. Completely focused on telecommunications, it was the clear global leader in mobile phone sales and a strong player in providing the supporting network equipment. Its margins on phones were estimated to exceed 20 percent, while those of its chief rivals—Ericsson and Motorola—were at best in the low single digits. Nokia had achieved this transformation by consistently leading the industry in developing new models with better technology, features, and design at the same time that it maintained the strict control over operations necessary to keep meeting the exploding demand for its products. Even after the boom in telecommunications collapsed and many firms in the telecommunications equipment industry ran into severe difficulties, Nokia continued to thrive.

Nokia chose in 1992 to focus all its energies and attention on telecommunications, and over the next few years it exited all its other businesses, including ones with global scale and good performance. As deregulation and privatization opened telecommunications services markets in Europe, Nokia allied with the upstart new entrants that were challenging the established national monopoly service providers. Paying careful attention to the final users, Nokia developed new features for its phones that gave its clients points of differentiation that the established service providers were slow to match. This pattern of innovation was a result of Nokia's early recognition that mobile phones were a consumer product. This recognition also led it to focus on design, aiming for both appealing looks and ease of use, and on branding. At the same time, Nokia was quick to recognize the possibilities for developing common platforms that would allow offering a wide variety of models while saving on product development, procurement, and manufacturing costs.

Nokia's sales more than doubled year-on-year from 1992 through 1995. Growth at these rates presented immense operational challenges, and in 1995 logistics problems led to severe difficulties in meeting demand for its latest products. Meanwhile, older products sat unsold. The firm's stock market valuation was cut in half. Rallying from this new crisis, Nokia introduced new information and decision support systems and stronger operating controls that allowed it to triple its sales revenue between 1996 and 1999 while maintaining its pace of innovation.

The organizational design that Nokia adopted was crucial to this success. In the early days, employees throughout the firm were motivated by the desire to save the company and then to build it to be something special for themselves and their country. The successes they collectively achieved were a source of real, personal pride. The vision first offered by the leadership—that voice would go wireless—was an additional source of inspiration, as, later, was the announced intention to supplant Motorola as the industry leader. The excitement and fun of being part of a rapidly growing, internationally successful firm further strengthened employees' identification with the company.

Other aspects of the organizational design supported this identification and the motivation it provided. The architecture was kept fluid, with project teams forming and dissolving easily, so all had the opportunity to work on interesting things and to build networks across the firm. Growth meant there were potentially lots of opportunities for learning and taking on new responsibilities. The company encouraged taking these by posting all job openings internally and prohibiting the bosses of those who wanted to move from blocking transfers. The leaders of the company were open and very approachable, eating in the same cafeteria as the other employees. They clearly operated as a team and set an example of teamwork throughout the organization. "Value-based leadership," rather than control through rigorous processes, was the model, and the values of customer satisfaction, respect for the individual, achievement, and continuous learning were acted upon consistently.

Pay differences across the organization were muted. Bonuses were small and were typically paid on a team basis and on overall company performance, not individually. At the same time these low-powered explicit incentives were offered, stretch targets were set that shaped expectations and helped create norms of hard work and performance delivery. Meanwhile, innovation and experimentation were encouraged. More than a third of the employees were in R&D positions, but anywhere in the organization, if someone had an idea, it would be hard to find anyone who would block its being tried. Honest failures were not punished—for example, no one was fired over the 1995 logistics breakdown—and the leadership sought to remove fear from the organization, so that people would be willing to take risks. Politics and influence activities were strongly discouraged, and a norm of open, honest communication and debate was fostered. People at Nokia felt they could trust one another and their bosses, and this too made taking risk-taking easier.

In 1998 and 1999, Nokia made an even greater commitment to innovation, declaring its intent to lead the development of the "Mobile Information Society" that would put full access to the Internet on everyone's mobile phone. Nokia's previous innovations had been undertaken in the context of the externally established standards governing mobile voice communications. In contrast, no quasi-governmental body would set standards for the mobile Internet. Moreover, while mobile telephony in the 1990s had been largely concerned with voice communications, data and multimedia would likely drive the next generation of mobile communications. What constituted a better mobile phone for voice communications was pretty clear—smaller, better sound quality, longer battery life. Data communications involved much wider possibilities for developing services that could be delivered over the phone, from the provision of location-sensitive information tied to the Global Positioning Satellite system to interactive games and mobile commerce. Additionally, there were emerging technologies for wireless communications apart from the phone. Thus, the company's new innovation efforts could, and would have to be, much more far ranging and open-ended than before.

To deal with this need for more exploration, Nokia in 1998 established a separate unit, Nokia Ventures Organization (NVO). Its remit was to develop businesses that involved combining new technologies with new markets. Explicitly, the two existing core business units supplying mobile phones (Nokia Mobile Phones—NMP) and network equipment were charged with developing opportunities that extended existing technology into new markets or that sought to serve existing markets with new technologies. At the same time, responsibilities were reallocated among the group who together had led the corporation since 1992. The president, Jorma Ollila, became chairman while retaining the role of CEO. Pekka Ala-Pietilä, the head of NMP, was named to replace Ollila as president of the corporation and then assigned to head the fledgling NVO and the corporate Central Research Laboratories. Thus, the second-highest ranking executive took responsibility for driving exploration and growth. Meanwhile, the head of the networks business moved over to lead NMP.

NVO contained both internal venture units and a corporate venture capital fund, which was based in Silicon Valley. NVO was to function as an incubator for new businesses, which would, if they succeeded, return to the core business units, become new freestanding business units on their own, or be sold or spun off as independent companies. No business would stay in NVO indefinitely. This was to limit internal resistance and jealousies that many companies have experienced when they set up exploratory units. Ideas for new ventures might arise anywhere in the company. Whether they were moved into NVO or stayed in one of the core businesses, which had their own internal venturing units, was determined by the rule of whether the ideas involved both new technologies and new markets. Teams of engineers regularly moved between the operating businesses, NVO, and the Labs, so that narrowly defined interests were avoided. Governance of NVO was by a group involving the leaders of the operating businesses. This helped further ensure that NVO would be connected to the main businesses and not isolated from the corporation's center.

The collapse of the boom in telecommunications in 2000 has slowed adoption of new technologies by the telephone service operators and has been disastrous for many equipment suppliers. Still Nokia has continued to prosper. It has developed a range of new products and software platforms, both on its own and through consortia, spending over 10 percent of net sales on R&D. Meanwhile it has increased its market share to near 40 percent in mobile phones and maintained remarkable margins while its competitors are losing money.

Ollila attributed Nokia's success to the company's ability to balance exploration and exploitation: "Why have we been a successful company? If you want a very simple answer, it is getting the balance right between innovation and execution."[4]

Ollila's answer is simple, but actually achieving this balance is very hard. The key is good organizational design.

Notes

1. See, for example, Saloner, Shepard, and Podolny (2001: 271–84).
2. See Grinblatt and Titman (2002: 707–8) for a discussion of the literature in this area.
3. See Day *et al.* (2001) for a discussion of this architectural solution and Burgelman (1984) for a broad analysis of alternative models for organizing new business development initiatives.
4. Quoted in Doornik and Roberts (2002).

7

Creating the Modern Firm: Management and Leadership Challenges

This book has offered a set of frameworks, concepts, and tools to help meet the challenges of designing effective organizations. It has also offered a number of examples of firms that have developed strategies and organizational designs that allowed them to deliver exceptional performance and growth. Yet, the fact remains that it is very difficult to develop a winning strategy and an effective organization. Doing so is fundamentally a creative act that requires both the analytical problem-solving that characterizes management and the vision, communication, and persuasion that are essential features of leadership.[1]

For success, the elements of the firm's strategy and organization must be aligned with one another and must fit the environment in which the firm operates. This need for alignment and fit, combined with the many interdependencies among the elements of the strategy and organizational design, means the strategy and organization really must be developed in tandem, in a holistic fashion.

Structure does not follow strategy any more than strategy follows structure. This simultaneity implies that the problem of creating a strategy and an organization that will allow the firm to succeed is immensely complex, because it involves so many dimensions that interact with one another.

Many of these interactions are dynamic. Especially for a large firm, a change in strategy can easily affect the industry and bring a reaction that leads to the need for further changes in strategy and organization. The same is true internally: Changes in one aspect of the organization aimed at effecting one particular change in behavior can alter other aspects of behavior in ways that necessitate further changes on other dimensions of the design. Thus, the usual approach to fixing the problems that arise as organizations evolve—find an intervention whose first-order effect is to solve the problem, take everything else as given, and pull the lever—is fundamentally flawed. It only sets off a potentially unending stream of response, intervention, further unanticipated response, and yet another intervention.

Instead, strategic and organizational choices must be made holistically, recognizing the interdependencies. The scope of the firm—what it is going to do, where, how, and for whom—must be decided. How it is going to distinguish itself from the competition, gain competitive advantage, and create value must be determined. The right people must be attracted, retained, and assigned to different roles. The formal architecture must be crafted to allow effective coordination and motivation of these people. The processes, procedures, and routines that guide and control behavior must be developed. The fundamental values, beliefs, and norms that will be shared across the firm must be created, transmitted, and adopted. And all these must mesh properly with one another, so the organization really does allow the strategy to be executed.

The people, the networks among them, and the routines they follow must give the firm the capabilities it needs to create value. The system of incentives must motivate the particular people that have been attracted to the firm to supply the right mix of behaviors needed to deliver on the strategy and let the firm reach its goals. The formal structure and the allocation of decision authority need to be aligned with where expertise lies and with what motivates the people in the organization. Finally, all the elements of the strategy and organization need to fit with the competitive, technological, social, legal, and regulatory realities the firm faces.

Then, as the world and the organization itself evolve, the fit must be maintained by adjusting—or even radically changing—the strategy and the organizational design.

Recognizing the complementarity and substitution relationships that exist among the design variables can help suggest the shape of potentially coherent patterns, and thus reduce the design problem's complexity. Still, it remains very hard. People throughout the firm must be involved, because in a firm of any size the knowledge of how things really work, how customers really behave, how choices really interact, is highly dispersed. Managers throughout the firm must participate in the design task, completing the details of the parts of the strategy and organization they know best while cooperating to ensure that the overall result remains coherent.

Solving the organizational design problem then fundamentally requires both management and leadership.

Much of the actual design work is management—putting together budgeting processes, specifying reporting relationships, determining what will be outsourced, setting up governance procedures, creating and staffing departments, establishing the financing model. This is vitally important, but it is not enough. Leadership is needed too. Leaders offer direction and then motivate others to believe and to follow. The basic conception of the strategy and organizational design is thus a matter of leadership. The leaders must provide a vision of the strategy and organization, indicating the underlying principles and how the basic trade-offs are to be resolved. They also need to communicate the model in a clear and compelling way, so that others understand and embrace it and are motivated to try to realize it in designing their parts of the organization.

Leadership is involved in a second way in solving the design problem. While managers across the firm can craft and institute the formal aspects of the design, they cannot directly control the networks and culture. The people in the organization, individually and collectively, determine what they are going to believe, what they will value, what behavioral norms they will adopt, and with whom they will connect informally. Yet, these features may be the most important ones for determining behavior, and thus how well the firm performs. Leadership can shape these choices.

The formal elements of the design can influence the networks and culture, so managers can have some indirect control over them. For example, BP's establishing peer groups helped create networks that were important even after the original members had moved on to new jobs and were no longer in the same peer group. Nokia's choosing not to fire anyone after its logistics disaster in 1995 helped create the absence of fear in the organization that strongly promoted people's willingness to take risks. Still, leadership must play a crucial role in successfully shaping the culture.

Enunciating corporate values is the easy part and, on its own, not very effective. Most statements of values are too vague and too abstract to have much impact. Organizations all say that they care about their customers, but what does that mean in terms of behavior? Leaders must give specific meaning to the values, which then sets the basis for their generating norms of expected behavior.

The first step is for the leaders themselves to act in accordance with the values and to model the sort of behavior that is wanted. A CEO who personally handles a sampling of customer complaints on a regular basis is indicating in a forceful way how important customer care really is. The leaders should also celebrate and reward those who act in appropriate ways and correct those who do not.

Stories can be an especially powerful tool for communicating what is wanted and thus for shaping what happens. For example, the 3M CEO's telling stories about the scientist who ignored his orders to drop a project and brought it through to a successful product moulds the culture by signaling very clearly what is important. Even more powerful is the story told every new employee at Nordstrom, the U.S. retailer renowned for its customer service. A customer carrying a very worn set of tire chains approached a clerk and complained that the chains had not proven satisfactory. Although the customer had no receipt, the clerk immediately refunded the claimed purchase price without question. This was despite the fact that Nordstrom has never sold tire chains, or any other kind of automobile supplies!

Thus, organizational design involves both management and leadership. Beyond that, it is fundamentally a creative process. To succeed, a firm must create value and keep some of it. This can happen only if the firm's strategy and organization together allow the firm to be better than the competition, to offer products or services that meet its target customers' needs more effectively or more cheaply. A firm that does the same things in the same ways as the competition cannot be better than its rivals, and the head-to-head competition that will ensue will guarantee it gets to keep very little of any value it might create.

This means that inherently there must be something distinctively different about a successful firm's strategy and organization. For this reason, solving the problems of strategy and organization is an act of real creativity. It involves finding something new and different that works.

Clearly, much of this creativity can take the form of putting existing things together in novel ways. Not every element of the strategy and organizational design has to be absolutely new and unique, and there is much to be learned from experience. But chasing after apparent best practices is largely futile if the aim is to achieve distinctiveness. At best it may make the firm as good as the competition, and this is not enough to win. The more likely outcome is that it results in a monstrosity, a patchwork of ill-fitting organizational features that do not add up to a coherent design. This is a recipe for failure.

Creativity involves originality, imagining new things, seeing new patterns and connections. Yet, as important as this originality is, it is not enough. For the point is not just to come up with something new, but instead something distinctive that works. For this, understanding of the fundamental logics governing organizational design is required. The ideas and examples offered in this book are meant to be a start on providing this understanding.

Note

1. See Kotter (1990) on this differentiation between management and leadership.

References

Abreu, D., Pearce, D., and Stacchetti, E. (1990). "Towards a Theory of Discounted Repeated Games with Imperfect Monitoring." *Econometrica*, 58: 1041–63.

Aghion, P., and Tirole, J. (1997). "Formal and Real Authority in Organizations." *Journal of Political Economy*, 105: 1–29.

Akerlof, G. A. (1970). "The Market for Lemons: Quality Uncertainty and the Market Mechanism." *Quarterly Journal of Economics*, 89: 488–500.

Alchian, A., and Demsetz, H. (1972). "Production, Information Costs, and Economic Organization." *American Economic Review*, 62: 777–95.

Anderson, E. (1985). "The Salesperson as Outside Agent or Employee: A Transactions Cost Analysis." *Marketing Science*, 4: 234–54.

——, and Schmittlein, D. C. (1984). "Integration of the Sales Force: An Empirical Examination." *The RAND Journal of Economics*, 15: 385–95.

Arrow, K. (1974). *The Limits of Organization*. New York: W. W. Norton & Company.

Asanuma, B. (1989). "Manufacturer–Supplier Relationships in Japan and the Concept of Relation-Specific Skill." *Journal of the Japanese and International Economies*, 3: 1–30.

References

Asanuma, B., and Kikutani, T. (1992). "Risk Absorption in Japanese Subcontracting: A Microeconometric Study on the Automobile Industry." *Journal of the Japanese and International Economies*, 6: 1–29.

Athey, S., and Roberts, J. (2001). "Organizational Design: Decision Rights and Incentive Contracts." *American Economic Review: Papers and Proceedings*, 91: 200–5.

Avery, C., Chevalier, J. A., and Schaefer, S. (1998). "Why Do Managers Undertake Acquisitions?: an Analysis of Internal and External Rewards to Acquisitiveness." *Journal of Law, Economics, and Organization*, 14: 24–43.

——, Roberts, J., and Zemsky, P. (1993). "Sony Corporation Enters the Entertainment Business." Stanford, CA: Stanford University Graduate School of Business, case S-BP-265.

Baker, G. (2000). "The Use of Performance Measures in Incentive Contracting." *American Economic Review: Papers and Proceedings*, 90: 415–20.

——, Gibbons, R., and Murphy, K. (1994). "Subjective Performance Measures in Optimal Incentive Contracts." *Quarterly Journal of Economics*, 109: 1125–56.

—— —— —— (2001). "Relational Contracts and the Theory of the Firm." *Quarterly Journal of Economics*, 117: 39–83.

Baron, J., and Kreps, D. M. (1999). *Strategic Human Resources: Frameworks for General Managers*. New York: John Wiley & Sons.

——, Burton, D., and Hannan, M. T. (1996). "The Road Taken: Origins and Early Evolution of Employment Systems in Emerging Companies." *Industrial and Corporate Change*, 5: 239–76.

Barnett, W., and Reddy, P. (1995). "Newell Company (A)." Stanford, CA: Stanford University Graduate School of Business, case S-SM-16A.

Bartlett, C. A. (1993). "ABB's Relays Business: Building and Managing a Global Matrix." Boston: Harvard

References

University Graduate School of Business Administration, case 9-394-016.

——, and Mohammed, A. (1995). "3M: Profile of an Innovating Company." Boston: Harvard University Graduate School of Business Administration, case 9-395-016.

——, and O'Connell, J. (1998). "Lincoln Electric: Venturing Abroad." Boston: Harvard University Graduate School of Business Administration, case 3-398-095.

Berg, N. A., and Fast, N. D. (1975). "Lincoln Electric Co.." Boston: Harvard University Graduate School of Business Administration, case 9-376-028.

Berger, P., and Ofek, E. (1995). "Diversification's Impact on Firm Value." *Journal of Financial Economics*, 37: 39–65.

—— —— (1996). "Bustup Takeovers of Value-Destroying Diversified Firms." *Journal of Finance*, 51: 1175–200.

Berzins, A., Podolny, J., and Roberts, J. (1998*a*). "British Petroleum (A): Performance and Growth." Stanford, CA: Stanford University Graduate School of Business, case S-IB-16A.

—— —— —— (1998*b*). "British Petroleum (B): Focus on Learning." Stanford, CA: Stanford University Graduate School of Business, case S-IB-16B.

Brady, D., and de Verdier, A.-K. (1998). "Nike: A History." Stanford, CA: Stanford University Graduate School of Business, case S-IB-14A.

Bresnahan, T., Brynjolfsson, E., and Hitt, L. M. (2002). "Information Technology, Workplace Organization and the Demand for Skilled Labor: Firm-level Evidence." *Quarterly Journal of Economics*, 117: 339–76.

Brynjolfsson, E., and Hitt, L. M. (2000). "Beyond Computation: Information Technology, Organizational Transformation and Business Performance." *Journal of Economic Perspectives*, 14/4: 23–48.

References

Burgelman, R. (1984). "Designs for Corporate Entrepreneurship in Established Firms." *California Management Review*, 26: 154–66.

—— (2002). *Strategy is Destiny: How Strategy-Making Shapes a Company's Future*. New York: Free Press.

Burt, T. (2002). "Auditors Drive a Hard Bargain at Ford." *Financial Times*, January 14, U.S. edition, 14.

Campa, H., and Kedia, S. (2002). "Explaining the Diversification Discount." *Journal of Finance*, 57: 1731–62.

Chandler, A., Jr. (1962). *Strategy and Structure*. Cambridge, MA: MIT Press.

—— (1977). *The Visible Hand: The Managerial Revolution in American Business*. Cambridge, MA: Belknap Press.

Chevalier, J. (2002). "Why do Firms Undertake Diversifying Mergers? An Examination of the Investment Policies of Merging Firms." Chicago: University of Chicago Graduate School of Business, working paper.

Coase, R. (1937). "The Nature of the Firm." *Economica*, 4: 386–405.

—— (1960). "The Problem of Social Cost." *Journal of Law and Economics*, 3: 1–44.

Comment, R., and Jarrell, G. (1995). "Corporate Focus and Stock Returns." *Journal of Financial Economics*, 37: 67–87.

Day, J., Mang, P., Richter, A., and Roberts, J. (2001). "The Innovative Organization: Why New Ventures Need More than a Room of their Own." *The McKinsey Quarterly*, (Second Quarter): 20–31.

—— —— —— —— (2002). "Has Performance Pay Had its Day?" *The McKinsey Quarterly* (Fourth Quarter): 46–55.

Doornik, K. (2001). "Relational Contracting in Partnerships." Stanford, CA: Stanford University Graduate School of Business, working paper.

References

—— (2002). "Incentive Contracts with Dispute Costs." Stanford, CA: Stanford University Graduate School of Business, working paper.

—— (2003). "Dispute Costs and Reputation." Oxford: Oxford University Saïd School of Business, working paper.

Doornik, K., and Roberts, J. (2001). "Nokia Corporation: Innovation and Efficiency in a High-Growth Global Firm." Stanford, CA: Stanford University Graduate School of Business, case S-IB-23.

Gibbons, R., (1997). "Incentives and Careers in Organizations." In D. Kreps and K. Wallis (eds.), *Advances in Economic Theory and Econometrics*, vol. II. Cambridge: Cambridge University Press, 1–37.

——, and Murphy, K. (1990). "Relative Performance Evaluation for Chief Executive Officers." *Industrial and Labor Relations Review*, 43: 30S–51S.

—— —— (1992). "Optimal Incentive Contracts in the Presence of Career Concerns: Theory and Evidence." *Journal of Political Economy*, 100: 468–505.

Gibbons, R., and Waldman, M. (1999). "Careers in Organizations: Theory and Evidence." In O. Ashenfelter and D. Card (eds.), *Handbook of Labor Economics*, vol. 3B. Amsterdam: Elsevier, 2373–437.

Gomes-Casseres, B., and McQuade, K. (1991). "Xerox and Fuji Xerox." Boston: Harvard University Graduate School of Business Administration, case 9-391-156.

Grinblatt, M., and Titman, S. (2002). *Financial Markets and Corporate Strategy*. Boston: McGraw-Hill Irwin.

Grossman, S. J., and Hart, O. (1986). "Costs and Benefits of Ownership: A Theory of Vertical and Lateral Integration." *Journal of Political Economy*, 94: 691–719.

Hart, O. (1995). *Firms, Contracts, and Financial Structure*. Oxford: Clarendon Press.

References

Hart, O., and Holmström, B. (1987). "The Theory of Contracts." In T. Bewley (ed.), *Advances in Economic Theory: Fifth World Congress*. Cambridge: Cambridge University Press, 71–155.

——, and Moore, J. (1990). "Property Rights and the Nature of the Firm." *Journal of Political Economy*, 98: 1119–58.

Hellmann, T. (1998). "The Allocation of Control Rights in Venture Capital Contracts." *RAND Journal of Economics*, 29: 57–76.

Helper, S., MacDuffie, J. P., and Sabel, C. (1998). "The Boundaries of the Firm as a Design Problem." Proceedings, Conference on Make versus Buy: Emerging Structures. New York: Columbia University School of Law Sloan Project in Corporate Governance.

Holmström, B. (1979). "Moral Hazard and Observability." *Bell Journal of Economics*, 10: 74–91.

—— (1982a). "Managerial Incentive Problems—A Dynamic Perspective." In *Essays in Economics and Management in Honor of Lars Wahlbeck*. Helsinki: Swedish School of Economics. Reprinted in *Review of Economic Studies*, 66 (1999): 169–82.

—— (1982b). "Moral Hazard in Teams." *Bell Journal of Economics*, 13: 324–40.

—— (1999). "The Firm as a Subeconomy." *Journal of Law, Economics, and Organization*, 15: 74–102.

——, and Milgrom, P. (1991). "Multitask Principal-Agent Analyses: Incentive Contracts, Asset Ownership and Job Design." *Journal of Law, Economics, and Organization*, 7: 24–52.

——, and Roberts, J. (1998). "The Boundaries of the Firm Revisited." *Journal of Economic Perspectives*, 12: 73–94.

Horngren, C. T. (1999). *Cost Accounting: A Managerial Emphasis*, 5th edn. Englewood Cliffs, NJ: Prentice Hall.

References

Ichniowski, C., Shaw, K., and Prennushi, G. (1997). "The Effects of Human Resource Management Practices on Productivity: A Study of Steel Finishing Lines." *American Economic Review*, 87: 291–313.

Jaikumar, R. (1986). "Postindustrial Manufacturing." *Harvard Business Review*, 64: 61–8.

Jensen, M., and Meckling, W. (1976). "Theory of the Firm: Managerial Behavior, Agency Costs and Ownership Structure." *Journal of Financial Economics*, 3: 305–60.

Joskow, P. L. (1985). "Vertical Integration and Long Term Contracts: The Case of Coal Burning Electric Generating Plants." *Journal of Law, Economics, and Organization*, 1: 33–80.

—— (1987). "Contract Duration and Relationship Specific Investments: Empirical Evidence from Coal Markets." *American Economic Review*, 77: 168–85.

—— (1988). "Asset Specificity and the Structure of Vertical Relationships: Empirical Evidence." *Journal of Law, Economics, and Organization*, 4: 95–117.

Kamper, A., Podolny, J., and Roberts, J. (2000). "Novo Nordisk: Global Coordination." Stanford, CA: Stanford University Graduate School of Business, case S-IB-20A.

Kawasaki, T., and McMillan, J. (1987). "The Design of Contracts: Evidence from Japanese Subcontracting." *Journal of the Japanese and International Economies*, 1: 327–49.

Kennan, J., and Wilson, R. (1993). "Bargaining with Private Information." *Journal of Economic Literature*, 31: 45–104.

Klein, B., Crawford, R., and Alchian, A. A. (1978). "Vertical Integration, Appropriable Rents, and the Competitive Contracting Process." *Journal of Law and Economics*, 21: 297–326.

Kotter, J. (1990). "What Leaders Really Do." *Harvard Business Review*, 68: 103–11.

References

Kreps, D. (1990). "Corporate Culture and Economic Theory." In J. Alt and K. Shepsle (eds.), *Perspectives on Positive Political Economy*. Cambridge: Cambridge University Press, 90–143.

Lang, L. H. P., and Stulz, R. M. (1994). "Tobin's q, Corporate Diversification and Firm Performance." *Journal of Political Economy*, 102: 1248–80.

Lazear, E. (2000). "Performance Pay and Productivity." *American Economic Review*, 90: 1346–61.

——, and Rosen, S. (1981). "Rank-Order Tournaments as Optimum Labor Contracts." *Journal of Political Economy*, 89: 841–64.

Levin, J. (2003). "Relational Incentive Contracts." *American Economic Review*, 93: 835–57.

Levinthal, D. A. (1997). "Adaptation on Rugged Landscapes." *Management Science*, 43: 934–50.

Lichtenberg, F. (1992). "Industrial De-Diversification and its Consequences for Productivity." *Journal of Economic Behavior and Organization*, 18: 427–38.

Lins, K., and Servaes, H. (1999). "International Evidence on the Value of Corporate Diversification." *Journal of Finance*, 54: 2215–40.

McMillan, J. (1995). "Reorganizing Vertical Supply Relationships." In H. Siebert (ed.), *Trends in Business Organization: Do Participation and Cooperation Increase Competitiveness?* Tübingen: J. C. B. Mohr, 203–22.

—— (2002). *Reinventing the Bazaar: The Natural History of Markets*. New York: W. W. Norton & Company.

——, and Woodruff, C. (1999a). "Dispute Prevention Without Courts in Vietnam." *Journal of Law, Economics, and Organization*, 15: 637–58.

—— —— (1999b). "Interfirm Relationships and Informal Credit in Vietnam." *Quarterly Journal of Economics*, 114: 1285–20.

References

March, J. (1991). "Exploration and Exploitation in Organizational Learning." *Organization Science*, 2: 71–87.

Masten, S. E. (1984). "The Organization of Production: Evidence from the Aerospace Industry." *Journal of Law and Economics*, 27: 403–17.

——, Meehan, J. W., and Snyder, E. A. (1989). "Vertical Integration in the US Auto Industry: A Note on the Influence of Transactions Specific Assets." *Journal of Economic Behavior and Organization*, 12: 265–73.

Matsusaka, J. (1993). "Takeover Motives During the Conglomerate Merger Wave." *RAND Journal of Economics*, 24: 357–79.

Meyer, M., Milgrom, P., and Roberts, J. (1992). "Organizational Prospects, Influence Costs and Ownership Changes." *Journal of Economics and Management Strategy*, 1: 9–36.

Milgrom, P., and Roberts, J. (1988a). "Communication and Inventories as Substitutes in Organizing Production." *Scandinavian Journal of Economics*, 90: 275–89.

—— —— (1988b). "An Economic Approach to Influence Activities in Organizations." *American Journal of Sociology*, 94 Suppl.: S154–79.

—— —— (1990a). "Bargaining Costs, Influence Costs and the Organization of Economic Activity." In J. Alt and K. Shepsle (eds.), *Perspectives on Positive Political Economy*. Cambridge: Cambridge University Press, 57–89.

—— —— (1990b). "The Economics of Modern Manufacturing: Technology, Strategy and Organization." *American Economic Review*, 80: 511–28.

—— —— (1990c). "The Efficiency of Equity in Organizational Decision Processes." *American Economic Review: Papers and Proceedings*, 80: 154–9.

—— —— (1992). *Economics, Organization and Management*. Englewood Cliffs, NJ: Prentice Hall, 1992.

References

Milgrom, P., and Roberts, J. (1993). "Johnson Controls, Inc., Automotive Systems Group: Georgetown, Kentucky Plant." Stanford, CA: Stanford University Graduate School of Business, case S-BE-9.

—— —— (1994). "Complementarities and Systems: Understanding Japanese Economic Organization." *Estudios Economicos*, 9: 3–42.

—— —— (1995). "Complementarities and Fit: Strategy, Structure and Organizational Change in Manufacturing." *Journal of Accounting and Economics*, 19: 179–208.

—— —— (1998). "The Internal Politics of the Firm." In S. Bowles, M. Franzini, and U. Pagano (eds.), *The Politics of Exchange and the Economics of Power*. London: Routledge, 46–62.

Monteverde, K., and Teece, D. (1982). "Supplier Switching Cost and Vertical Integration in the U.S. Automobile Industry." *Bell Journal of Economics*, 13: 206–13.

Montgomery, C. A., and Wernerfelt, B. (1988). "Diversification, Ricardian Rents and Tobin's q." *RAND Journal of Economics*, 19: 623–32.

Myerson. R., and Satterthwaite, M. (1983). "Efficient Mechanisms for Bilateral Trading." *Journal of Economic Theory*, 29: 265–81.

Nagar, V. (2002). "Delegation and Incentive Compensation." *Accounting Review*, 77: 379–95.

Newman, P. C. (1985). *Company of Adventurers, Vol. I*. Markham, ON: Penguin.

—— (1987). *Company of Adventurers, Vol. II: Caesars of the Wilderness*. Markham, ON: Penguin.

—— (1991). *Company of Adventurers, Vol. III: Merchant Princes*. Markham, ON: Penguin.

Nickerson, J. (2003). "Being Efficiently Fickle: A Dynamic Theory of Organizational Choice." *Organization Science*, 13: 547–66.

References

Ohno, T. (1988). *Toyota Production System: Beyond Large-Scale Production*. Cambridge, MA: Productivity Press.

O'Reilly III, C. (1998). "Cisco Systems: The Acquisition of Technology is the Acquisition of People." Stanford, CA: Stanford University Graduate School of Business, case S-HR-10.

Oyer, P. (1998). "Fiscal Year Ends and Nonlinear Incentive Contracts: The Effect on Business Seasonality." *Quarterly Journal of Economics*, 113: 149–85.

Pearson, A., and Hurstak, J. (1992). "Johnson and Johnson: Hospital Services." Boston: Harvard University Graduate School of Business Administration, case 9-392-050.

Pfeffer, J. (1996). *Competitive Advantage Through People: Unleashing the Power of the Work Force*. Boston: Harvard Business School Press.

Porter, M. (1980). *Competitive Strategy: Techniques For Analyzing Industries And Competitors*. New York: Free Press.

—— (1985). *Competitive Advantage: Creating And Sustaining Superior Performance*. New York: Free Press.

Prendergast, C. (1999). "The Provision of Incentives in Firms." *Journal of Economic Literature*, 37: 7–63.

—— (2000). "What Trade-off of Risk and Incentives?" *American Economic Review: Papers and Proceedings*, 90: 421–5.

Rajan, R., Servaes, H., and Zingales, L. (2000). "The Cost of Diversity: The Diversification Discount and Inefficient Investment." *Journal of Finance*, 60: 35–80.

——, and Wulf, J. (2002). "The Flattening Firm: Evidence from Panel Data on the Changing Nature of Corporate Hierarchies." Philadelphia: University of Pennsylvania Wharton School of Finance, working paper.

——, and Zingales, L. G. (1998). "Power in a Theory of the Firm." *Quarterly Journal of Economics*, 113: 387–432.

References

Roberts, J. (1998). "Value Maximization." In P. Newman (ed.), *The New Palgrave Dictionary of Economics and the Law*, vol. 3. London: Macmillan Reference.

——, and Van den Steen, E. (2001). "Human Capital and Corporate Governance." In J. Schwalbach (ed.), *Corporate Governance: A Volume in Honor of Horst Albach*. Berlin: Springer Verlag, 128–44.

Rotemberg, J., and Saloner, G. (1994). "The Benefits of Narrow Business Strategies." *American Economic Review*, 84: 1330–49.

—— —— (2000). "Visionaries, Managers and Strategic Direction." *RAND Journal of Economics*, 31: 693–716.

Roy, D. (1952). "Quota Restriction and Goldbricking in a Machine Shop." *American Journal of Sociology*, 57: 427–42.

Ruigrok, W., Pettigrew, A., Peck, S., and Whittington, R. (1999). "Corporate Restructuring and New Forms of Organizing: Evidence from Europe." *Management International Review*, 39 (Special Issue): 41–64.

Saloner, G., Shepard, A., and Podolny, J. (2001). *Strategic Management*. New York: John Wiley & Sons.

Schaefer, S. (1988). "Influence Costs, Structural Inertia and Organizational Change." *Journal of Economics and Management Strategy*, 7: 237–63.

Scharfstein, D. (1998). "The Dark Side of Internal Capital Markets II: Evidence from Diversified Conglomerates." Cambridge, MA: National Bureau of Economic Research, working paper 6352.

——, and Stein, J. (2000). "The Dark Side of Internal Capital Markets: Divisional Rent-Seeking and Inefficient Investment." *Journal of Finance*, 55: 2537–64.

Shin, H.-H., and Stultz, R. (1998). "Are Internal Capital Markets Efficient?" *Quarterly Journal of Economics*, 112: 531–52.

Simon, H. (1951). "A Formal Theory of the Employment Relationship." *Econometrica*, 19: 293–305.

References

—— (1991). "Organizations and Markets." *Journal of Economic Perspectives*, 5: 25–44.

Smith, A. (1776/1937). In E. Canaan (ed.), *An Inquiry into the Nature and Causes of the Wealth of Nations*. New York: The Modern Library.

Spence, A. M. (1973). "Job Market Signaling." *Quarterly Journal of Economics*, 87: 355–74.

Spraakman, G. P. (2002). "A Critique of Milgrom and Roberts' Treatment of Incentives vs. Bureaucratic Controls in the British North American Fur Trade." *Journal of Management Accounting Research*, 14: 135–52.

Stevenson, H., Martinez, J., and Jarillo, J. C. (1989). "Benetton S.p.A." Boston: Harvard University Graduate School of Business Administration, case 9-389-074.

Vance, R., Bhambri, A., and Wilson, J. (1980). "IBM Corp.: The Bubble-Memory Incident." Boston: Harvard University Graduate School of Business Administration, case 9-180-042.

Van den Steen, E. (2002). "Organizational Beliefs and Managerial Vision." Cambridge, MA: Massachusetts Institute of Technology Sloan School of Management, working paper.

Villalonga, B. (2002*a*). "Diversification Cost or Premium? New Evidence from BITS Establishment-Level Data." Boston: Harvard University Graduate School of Business Administration, working paper.

—— (2002*b*). "Does Diversification Cause the 'Diversification Discount'?" Boston: Harvard University Graduate School of Business Administration, working paper.

Whang, S., and de Verdier, A.-K. (1998). "Nike: Global Supply Chain." Stanford, CA: Stanford University Graduate School of Business, case S-IB-14D.

Whinston, M. (2003). "On the Transaction Cost Determinants of Vertical Integration." *Journal of Law, Economics, and Organization*, 19: 1–23.

Whittington, R., Pettigrew, A., Peck, S., Fenton, E., and Conyon, M. (1999). "Change and Complementarities in the

References

New Competitive Landscape: A European Panel Study, 1992–1996." *Organization Science*, 10: 583–600.

Williamson, O. (1975). *Markets and Hierarchies: Analysis and Antitrust Implications*. New York: Free Press.

—— (1985). *The Economic Institutions of Capitalism*. New York: Free Press.

Womack, J. P., Jones, D. T., and Roos, D. (1990). *The Machine that Changed the World*. New York: Harper Perennial.

Index

Figures, tables, and notes are indicated by **f**, **t**, and **n** respectively.

Index

Index

Index

Index

Index

Index

Index

Index

Index

313

Index

Index

processes, control of 255
Proctor & Gamble 257
  innovation in 266–7
procurement 199
production 167–8
  in BP 185
  in Lincoln Electric Company 43
  lines in Japan 63
productivity 38, 45–6, 63
  in Lincoln Electric Company 45–6
products 47, 261
  development of 167–8
  in Sony 220–1
profitability 245
property rights 95, 105
public goods 79–80, 87
  excludable 79–80
public traded corporations 171
purpose of the firm 74–115

quality:
  circles 63
  control 203
  in Lincoln Electric Company 144
  in manufacturing 148
  of goods 82
quasirents 92, 116 n

R&D groups 259
  in Proctor and Gamble 266
Rajan, R. 104, 225
recruitment:
  in North West Company (NWC) 5
  of employees 164–5
Reddy, P. 250
relational contracts see contracts,
    relational
relationships between firms 209, 213
  long-term 209, 213–14
renegotiation:
  of contracts 86–7, 92, 115 n
  of employment 85–7
rents 116 n
reputations 121–2, 125, 160–4
  and contracts 120–1

as motivation 161
formation of 162
in agency context 242 n
in reward systems 163
in Toyota 206
in Vietnam 163
Research and Development groups 259
results, measurement of 140
rewards 124, 128, 130–1, 139, 142–4,
    154–5, 158–9, 165
  for subjective evaluations 270–1
  in 3M 259
  non-contractual 161
  outcomes-based 126
  performance-based 144, 176
    measures 176
  schemes 131, 140, 150, 154, 158–9
    and behavior 159
    for sales staff 138
    formulaic 158
  systems 138, 154, 165
    in North West Company (NWC) 5
    politicization of 160
    reputations in 163
risk 134–5, 151, 216, 234, 263, 266
  aversion 131–4, 165, 262, 265–6
  manage 255
  reduction 215, 242 n
  sharing 129–30
  taking 171, 268
  and managers 120
risk-neutrality 132, 178 n
Roberts, J. 25, 28, 31 n, 35, 41, 47,
    73 n, 99, 113, 115 n, 116 n, 141,
    146, 169, 170, 177 n, 178 n, 201,
    218, 225, 226, 233, 242 n, 280 n
Roos, D. 197
Rosen, S. 139
Rotemberg, J. 164
Roy, D. 154
Rubbermaid 250
Ruigrok, W. 240

Sabel, C. 202
sabotage of projects 224

315

Index

Index

Index